LENI RIEFENSTAHL
The Fallen Film Goddess

LENI RIEFENSTAHL
The Fallen Film Goddess

By Glenn B. Infield

THOMAS Y. CROWELL COMPANY
Established 1834   New York

ᘯ17698   ACKNOWLEDGMENTS

The exploration of a complex and controversial subject such as the one examined in this book requires the opinions of many individuals and organizations and a large amount of documented material before the author can come to any definite conclusions. I was very fortunate in receiving such help from many sources, but I want to emphasize that not all sources are named here. Some people have preferred not to have their opinions publicized, although the documentation for their statements, which I personally examined, is authentic.

Among those in the film industry who worked with Leni Riefenstahl and who were very helpful to me were Luis Trenker, Harry Sokal, Willy Zielke, and Karl Ritter. Many of her associates, of course, have passed away. During my various trips to Germany I visited with Otto Skorzeny in Madrid, Albert Speer in Heidelberg, Hans Barkhausen in Koblenz, and many others who had knowledge of the times and the works of Leni Riefenstahl and her associates during the Third Reich. Erwin Leiser of Zurich, who produced the excellent documentary Mein Kampf, provided valuable documentation, as did Dr. Giessler of the Bundesarchiv in Koblenz, Dr. Ebhard Spiess of the Deutsches Institut für Filmkunde in Wiesbaden-Biebrich, and Richard Bauer of the Mission of the United States in Berlin.

Charles Silver of the Film Study Center, The Museum of Modern Art; George C. Pratt of the International Museum of Photography at George Eastman House; Robert S. Young of the Central Intelligence Agency; Jerry Rosenfeld, mayor of Telluride, Colorado; Paul Myers of the Library and Museum of the Performing Arts at Lincoln Center, New York; Walter Laqueur of the Wiener Library, London; Jean Favier of the Secretariat d'État à la Culture, Paris; Arthur G. Kogan of the U.S. Department of State; Gottfried Reinhardt, Salzburg, Austria; Margaret J. Cox of the British Broadcasting Corporation, London; Renate Strasser of the Institut für Zeitgeschichte, Munich; Jerry L. Kearns of the Library of Congress; William B. Fraley and William H. Cunliffe of the National Archives, Washington, D.C.; Marcel Ophuls, filmmaker; and Hanna Reitsch of Frankfurt were all very cooperative and helpful.

Dr. T. Johnson of Geneva College, who did the German translation, was of invaluable aid to me.

Without the help of my wife, Peggy, the book would not have been completed.

To those whom I have not mentioned and to those who asked me not to mention their names—thanks!

Copyright © 1976 by Glenn B. Infield

Published simultaneously in Canada by Fitzhenry & Whiteside Limited, Toronto.

Designed by Spencer Drate

Manufactured in the United States of America

Library of Congress Cataloging in Publication Data

Infield, Glenn B   Leni Riefenstahl, the fallen film goddess.
Bibliography: p.   Includes index.   1. Riefenstahl, Leni.   I. Title.
PN1998.A3R528   791.43'028'0924   [B]   76-7084
ISBN 0-690-01167-9

1 2 3 4 5 6 7 8 9 10

FOR
Judi and Sally

Books by the author:

Unarmed and Unafraid
Disaster at Bari
The Poltava Affair
Big Week
Eva and Adolf
Leni Riefenstahl:
The Fallen Film Goddess

Contents

part four: The Postwar Years

Foreword

Leni Riefenstahl, Adolf Hitler's favorite filmmaker, has long
been cinema's foremost figure in the conflict between art and
morality. There is little or no controversy about her talents. Her
films *Das blaue Licht*, *Triumph des Willens*, and *Olympia* are
evidence of her creative ability as an actress and as a director.
Yet these same films, particularly the last two, are considered by
many also to be propaganda masterpieces. They were made by
the order of Adolf Hitler and glorified the Nazi party and the
Führer. For that reason she has been called a "faithful servant of
Nazism" and "a genius glorifying the wrong cause."

Was she?

There are many who believe that she was an artist who
made near-perfect films with no thought about politics or any effect the films might have on her audiences but the aesthetic. To
them she is a modern-day cult figure idolized for achievements
on the screen. They believe that her genius was based on a
romantic dream and that she wanted to show human beings not
as they often are but as they should be, that she wanted not
merely to record but to enhance. Her supporters insist that she
should be judged solely on her artistry. They believe in the
adage "Politics and art should never be confused."

Are they correct?

This book is not a biography of Leni Riefenstahl but an investigation of her filmmaking during the Third Reich, of her
close association with Hitler and other Nazi officials, and of the

effect that this close association may have had on the content of her films. The question of the moral responsibility of the artist is of prime importance in the light of Watergate, Vietnam, and recent disclosures of CIA abuses. The artist can project images that mislead the public, sometimes so cleverly that the public is never aware that it has been shown fantasy and not reality. Did Leni Riefenstahl compromise her moral principles to advance her career? Was she an ardent Nazi supporter? Was she Adolf Hitler's mistress? Is she guilty of having contributed to Hitler's anti-Semitic policies with her films? Was she the only truly liberated woman in Nazi Germany?

These questions and others are thoroughly investigated here and the answers documented. This book is not intended to be an indictment of an individual but an overall study of the important factors involved in the fusion of filmmaking and politics, factors that can help change the course of a nation just as they did in Nazi Germany.

part one

The Early Years

1
Legend in the Shadows

Early on the evening of March 28, 1935,[1] a crowd began entering the Ufa-Palast-am-Zoo, Berlin's largest theater. It was a well-dressed audience. Many of the men wore black tie, while most of the women were dressed in long, expensive gowns. Shortly before the festivities began, the beautiful German actress and director Leni Riefenstahl stepped from a limousine and greeted the huge crowd of onlookers in front of the theater. Wearing a white fur coat and a low-cut gown that revealed the upper half of her ample breasts, Riefenstahl smiled and waved to the cheering throng. Many of the onlookers reached across the restraining ropes and tried to touch her; others threw kisses. They knew her well from seeing her movies during the past nine years—films such as *Der heilige Berg, Der grosse Sprung, Die weisse Hölle vom Piz Palü,* and her famous masterpiece, *Das blaue Licht.* She was at the Berlin theater this night to attend the premiere of her latest production, *Triumph des Willens,* the film she had made for the chancellor of Germany, Adolf Hitler.

After Riefenstahl had waved to the people on all sides of her and given the photographers plenty of time to take their pictures, she moved into the theater, where the first-nighters awaited her arrival. When the members of the audience saw her enter, they rose from their seats and applauded for several minutes. Riefenstahl accepted their applause, just as she had accepted the shouts and praise of the crowd outside: with a smile and a wave of her hand that indicated that she not only appreci-

3

ated the acclaim but was accustomed to it and felt entitled to it.

A short time after Riefenstahl took her place in her private box with her companions, a black Mercedes-Benz pulled up at the curb outside. The driver hurried around to open the rear door. A moment later a roar went up from the people outside the theater as Chancellor Adolf Hitler got out of the limousine. The roar had a different quality from that of the cheers and shouts that had greeted Riefenstahl. It was more of a regimented greeting, as though some unseen cheerleader had given the signal and everyone had shouted at once, in the same key, and for the same length of time. It wasn't the friendly, spontaneous ovation given the actress-director. It sounded restrained, even forced, as though the German citizens were not quite certain how they felt about Hitler. Hitler gave the now-familiar Nazi salute, his right arm extended, and quickly walked into the Ufa-Palast-am-Zoo.

The crowd's restraint was understandable. Although he had been appointed chancellor by President Paul von Hindenburg on January 30, 1933, Hitler was not yet well known to the average German citizen. He spent much of his time at his compound in the mountains near Berchtesgaden or in Munich or traveling around Germany. The only films the Germans ever saw of him were newsreel shots, and these revealed little of his true character. They knew of some of his actions since taking over the chancellorship: the March 24, 1933, "Enabling Act"; the boycott of Jewish shops; his meeting with Mussolini in Venice; his murderous purge of his longtime friend and supporter Ernst Röhm and other SA (Sturmabteilung) officers; his assumption of the presidency when Hindenburg died in August 1934; and his vow to reestablish Germany as a world power. But they were not certain what type of man he was, and most hoped that Riefenstahl's film would answer that question.

Just before the scheduled start of *Triumph des Willens,* another limousine stopped in front of the theater and Dr. Joseph Goebbels emerged. This time the spectators were silent. They watched as the crippled Goebbels walked slowly toward the entrance, staring at his shrunken frame and stooping shoulders. Goebbels' physical appearance was not the sort to arouse the admiration of a crowd, and the Germans were not yet won over by his rhetoric. Yet they showed him silent respect, knowing that this was the man who had been chosen by Hitler to be his minister for "people's enlightenment and propaganda." They knew, too, that Goebbels controlled all filmmaking in the Third Reich . . . except for the productions of Leni Riefenstahl. Hitler personally gave Riefenstahl her orders, much to Goebbels' chagrin, it was said. In fact, many of the onlookers were amazed that the stern-faced Goebbels had left his office on the Wilhelmplatz to attend the premiere, knowing how he felt toward the actress-director. Goebbels was there because Hitler had ordered him to attend.

Triumph des Willens lasted approximately 110 minutes,[2] and long before the film ended, Hitler, Goebbels, other Nazi officials in the audience, and Riefenstahl herself knew it was an outstanding success. The film was about the 1934 Nazi party rally at Nuremberg and it had been produced at Hitler's order. Hitler had titled this sixth party congress "The Party Day of Unity," and he wanted the spectacular events of the rally, attended by 700,000 people, to convince all Germans—and the world—that Germany was united under his rule, that the unanimity in the Nazi hierarchy was undisturbed by the murder of Röhm and his associates. Both Hitler and Goebbels recognized that the film had projected the desired image of the party and of Hitler, that it would tell audiences what they wanted them to believe.

Riefenstahl took several curtain calls, a jubilant beauty who was well aware that she had the confidence and support of the most powerful man in Germany, Adolf Hitler. Only once did her poise falter, and that was when the Führer presented her with a huge bouquet of flowers. She stumbled and started to sag to the stage in a faint, but recovered quickly. Later she said it was because she was so tired, not because she was overwhelmed by Hitler's gesture.

Though Goebbels was not fond of Riefenstahl, he recognized her artistic genius and was gratified that she had used this great talent to make a film that would further the aims of the Nazi party. On May 1, 1935, at the Festival of the Nation in

Berlin, he presented Riefenstahl with the National Film Prize for *Triumph des Willens,* stating:

> This film represents an exceptional achievement in the film production of the past year. It is closely relevant to us because it reflects the present; it describes in unprecedented scenes the gripping events of our political existence. It is a filmed grand vision of our Führer, who is shown here for the first time on the screen in the most impressive manner. The film successfully overcomes the hazard of becoming a mere propaganda feature. It has lifted up the harsh rhythm of our great epoch to extreme heights of artistic achievement. It is a monumental film, thundering with the tempo of marching columns, based on iron principle, steaming with creative [style].[3]

The phrase "filmed grand vision of our Führer" especially pleased the beautiful Riefenstahl in 1935, but it was to haunt her in postwar years and make her one of the most controversial women in the film industry.

Her *Triumph des Willens* brought her closer to the center of Nazi party power and to Hitler himself. Riefenstahl enjoyed her position as "Hitler's favorite filmmaker" and the benefits that went with it: financing, excellent film crews, protection from Goebbels' interference, and worldwide recognition that she was a confidant of a world leader. She was a star in films and a star in the Third Reich social scene.

But ten years after the triumphant premiere at the Ufa-Palast-am-Zoo, Riefenstahl lost her supporting cast in a bunker near Potsdamerplatz. It was there, in April 1945, that both Adolf Hitler and Joseph Goebbels committed suicide in the last moments of the war they had lost. Their deaths ended the reign of the Third Reich—and the reign of Leni Riefenstahl as the Third Reich film goddess—and revived the perennial controversy about the moral responsibility of an artist of great talent. How should artistic ability be used when it is powerful enough to influence the minds and hearts of millions of people?

During the more than three decades since the end of the Third Reich, the part that Leni Riefenstahl played in it has been disputed all over the world and by people in all walks of life, not only by those in the film industry. It has been a subject of controversy because the question to be answered goes far beyond the Riefenstahl-Hitler association. The debate about whether Leni Riefenstahl is a tarnished film goddess or an innocent martyr because of her relations with Adolf Hitler is an attempt to establish the limits to which an artist can go without assuming responsibility for the effects of artistic achievement on the human race as a whole.

When the government-subsidized British Film Institute invited Riefenstahl to lecture at the National Film Theatre in London in 1960, fifteen years after the end of the Third Reich, the officials thought the world was ready to forget about her close association with Hitler. They were wrong. So many protests were received that the institute was forced to withdraw the invitation. Many of the letters and telegrams protested the honoring in Britain of the actress Hitler had called "the perfect example of German womanhood." Ivor Montague, the British director, and Peter Sellers, the well-known British actor, were scheduled to appear with her, and their different viewpoints about Riefenstahl's career point up the controversial nature of the issue of the artist's moral responsibility.

Montague, winner of the Lenin Peace Prize and known for his Communist sympathies, wrote to Sellers: "I could not possibly agree to giving a lecture as a part of a series including Leni Riefenstahl." [4] He asked Sellers to withdraw from the program, as he intended to do, if the British Film Institute insisted on presenting her.

Sellers, however, refused to withdraw. His reasons were related to the artistic merit of her films. He replied:

> Miss Riefenstahl has presumably been invited to lecture because of her outstanding talents as a filmmaker. Alongside her contributions to the art of filmmaking our efforts, if I may say so, appear very puny. Are you seriously proposing that in a civilized society the artist as an artist isn't entitled to be heard because of popular objections to his or her political associations or personal morality? [5]

The last sentence of Sellers' letter is, of course, the crux of the problem and the opinion held by the cult supporting Riefenstahl. Even the board of the British Film Institute, which ultimately withdrew Riefenstahl's invitation, stated in its announcement:

> The Institute stands by its rights to invite artists to lecture at the National Film Theatre on the basis of their artistic achievements regardless of their political attachments. But in the present circumstances it is felt that Miss Riefenstahl's visit would not be capable of fulfilling the intentions of the Institute and her invitation is therefore being withdrawn.[6]

Survivors of the Hitler holocaust and friends and relatives of those who did not survive created the "present circumstances" to which the British Film Institute referred.

In May 1972, more than a quarter of a century after Hitler died, Riefenstahl was invited to show *Olympia*, another of her films produced during the Third Reich, in Berlin.[7] This was a version edited at the order of the German Voluntary Self-Control (FSK) in Wiesbaden. Riefenstahl was scheduled to show the film in the Ufa-Palast-am-Zoo, the same theater where she had scored her glorious success with *Triumph des Willens* in 1935. This time there were no triumphant moments for her to savor. Protests streamed into all newspaper offices, radio stations, television stations, and the office of the mayor of Berlin, saying that Riefenstahl's appearance would cause violent demonstrations. These protests were so vehement that the film was canceled. When Riefenstahl's life was threatened she quickly left Berlin.

Two years later, in September 1974, plans were made to honor Riefenstahl at the First Telluride Film Festival at Telluride, Colorado.[8] This was forty years to the month after she had filmed the Nazi party rally at Nuremberg for Hitler and produced her film *Triumph des Willens*. Other guests scheduled to be honored with her at Telluride included Francis Ford Coppola, director of *Conversation* and *The Godfather*; Gloria Swanson, star of silent screen and contemporary movies; and Henry Langlois, curator of the Cinémathèque Française. They too were asked to withdraw from the festivities, just as Montague and Sellers had been, but they refused.

When Gloria Swanson was asked about the controversy surrounding Riefenstahl, the former Mack Sennett bathing beauty, who is one of the most celebrated movie actresses in the history of films, was annoyed.

"Why should I withdraw? Is Leni Riefenstahl waving a Nazi flag? I thought Hitler was dead. I don't want to talk about scandal." [9]

Coppola, advised of the protests being made by various Jewish organizations, had dinner with Riefenstahl so he could ask his own questions. Evidently her answers were satisfactory to him because he did not withdraw. He said later that he would have been interested in seeing additional Riefenstahl work and wondered what she might have accomplished since the end of World War II if she had been permitted to remain active in the film industry. [10]

Jerry Rosenfeld, Telluride's thirty-four-year-old mayor and a Jew, was more explicit: "We are honoring the artist, not the individual." [11]

As usual, those supporting Riefenstahl made no mention of her moral responsibility for the content of her films, and did not raise the issue of whether an artist can be expected even to consider the question of moral responsibility in regard to his or her art.

Not all the people gathered at the Telluride festival agreed with Swanson, Coppola, and Rosenfeld, however. Many protesters were in the crowd surrounding the Sheridan Opera House, and most of them carried signs. One woman had a placard reading:

I object as a woman.
I object as an American.
I object as an active Coloradan.
I object as a Jew. [12]

A young man nearby carried a sign that read: "Every fine artist knows that the Nazis were anti-art." [13]

Another woman, not a Jew, had a thought-provoking message printed on her cardboard sign: "The greater the artist, the greater the responsibility. When she serves evil, the greater the crime." [14]

The American Jewish Congress attacked the ceremony as "morally indefensible." Rabbi Yaakov Rosenberg, chairman of the Congress Commission on Jewish affairs, stated:

> Miss Riefenstahl put her talents as a propagandist at the service of a monster, helping thereby to seduce the German people and hypnotize an unsuspecting world. Any award to such a filmmaker is morally indefensible.
>
> *Triumph des Willens* could only have been created by a Nazi fanatic. It has rightly been called a profoundly subversive work and its creator Nazism's most effective film propagandist. It is perhaps understandable that Miss Riefenstahl in recent years has sought to absolve herself of personal culpability for the horrors of Nazism. What is incredible is that she has so many defenders and willing listeners. To honor Leni Riefenstahl is to insult all those who suffered at the hands of the Nazi tyranny she so effectively promoted. [15]

Julius Schatz, director of the American Jewish Congress, explained the organization's feelings toward the proposed honoring of Riefenstahl:

> It is an insensitive act to decorate a talented artist whose fanaticism and support of Hitler and the Nazi war machine and genocidal pogroms encouraged her to produce the famous film epic, *Triumph des Willens*. She lent her name, her fame, her talent to the Nazi murderers. Whether or not she was a card-carrying Nazi party member is immaterial. She shares in the collective blame of those few German artists who prostituted themselves for the greater glory of Hitler's Reich.
>
> Hundreds and thousands of German writers, artists and filmmakers died or chose exile rather than allow themselves to serve Nazi criminality. She has consistently defended herself by saying she performed her duties artistically in the services of her nation and not for the Nationalist Socialist Party. But this is absurd. She knew what Hitler and his pals were doing and yet she

became an accomplice of the greatest deception and destruction in human history.[16]

The officials of the First Telluride Film Festival ignored the protests and gave Riefenstahl the silver medallion in an award ceremony inside the Sheridan Opera House on Saturday night. Riefenstahl, still vivacious and attractive at seventy-two, was obviously moved as she acknowledged the applause from the segment of the audience that approved of the award.

"It is like before the war," she murmured to a friend standing nearby. "They like me." [17]

When it came time for her to appear at a scheduled seminar, however, her chair was empty. A festival official announced: "Due to Miss Riefenstahl's warm reception in Telluride, we feel her appearance should not be marred." He later explained that Riefenstahl was frightened of the demonstrators, was hurt that there was a protest, and did not want her photograph taken with anti-Nazi and anti-Riefenstahl signs in the background.

Riefenstahl left Telluride immediately and returned to her home in Munich, leaving behind her in the United States, as she has in other parts of the world, the unanswered questions that have beset her since the end of World War II. Was she Hitler's lover? Was she aware of Hitler's programs, and did she approve of them? Are her films artistic masterpieces or propaganda masterpieces—or both? Is she a great and dangerous film artist because of her association with Hitler or is she an apolitical artistic genius who has been made a martyr because of her innocent acquaintance with the Führer?

A detailed study of her controversial career separates the myth from the reality and provides the answers.

2

Early Years

The outrage directed against Leni Riefenstahl after the end of World War II particularly shocked her because she had always basked in love and admiration. While the arrival of Helene Bertha Amalie (Leni) Riefenstahl at Hindenburgstrasse 97, Berlin, on August 22, 1902,[1] had none of the drama of the arrival of Adolf Hitler at Nuremberg in the film that she made thirty-two years later, it was a proud day for her parents.

Alfred Riefenstahl, her father, was a wealthy Berlin merchant who had made his money in the plumbing and heating business. He was a practical man, a businessman who hoped his first child might be a son he could train to take over his extensive business enterprise. Yet he certainly was not bitter over the birth of a daughter. In fact, he was delighted. He still intended to educate his child in business administration. Although he was a German father of the old school, who ruled his family with a firm hand and thought woman's place was in the home, he was practical; he knew he needed someone to take his place in the business, and he wanted that person to be his own child.

Riefenstahl's mother, the former Bertha Scherlach, loved her husband very much but was determined that their daughter would have a voice in her future, that Alfred would not dictate her career. Leni, her mother realized, might not be interested in the heating and plumbing business. Bertha Riefenstahl was exactly right. At first the young Leni showed a natural talent for painting, and during her early school years her mother was certain her daughter would be a fine artist. Later, however, while Leni was still very young, her interest turned from art to dancing.

"When I was six or seven years old I saw *Swan Lake* in the theater," Riefenstahl said, "and from that moment I only wanted to dance." [2]

When her father became aware of her ambitions, he was furious. He demanded that she take business courses in school, that she plan on entering his business as soon as she had completed her studies.

"You have no head for business," he said, "but I will train you. There will be no dancer in my family." [3]

Her mother sided with Leni, and while her father fretted about her "frivolous affair with the dance," Bertha Riefenstahl encouraged the young girl. She was happy that her daughter was interested in the arts, as she herself was artistic but had never developed her talents. Leni took dancing lessons secretly, supported by her mother, and gave the usual dancing school performances at recitals. When her father discovered what was going on behind his back, he decided on another strategy to thwart his daughter's ambition. If he could not change her mind, he would enroll her in the best dancing school in Berlin and let her find out for herself that she had no real talent.

The day after he learned she had been taking lessons secretly, he enrolled Leni in the famous Russian Ballet School in Berlin. After the very first lesson it was evident to teacher Jutta Klammt that her new pupil had a great talent. In later years, after his daughter had become world-famous, Alfred Riefenstahl was very proud of her and often explained that it was his idea that she train at the Russian Ballet School. [4] Only his daughter and his wife knew why he had sent her there.

Later, Leni was called upon to substitute for the well-known dancer Anita Berber at a performance in Berlin, and while she received only average notices, she was encouraged to continue her training. Even during these early years she showed the tenacious ambition that she exhibited during the Third Reich years.

"My desire was to dance alone, to dance to my own fantasies," she explained. "I was always different from the others. I designed my own costumes, choreographed my own performance." [5]

In her late teens she became interested in the new forms of dance that were introduced at that time. Isadora Duncan, who became tired of "artificial" dance forms, had developed a simple, natural style. Inspired by the art of ancient Greece, she advocated the natural use of the body clothed in loose garments, barefoot, on a stage with little or no scenery. One of the first great modern dancers was Mary Wigman, who used the new ideas of Rudolf von Laban of Germany. Wigman opened her own school and Riefenstahl became one of her outstanding students.

Before long she was appearing on stages all over Europe. Dresden, Munich, Berlin, Frankfurt, Prague, Zurich, Cologne . . . there was no rest for the ambitious and talented dancer. Accompanied by her mother and her pianist, Herbert Klamt, Riefenstahl couldn't satisfy the demand for performances in the various cities of the Continent. [6] The great German theater director Max Reinhardt engaged her for many productions, although he had never interviewed her personally.

"I was in a train, in the dining room, traveling to a location where my first film was to be made several years after I first danced for Max Reinhardt," Riefenstahl said, "when I noticed a man staring at me. He stared so long that I became nervous. Finally he came to the table and introduced himself. It was Max Reinhardt and he wanted to tell me how beautifully I danced. That was the first and only time I ever met him." [7]

That day on the train Reinhardt offered her a leading part in a play he intended to produce. She promised to join him as soon as she completed her film. Riefenstahl was never able to keep that promise. Two men, Dr. Arnold Fanck and Adolf Hitler, diverted her attention from Reinhardt.

During the period that Riefenstahl was developing into an excellent professional dancer and appearing on stages across the Continent, the infant German cinema was developing into a major industry. On November 1, 1895, only seven years before Riefenstahl was born, Max Skladanowsky presented the first moving pictures to a paying German audience in the Berlin Wintergarten. His system of projection was very complicated. It involved projecting two strips of films simultaneously through two projectors, which were alternately covered by shutters to allow alternate frames on the two strips to follow each other in logical sequence. Both rolls were projected at eight frames per second, producing, when combined, a frequency of sixteen frames per second.[8]

Skladanowsky's success was short-lived because of the complexity of the equipment, but other film pioneers built on the foundation he had established. One year later Oskar Messter opened his first "movement theatre," with artificial light, on the Friedrichstrasse in Berlin. After taking over his father's optical laboratory, Messter developed his own projection system, called *Kinematograph*, which transported the film through the camera without any jerking effect. Initially he produced short features in his studio, and at one time, early in his career, he had eighty-four such movies on the market. Later he produced *Andreas Hofer*, a full-length film about a Tyrolean folk hero of the Napoleonic period, which was filmed on location in the Tyrol rather than in a studio.

Messter even introduced "sound films" during the early years of the industry. Actually, he had entertainers before the camera mouth the words in synchronization with a gramophone hidden behind the screen. Crude as such productions were, they were very popular.[9]

Another pioneer filmmaker was Max Mack, a Jewish director well known in Berlin. He was one of the first to introduce closeups in German films and to use a hidden camera. His full-length feature *Der Andere* (*The Other One*) was one of the first films taken seriously by the critics.[10]

Young Riefenstahl, while busily engaged with her dancing career, was intrigued by these early films. Her parents, however, tried to discourage her from attending the movies. There was a good reason. The people who attended the early films were usually interested only in entertainment; unlike theater audiences, they were not artistically oriented. At least, that was the opinion of those German citizens who believed that a thorough background in the arts was a requirement for culture. Movie audiences did not have this background. They consisted mostly of unemployed men and women who had somehow managed to scrape together enough money for a ticket. They went to the movies because there was nothing else to do or because they could enjoy there some privacy and darkness with their lovers. For years the stage directors, actors, actresses, and writers of Germany ignored this new medium, thinking its requirements were far beneath their intelligence and skill. Consequently, the patrons of stage productions also ignored the film industry.

Riefenstahl attended a few movies despite her parents' objections, but she concentrated largely on her dancing. Her tours were very successful and she was making 600 and 700 marks for every performance.[11] She gave no thought to a film career. There was prestige to be gained in the theater, none in movies. As an accomplished professional dancer appearing in cities all over Europe, she felt that she was too artistic for filmmaking. She never regretted her early attachment to the stage. Many years later she admitted that her training as a dancer and her ability to paint had helped her achieve success in the cinema when at last she turned to it.

"These two elements, dance and painting, played a role in forming the style of composition and editing images that were mine," she said.[12]

Max Reinhardt also ignored the new medium as beneath his talents. Born Max Goldmann in Baden, near Vienna, he started as an actor and began directing plays in 1903, one year after Riefenstahl was born. He experimented with many new theatrical forms and styles, even transforming the inside of a theater to resemble a cathedral for one of his productions. He had his early stage training under Professor Emil Burde and appeared as an actor in several plays at Rudolfsheim and Salzburg. Later, Otto Brahm, who operated the Deutsches Theatre in Berlin, signed Reinhardt to a contract, and he appeared in Prague, Vienna, Budapest, and many other cities as well.

Reinhardt developed staging ideas of his own and decided he wanted to be a director instead of spending his entire career as an actor. In 1903 he broke his contract with Brahm and obtained assignments as director in the Klines Theatre and Neues Theatre productions. As his stage presentations became more ambitious, he bought his own group of theaters. He was constantly searching for new talent, and one of his discoveries was an excellent dancer with a "great shock of yellow hair," Leni Riefenstahl. Her hair was blonde at the time.

Dr. Arnold Fanck, who was also destined to play an important supporting role in Riefenstahl's controversial career, was one of the few who ignored stage presentations to study film techniques. Fanck was born in Freiburg in 1889, the same year that Adolf Hitler was born in the Austrian town of Braunau. A rather sickly young man, Fanck spent a great deal of time in the mountains. Skiing, mountain climbing, rugged living, the grandeur of the mountains fascinated him. Later, after he had earned a doctorate in geology, he combined vocation with avocation.

In 1920, the same year Riefenstahl began appearing regularly on stage as a dancer, Fanck decided that he wanted to produce films. With the help of some experienced camera crews he made a few short documentaries, but he was not satisfied with the results. It was then, while searching for a new idea for a film, that he thought of making a movie about mountain people, actually filmed in the mountains. Until that time, nearly all films were produced inside studios for reasons of cost and safety. Few actors were good skiers or climbers, and cameramen willing to risk their necks among the hazardous peaks in icy weather would be difficult if not impossible to find. Fanck, however, with his zeal for mountain life, was convinced that the Alpine terrain was ideal for cinematic effects, and that properly trained actors and actresses could produce a heightened tension there that would enthrall audiences.

In the end he had to develop his own crew of cameramen who were willing to conquer the new and hazardous technique of filming a scene while hurtling down a slope or hanging on the edge of a cliff. Hans Schneeberger, Sepp Allgeier, and Richard Angst were three of the most prominent cameramen to graduate from Fanck's Freiburger Kameraschule, and were not only experts in filming mountain scenes but skilled skiers as well. Once he had his crew trained to withstand the rigors of the mountains,

Fanck sought actors and actresses willing to perform under such dangerous and uncomfortable conditions. One of the best actresses he was to find was Leni Riefenstahl.

There were other Germans concentrating on their very different careers while Reinhardt, Fanck, and Messter developed new stage and film techniques and Riefenstahl flowered into a famous dancer. Two of these men would also play important parts in Riefenstahl's career.

Joseph Goebbels was born in Rheydt, a Rhineland textile center, in 1897. When he was four years old he contracted infantile paralysis, which left him with a permanently impaired foot. The illness also may have stunted his growth. As a young man he had a shrunken frame, stooped shoulders, and an unprepossessing appearance. Yet it was clear both to his parents and to those who jeered him that he was very intelligent. Straining the family budget to the utmost, Friedrich and Katherina Goebbels enrolled their son at the *Gymnasium*, the institution of higher learning in Rheydt. They didn't overestimate the brilliance of their son. One of the best scholars in the school, he often had the best record in his class. When he graduated from the *Gymnasium* in 1917 he passed the university entrance examinations with the highest honors.

Obtaining a loan from the Albertus Magnus Society, the important Catholic charitable organization, Goebbels entered Bonn University. Other universities followed: Freiburg, Würzburg, Cologne, Frankfurt, Munich, Berlin, and finally the University of Heidelberg, where he received a Doctor of Philosophy degree in 1921, at the age of twenty-four.

When Goebbels left the University of Heidelberg in 1921, the man who would one day put him in control of all artistic endeavors in Germany had just been elected the first president of the National Socialist German Workers' Party (NSDAP), which soon became known the world over as the Nazi party. Adolf Hitler was born in 1889. His parents, Alois and Klara, sent him to school in Linz, and they soon realized that he was not an excellent student. In fact, at the Linz *Realschule*, a technical school, he soon acquired an academic record that was so poor that he transferred to a second school to avoid suspension. He failed to graduate from this second school, too.

The poor grades neither embarrassed nor discouraged Hitler. He thought he had all the talent needed to become a great artist, and after his father died, he persuaded his mother to take part of her inheritance and enroll him in the Academy of Fine Arts in Vienna. Unfortunately for Hitler, a student had to prove his artistic skill before he could be enrolled, and, unlike Leni Riefenstahl, he had no talent as a painter. He was refused admittance. "Test drawing unsatisfactory" was the recorded decision.[13]

A second try in 1908 also failed, so Hitler gave up his artistic ambitions, although he was never convinced he could not have been a great artist. Radical politics became his passion instead. At the hostel on Meldemannstrasse in Vienna, where he stayed before World War I, he often argued politics so loudly that the porter had to warn him to quiet down so others could sleep. In a foretaste of the erratic behavior that would characterize him in later years, Hitler slipped out of Vienna in 1913 to avoid military service, only to write a formal letter to King Ludwig III of Bavaria requesting permission to join a Bavarian regiment as soon as the war began. The king never saw the letter but Hitler was granted his request and joined the First Company of the Sixteenth Bavarian Regiment, Infantry Reserve. Goebbels was refused permission to join the military because of his disability, but it was during this period that both men formed the political opinions that led them to join forces after the war and make their successful bid to control Germany.

Hitler was a fine soldier, much to the surprise of those who knew him before his military service. He was never promoted to a rank higher than corporal because of his eccentricities. He was incapable of small talk, was a loner, and unlike most soldiers, he volunteered for extra duties nearly every day. Yet he was awarded both the Iron Cross, Second Class, and the Iron Cross, First Class, and was commended by his commanding officers for bravery on several occasions. In 1918 he was treated at La Montagne after being gassed, then joined the guard detail at a prisoner-of-war camp at Traunstein.

As the political turmoil in postwar Germany became more violent, Hitler was assigned to the Commission of Inquiry of the Second Infantry Regiment in Munich. Actually, the members of this unit were informers checking on Communist sympathizers in the military and reporting them to their commanding officers.

As a member of the Commission of Inquiry, Hitler took a course of study at the University of Munich that explained the political philosophy of the various German military leaders. It was while he was attending the university that he first discovered his ability to sway an audience with his oratory. He joined the small German Workers' party, headed by Anton Drexler, a short time after completing his course of study at the university. With the financial aid of several German industrialists, he soon ousted Drexel and gained control of the party. He also raised enough money from his supporters to purchase the newspaper *Völkischer Beobachter* to propound his political views.

Hitler changed the name of his political party to the National Socialist German Workers' party ("Nazi" is derived from the German words *National* and *Sozialist*), enlarged the membership, and on the night of November 8, 1923, tried to seize control of Bavaria. The unsuccessful putsch started in the Bürgerbräukeller, a large beer hall, and was ever after known as the Beer Hall Putsch. The result was nineteen persons dead, many wounded, and a year's prison term at Landsberg Prison for Hitler. It was during his stay at the prison, fifty miles west of Munich, that he wrote *Mein Kampf*, his political blueprint for the future. Few Germans paid much attention to it. It was as clear as a Reinhardt or Fanck script, but few Germans believed then that this radical politician would ever amount to much. One man who read *Mein Kampf* and became convinced that Hitler would someday rule all of Germany was Ernst Röhm, who with Hermann Göring had organized Hitler's private army, the Sturmabteilung (SA). The relationship between Röhm and Hitler in the Nazi party's climb to power was to be an important feature of Riefenstahl's famous film *Triumph des Willens*.

The year 1924, a pivotal one for Riefenstahl, found those who were or would soon be involved in her controversial career in varying situations. Hitler was in Landsberg Prison writing *Mein Kampf* after his abortive putsch in Munich. He had resigned his leadership of the Nazi party for the duration of his imprisonment, and most Germans thought his political career was over. Goebbels, the future dictator of German artistic endeavors, was getting nowhere despite his numerous university degrees. After a stint as a clerk at the Cologne Stock Exchange, he failed to get work on the *Berliner Tageblatt,* and then sought a job in the theater. Finally he managed to become secretary to Franz Wiegershaus, Reichstag deputy of the People's Freedom party, and was permitted to write articles for the Nazi party journal. Dissatisfied with this position, he approached Karl Kaufmann, the Nazi *Gauleiter* for the Rhine-Ruhr district, and offered to work for him in hopes of rising in the party. Kaufmann, who always needed help in spreading the gospel of the struggling political party, appointed Goebbels to the staff of the northern Nazi party organization. Like Hitler, he was not considered a likely candidate for high political office in 1924.

In the arts, Riefenstahl's supporters and soon-to-be associates were doing much better. Max Reinhardt was general director of the Theater in der Josefstadt in Vienna. He was looking for an actress to play the part of Penthesilea, the last queen of the Amazons, in a play he was planning to produce. This was the part he offered Riefenstahl in 1924 when they met on the train to Switzerland. Dr. Arnold Fanck was completing a mountain film entitled *Der Berg des Schicksals (Peak of Destiny),* which he produced, directed, and wrote. He had been making his famous mountain films since 1921 and German audiences awaited each new one with eager anticipation. Working with him on *Der Berg des Schicksals* were Sepp Allgeier, Hans Schneeberger, and Luis Trenker.[14] The first two were his specially trained photographers, now expert in handling the movie cameras in the dangerous mountain terrain. Trenker, a former mountain guide, was an actor Fanck first hired in 1921 for his first mountain film, *Das Wunder des Schneeschuhs (The Marvel of Skis).* By 1924 he was a star. Fanck desperately needed an actress who could ski as well as act, and who had the courage to make a film in the uncomfortable mountain environment.

Fortunately for Fanck, Riefenstahl injured her knee while dancing. Despite treatments by the best doctors in Berlin, the knee refused to heal and the pain became worse. Finally a specialist told her that an immediate operation was necessary; delay might mean a permanently stiff knee. She agreed to the operation, which revealed she was suffering from torn cartilage and a bone tumor.[15] While convalescing, she went to the theater and saw *Der Berg des Schicksals*. It made a strong impression upon her. She was captivated by the terrain, by the challenge of real snow, real ice, real danger. It brought out her Teutonic admiration for the heroic idealism of Germans who sought to conquer the peaks. In addition, the film awakened in her an enthusiasm for movie-making that studio-made films had never aroused. She had no film experience, she could not ski, and she did not know Arnold Fanck; nevertheless, she determined to leave the hot lights of the stage for the frigid peaks of the Alps and films.[16]

3

Mountain Films

Much has been written about Dr. Fanck's mountain films and Riefenstahl's part in them. Siegfried Kracauer, an authority on the German cinema and the social and economic structures of the German middle classes, believed that the heroism depicted in the mountain films was "rooted in a mentality kindred to the Nazi spirit." [1] He was convinced that the German idolatry of glaciers and rocks was symptomatic of an antirationalism on which the Nazis could capitalize.

Susan Sontag, the prominent filmmaker, writer, and critic, agrees: "The mountain climbing in Fanck's pictures was a visual metaphor of unlimited aspiration toward the high mystic goal, both beautiful and terrifying, which was later to become concrete in Führer worship." [2] She denounced the films as proto-Nazi, although admitting they were probably not considered political when they were made, since Hitler was still a struggling radical politician at the time.

Others see no particular political ideology, direct or indirect, in the mountain films. Walter Laqueur, director of the Institute of Contemporary History and the Wiener Library in London, says that "if the films contained a political message it was carefully hidden." [3] He agrees that mountaineering was not then one of the favorite sports of German intellectuals, but does not agree that this made it a fascist activity. Many of those associated with Riefenstahl and Fanck during the filming of the mountain movies later refused to produce propaganda films for the Third Reich.

Certainly there were no political overtones to Riefenstahl's approach to Fanck. The beautiful, graceful dancer was ambitious, very ambitious, and when she recognized that the future of the film industry was far greater than the future of stage productions featuring dancers such as herself, she made her move. Riefenstahl's basic character has never really changed. She was, and is, an opportunist, a woman of courage who challenged men in a man's world, an intelligent person who always planned carefully and used every available resource to further her ambitions. Among her resources were her great beauty, warmth, and femininity, which often swayed the opinions of strong men. When she once made up her mind that she wanted to star in films, she permitted nothing to stand in her way. The politics of Hitler and his minor political party were far from her mind if, in fact, she had ever heard of them.

She arranged to meet Luis Trenker, the star of *Der Berg des Schicksals*. Trenker introduced her to Fanck, who was fascinated by the tall, sensual dancer and immediately recognized that she would be a definite asset on the screen. Fanck was aware that Riefenstahl was not an experienced skier or mountain climber, but he did decide to sign her to a contract to appear as a dancer in his next film, *Der heilige Berg (The Holy Mountain)*. Through past experience Fanck had learned that it was impossible to find an actress who could also ski and climb mountains like a professional. He always had to compromise. With Riefenstahl, of course, he far underestimated her stubbornness, determination, and ambition.

The operation on her injured knee was a success. Her knee healed much faster than the doctor had predicted, and there was no sign of stiffness.[4] The delight Riefenstahl felt over her complete recovery was lessened by the decision she faced once she was ready to go back to work. She was in great demand as a dancer. Contracts were offered her by producers in numerous cities of Europe, and her loyal fans were waiting patiently to see her again. Max Reinhardt was trying to persuade her to keep her promise to play the part of Penthesilea, the last queen of the

Amazons. At the same time, Fanck asked her to appear in *Der heilige Berg*. Riefenstahl evaluated the three opportunities carefully and finally decided that the mountain films of Arnold Fanck offered the best future. She signed the contract to appear in *Der heilige Berg*.

In this silent film she played a young dancer named Diotima who was converted to the ecstasies of the mountains. Appearing opposite her was the established film star Luis Trenker, whom Fanck relied upon to help Riefenstahl learn the nuances of acting before a camera. It was an intelligent decision, and the handsome actor and the sensual dancer were soon inseparable. In addition to having an experienced actor to aid her, Riefenstahl was fortunate in having three of the best directors of photography in the film industry working on the picture: Sepp Allgeier, Albert Benitz, and Hans Schneeberger. This trio was also captivated by the exuberant beauty, and in later years one or more of them almost always worked on her films. Fanck also gave her invaluable instruction in her first film role.

Fanck had an enormous amount of patience with her, and he needed it all. Before filming started, Riefenstahl set out to become an accomplished skier. Already she was looking into the future. She realized that Fanck would not need a dancer in every film, so she would have to be prepared to handle other roles if she were to appear in more of his pictures . . . and become a star.

She persuaded Luis Trenker to go with her to Cortina d'Ampezzo in Italy and give her skiing instructions. The second day she fell and broke a bone in her foot. The foot was put in a cast and she was ordered to stay off it for four weeks. Fanck was furious, but before he could make up his mind whether to get another dancer for her part, one of the male actors he was depending upon because of his skiing ability was also injured. In addition, the weather in the mountains turned bad, making filming impossible.[5]

Since the film was financed by Ufa (Universum Film Aktien Gesellschaft), the officers of this firm had a great deal of influence over the project. After the delay because of Riefenstahl's injury was compounded by the bad weather, it became obvious to them that the film would never be completed on schedule. They decided that to invest additional money in it would be a waste, so they withdrew from the project, leaving Fanck and his cast and crew abandoned in the middle of production. Fanck explained the situation to them: He could make the film if they would agree to advance their own expenses and wait for payment of their salaries until the picture was completed and began to earn money. They decided to go ahead. It was a gamble, but Riefenstahl never shied away from a gamble if she thought her chances of winning were good.

Even during this first film, she planned for the future. Not only did she become intimately acquainted with the excellent cameramen and with Trenker, but she watched every move Fanck made. When he gave orders to the crew or the cast, she didn't automatically do as he said, or stand idly by while the crew obeyed him. She asked Fanck the reason for the order, and sought information from him about every phase of filmmaking. In fact, her curiosity and ambition during the filming of *Der heilige Berg* nearly brought an abrupt end to her career. During the filming of a scene in which she did not appear, Riefenstahl stood beside a camera to watch the cameraman at work. It was a night scene and she was eager to learn the filming techniques used for darkness. Unfortunately, one of the lights exploded and burned one side of her face so seriously that a doctor who treated her shook his head and muttered, "Riefenstahl will never again be able to appear before the camera." [6]

"Never again" lasted six months. Her face healed; she made the long journey back to the mountains and completed her scenes in *Der heilige Berg*. When Ufa officials saw the edited film, they were so overjoyed by it that they took over distribution. The movie was a financial success, but more important to Riefenstahl, the critics praised her performance and the audiences loved her.

Fanck, of course, was delighted with his new discovery and quickly arranged for her to appear in his next film, *Der grosse Sprung (The Great Leap)*. This film was released in 1927. The director was so engrossed in his own filmmaking and so enthusiastic about his new star that he paid little attention to Riefenstahl's extraordinary interest in every phase of the production. When he did notice her seemingly endless stream of questions, he thought it was only because she was new to the medium and movie-making fascinated her. He didn't realize that Riefenstahl was thinking far into the future, that she wanted to direct as well as star in her own films.

"I had to learn to ski, to climb, and, by the press of circumstances," Riefenstahl said, "I also found myself involved with the camera work and at times I collaborated with the director's crew. I never stopped watching, observing, asking questions." [7]

As she became more experienced, Riefenstahl began to see things somewhat differently than Fanck did, and when the director dismissed her suggestions with a wave of his hand, she became more determined than ever that one day she would make her own films in her own way. Yet Germany in the late 1920s was hardly the place for a woman to launch a career as a film director. All film directors, producers, and executives were men; any woman who tried to scale the heights in a man's world was certain to create enemies. Women were expected to concern themselves with *Küche, Kinder, Kirche* (kitchen, children, church), and when a few women invaded the fields of medicine, law, and industrial management, there was an uproar that lasted until the Nazi party came to power in 1933. Hitler, of course, did not approve of professionally trained women. Women were excluded from membership in the Nazi party executive as early as 1921. He believed that motherhood or work consonant with women's "natural" inclinations, like domestic service, saleswork, farmwork, and, during the war, factory work, was the proper activity for women. This attitude, of course, only makes Riefenstahl's later career the more remarkable.

In her third mountain film, *Die weisse Hölle vom Piz Palü (The White Hell of Pitz Palu)*, Riefenstahl showed great improvement as an actress. By this time she was also well on her way to becoming an accomplished skier and mountain climber, so that her overall performance in the film drew raves. In this 1929 film she plays the part of a young woman trapped on a ledge with her husband and a doctor. The young husband wants to kill himself to end the ordeal, but in the end the doctor sacrifices himself to save the couple. This simple story was filmed in some of the most dangerous terrain in Europe and under weather conditions that would have discouraged most actresses from ever completing the movie.

"The difference between our mountain films and those made by other directors," Riefenstahl explained, "is that Dr. Fanck never wanted to use a double, didn't use tricks. He wanted everything to be real. Sometimes the scenes were so real, like the time I was buried in an avalanche, that the critics in Berlin wrote that it can't be true, that it was 'faked' in a studio." [8]

Die weisse Hölle vom Piz Palü was not entirely Fanck's own production. Ladislaus Vajda coscripted the screenplay and G. W. Pabst, a leading figure in German cinema, controlled the overall film. The assistant director was Marc Sorki, who later described his feelings about the production:

> That was a wonderful picture. The original was shot on location in Switzerland, and it was terribly cold in the mountains in winter. Most of the cast and the crew came down with pneumonia. Pabst and Fanck both had a sadistic drive. We really froze. All night long we drank hot wine and punch just to keep breathing. And I must say, Riefenstahl was wonderful. Never mind what she did later during the Third Reich, but in this picture she was driving herself as hard as anybody and more. She worked day and night. Schneeberger was in love with her and she with him and they were an excellent team. She would work extremely hard, harder than anybody. Even Pabst had to admire her. He said: "It's terrible. What a woman!" [9]

The film was very successful. A review that appeared in a Swiss newspaper stated:

> Here, as never before, is the living spirit of the mountains, vivid, rare, terrifying and lovely. Other mountain films we have had but we have never had *mountains*—almost personifiable, things of wild and free moods, forever changing. Nobody who loves the hills could fail to be held by this tribute to their splendor. The heroine is Leni Riefenstahl, renewed and unexpectedly fresh,

unexpectedly charming. There is a flowing, free rhythm, breath-catching beauty, genuine suspense.[10]

The critic Alexander Bakshy, who reviewed the film when it appeared in the United States, liked it, too.

> Although a great deal of the danger in which characters in screen thrillers are so frequently found is nothing but screen illusion, there is no denying the purely physical appeal of such a record of Alpine adventure as *The White Hell of Pitz Palu.* Here nature itself is alive with drama as it bares its gaping abysses, rises in towering walls of ice or breaks into the fury of blizzards and avalanches. Added to this is a visual loveliness that casts a sweet enchantment even over the perils of Alpine mountaineering or at least so it appears to one ensconced in a comfortable chair as he watches the Alpine glories so amazingly recorded in this German film.[11]

It was obvious by this time that Riefenstahl had arrived at film stardom, and her services were in demand by many movie producers besides Fanck. Yet, except for *Das Schicksal derer von Habsburg* (*The Destiny of the Hapsburgs*), in which she appeared in 1929, Riefenstahl stayed with the mountain films of Fanck. He became her Svengali, she his rapt pupil. In 1930 she appeared in the Fanck film *Stürme über dem Montblanc* (*Storms over Mont Blanc*), her first sound film. She conquered this hurdle very easily, since she had a fine speaking voice. The following year she starred in *Die weisse Rausch* (*The White Frenzy*), another Fanck film.

By this time Riefenstahl had established herself firmly as a star. She was world-famous, beautiful, self-assured, and an excellent trouper who knew filmmaking before and behind the camera, thanks to Arnold Fanck. She felt that it was time she broke from her Svengali and made a film on her own.

"I set about seeking a thread, a theme, a style, in the realm of legend," she explained. "Something that might allow me to give free rein to my juvenile sense of romanticism and the beautiful image." [12]

She selected an idea that she had first thought of while she was still a dancer. One of her dancing successes was called *The Blue Flower,* and when she combined the theme of the dance with the beauty and hazards of the mountains, the result was the initial script for her first try as a director, *Das blaue Licht (The Blue Light).* The story line was based on a legend from the Dolomites. According to the legend, on nights of the full moon a blue light shone from the mountain and lured young men from the villages below to their deaths. Riefenstahl plays Junta, a mountain girl, who alone of the villagers knows that the blue light on Mount Cristallo is a glimmering beam emitted when moonlight strikes the crystalline rocks in a grotto. When others try to follow Junta as she climbs a secret path to the grotto, they fall to their deaths or are lost. Eventually Vigo, an artist who had moved to the village and fallen in love with Junta, successfully follows her up the path. When he discovers the valuable crystal rocks, he tells the villagers about them in the belief that they will stop considering Junta a witch and persecuting her. But the villagers greedily strip the grotto of the valuable rocks, leaving not even one for Junta. Junta, convinced that her lover has betrayed her, leaps to her death from the top of Mount Cristallo.

Riefenstahl has said:

> Junta was happy with the blue light. It was a symbol to her, an ideal. Vigo was a good man but he was a realistic person. He didn't understand her idealism. When her ideal was destroyed, Junta no longer wanted to live. I have seen this in life very often. People who love beauty and have an ideal, when they must face the realistic world, they are broken. [13]

The idealism of *Das blaue Licht,* the methods Riefenstahl used to obtain the necessary financing to make the movie, and the way she assembled her cast and crew revealed her true character. Riefenstahl's "blue light" was her determination to direct and produce her own film and she was willing to go to practically any length to achieve this dream . . . just as she was later, during the Third Reich, in an effort to fulfill her craving for recognition in the film world. She learned all of Fanck's techniques, all his secrets of filmmaking. She made friends with his best cameramen, his actors and actresses, his financial advisers. When she decided to go out on her own, she felt no remorse about raiding Fanck's production unit.

One of the first of Fanck's crew to join her venture was Hans Schneeberger, the skilled cameraman upon whom the producer depended. It was easy for Riefenstahl to gain his services as cameraman, as she and Schneeberger had been lovers for several years. She asked Walter Traut to supervise the production activities of *Das blaue Licht,* and he too did not hesitate to leave the Fanck fold. Traut would perform this function on all future Riefenstahl films. Another Fanck employee who joined the *blaue Licht* crew was young Heinz von Jaworsky, a camera assistant to Schneeberger, who later said: "Salary was rock-bottom minimum—low-budget production and no unions involved—but everyone in the company was in the same situation. We all just loved what she did."

Guzzi Lantschner, a world champion skier, readily agreed to appear in the film. He was one of her former boy friends, one of her many romances. In fact, the production became cluttered with Riefenstahl's fiancés, boy friends, and former boy friends. When she needed money she went to Harry Sokal, a former fiancé, who agreed to subsidize her new film company, Riefenstahl-Film GmbH. She needed about 50,000 additional marks over her own savings to produce *Das blaue Licht* and Sokal provided this amount.

In addition to Fanck's personnel and filmmaking techniques, Riefenstahl gained another advantage from her association with Fanck. Béla Balázs was one of the leaders of the German avant-garde, a respected intellectual who liked Fanck's mountain films despite their simplistic story lines. Fanck became acquainted with Balázs and eventually introduced him to Riefenstahl. When she began preparations for *Das blaue Licht,* she brazenly asked the well-known writer and theorist to help her with the scenario. He not only agreed to help her with the script, but when the actual shooting began, Balázs traveled to the mountains to supervise.

"I was very lucky that he could take off three or four weeks to be present and in control for the most important scenes in which I acted." Riefenstahl admitted.[14]

Balázs, a Jewish Marxist, later regretted his association with

Riefenstahl on *Das blaue Licht,* and Riefenstahl eventually forgot her appreciation of his assistance. But at least she acknowledged his help in the credits. Another renowned film writer who helped Riefenstahl with the script for this picture was not so fortunate. Carl Mayer was one of the greatest screenwriters in Germany during the silent film era, responsible for such screenplays as *Berlin: Die Symphonie einer Grosstadt* (*Berlin: A City of Symphony*), Sonneraufgang (*Sunrise*), and the famous *Das Kabinett des Dr. Caligari.* He was a close friend of Riefenstahl's and spent a great deal of time with her while she was making this movie, but she did not give him a single line of credit. The credits for *Das blaue Licht* read: "A mountain legend of the Dolomites transformed into pictures by Leni Riefenstahl, Béla Balázs, Hans Schneeberger." Of course, there was no mention of Arnold Fanck's indirect and direct contribution to the film.

There is no denying, however, that Riefenstahl was in charge of the production and that she originated many of the techniques that made this film such an outstanding success. Her innovations were many and were copied by other filmmakers in later years. She even surprised her former Svengali. She showed Fanck a copy of the script before she started shooting and he told her that it would be impossible to infuse mysticism into Junta's climbing of Mount Cristallo unless she had a large studio and a lot of money, and didn't use outside arc lights. Riefenstahl recalled:

> Dr. Fanck was very pessimistic. I didn't give up, however, and after three days I got the idea that if I make the mountain full of fog and she climbs through this fog it will add the unrealistic effect that I want. The problem was how to do it. I decided to use smoke bombs but we had to wait until it was not too stormy. The smoke bombs were very successful. They put the whole mountain in "fog." [15]

She even had an argument with Schneeberger, who loved her very much but didn't want her to tell him how to use the camera. He had years of experience behind a movie camera and was recognized throughout the film industry as one of its top cameramen. So when Riefenstahl suggested that he put a green filter with a red filter, he refused; such an arrangement would result in no picture at all, he said. Riefenstahl, always stubborn, insisted, and finally the angry Schneeberger did as she wanted. Instead of no picture, the combination of filters resulted in the new, unexpected magical effect that made *Das blaue Licht* so different. Eventually she and Schneeberger resumed their former relationship, the argument forgotten.

Jaworsky, who worked with her on this and other films, characterized her this way:

> She was very hard to work with because she had a source of energy that was incredible. Her mind was always unwinding. She was always thinking about what she was doing night and day. We would be dead tired after a day of shooting in the mountains in bitter cold weather but she would get us all together that night and review what we did and tell us about the plans for the next day. I had great respect for her but it was hard working with her. [16]

It was not all work, however. One of the main problems during the long stay in the mountains was the dissension among the male members of the production unit caused by the rapid turnover among her lovers. At one time or another she was rumored to be in love with Schneeberger, Sokal, Trenker, and Lantschner, and there were others.

"It was sometimes very difficult," she admitted, "because we stayed in the mountains for many months and I was the only woman."

Yet she had no difficulty getting the men to take directions from her even if they were jealous of each other. She had the ability to have a relationship with a man for awhile and then, when the relationship ended, to keep his friendship. In the crew of her *Das blaue Licht,* as well as in the crews of later films she directed, Riefenstahl managed to have lovers and former lovers working together smoothly. She later explained:

> In the selection of a staff I always had to have the feeling that we would find each other sympathetic so that we would be able to go

through thick and thin together. Throughout the whole three months of shooting, there were never any bad moods, nagging or even dissatisfaction. It was really ideal togetherness. We were just like a family of eight. Everything was paid out of a common pot. Everyone tried to spend as little as possible to keep the pot alive as long as possible. If anyone had torn shoes or needed anything urgently, it was paid from the pot. I myself abstained from any personal purchases for fourteen months.[17]

Das blaue Licht was released in 1932 and was an outstanding success. Riefenstahl's beauty, the magnificent scenery, and the unusual visual effects captivated audiences in Germany and abroad. The *New York Sun*, in a review published on May 9, 1934, called it "one of the most pictorially beautiful films of the year. Leni Riefenstahl—author, director and star—is an expert climber as well as a handsome woman."

Marguerite Tazelaar said in the *New York Herald Tribune* that same day, ". . . for sheer pictorial beauty, [the film] is perhaps unexcelled. Told with absorbing intensity . . . How flawlessly this girl, who plays the lead and also wrote and directed, accomplished her task."

The film won the gold medal at the Venice Film Festival in 1932. At thirty years of age Leni Riefenstahl had reached a stature that made her famous not only in the film industry but among people in all walks of life. Politicians went to the movies, and one politician in particular, Adolf Hitler, had long loved the mountains. Although he still had not reached his goal of becoming chancellor ·of Germany, Hitler had already acquired his retreat in the mountains near Berchtesgaden, south of Munich. Called Haus Wachenfeld, the cottage had originally been built for a German industrialist and was later to become the world-renowned Berghof. Whenever he had the time, Hitler would leave the political turmoil and spend several days in the mountains he loved. When he learned in 1932 that *Das blaue Licht* was considered excellent, he arranged to see it. He too was fascinated by the scenery and visual effects of the movie. He was also fascinated by the star, Leni Riefenstahl. He did not forget her name.

Another movie fan who would spend a great deal of time at Hitler's retreat in the Bavarian Alps during the ensuing years was having his problems in 1932. In February, Joseph Goebbels was barred from the Reichstag for causing an uproar and insulting President Hindenburg. Later in the year he was indicted for high treason, but the charge was quashed when he accepted the mandate of the Prussian Diet. Even this turmoil was not permitted to interfere with Goebbels' admiration of a beautiful woman. He was well aware of Leni Riefenstahl and the acclaim she received after the release of *Das blaue Licht*. One of his most enjoyable pastimes was bedding beautiful women, an avocation he followed with great glee after he became czar of the Nazi cinema and could contol the careers of lovely actresses. The one actress who would not take his orders in later years when he gained such power was Leni Riefenstahl. She would take her orders directly from Hitler.

Riefenstahl starred in another Fanck film after *Das blaue Licht*. *S.O.S. Eisberg* (*S.O.S. Iceberg*) was made under the auspices of the Danish government on location in Greenland and coproduced by Fanck, Ernst Sorge of Deutsche Film, and Carl Laemmle of Universal.

"I only acted in it," Riefenstahl said. "When Dr. Fanck agreed to do the film, he couldn't find anyone who could handle the role because it required great physical effort. This was the last film in which I was only an actress." [18]

She was not exaggerating when she said that the role "required great physical effort." A cablegram from Dr. Fanck at Umanak, Greenland, to Carl Laemmle at Universal described some of the hazards:

A true miracle saved the lives of Fanck and associates making *S.O.S. Eisberg* among icebergs off west Greenland coast. Ernst Udet, the pilot, making a low flight over huge icebergs for the benefit of the cameras located on top of an iceberg, lost power on the engine of the plane and he crashed at the base of the iceberg. Only the propeller was broken and Udet was rescued by Eskimos. Within a few minutes after Udet was brought ashore, the iceberg on which Dr. Fanck, Hans Schneeberger and August Zogg were established with their cameras and sound recording equipment broke up. Half of the gigantic icy mass crumbled to bits, carrying men and equipment into the water below. The production unit ship anchored nearby was so severely shaken by the falling ice mass that the main mast top came within a few feet of the water and the ship very nearly capsized. Several persons standing along the rail were thrown into the water. Eskimos in their kaiaks and members of the ship's crew in motorboats rescued ten men and two women of the unit from drowning but considerable sound equipment was destroyed.[19]

S.O.S. Eisberg was another melodrama of the frozen wilds. Besides Riefenstahl, the principals in the cast were Gibson Gowland, Rod La Rocque, and Walter Riml. La Rocque plays Dr. Carl Lawrence, who heads a search party hunting for an expedition that has been missing for a year in the wilds of the frozen north. Riefenstahl, as his wife, eventually has to save him after he becomes lost and exhausted.

Much of Riefenstahl's time was spent in a plane making daring flights over the icebergs and glaciers. While it appeared that she was piloting the aircraft, the famous World War I ace Ernst Udet was actually at the controls, crouched low in the cockpit so the cameras would not reveal his presence. Udet and Riefenstahl became intimate friends during the making of this film and remained close after he became a general in the *Luftwaffe* during the Third Reich.

S.O.S. Eisberg was released in 1933 and was the last film Riefenstahl made before the establishment of the Third Reich, which so drastically changed her life. By the time this film was shown to audiences around the world, her image as an innocent young girl was established. The cult that had grown up around Riefenstahl revered this image of her, convinced that she stood for idealism, love of beauty, the clean life of the simple mountain people who were strangers to greed and sin. People found her a refreshing contrast to the new sex wave that swept Germany before the Third Reich. Nude shows, hard pornography, and moral corruption permeated Berlin, which became known as the entertainment capital of Europe during the 1920s and early 1930s. There were also flourishing trades in drugs, prostitution, and gambling. Venereal disease was widespread. It was a period of escapism, an era of "anything goes."

At the beginning of 1933, when Adolf Hitler was maneuvering himself toward the chancellorship, the millions of Germans who idolized Leni Riefenstahl thought she could do no wrong. They were dedicated to her film image, thinking that this was also her off-screen image.

They were wrong!

4

The New Führer

During 1932, while Leni Riefenstahl enjoyed great popularity and acclaim, Adolf Hitler and the Nazi party were in deep trouble. He had thought the chancellorship would be his long before this, or, as he so enjoyed stating, he would be in power through *Machtergreifung* (seizure of power). Yet neither legally nor illegally had he been able to assume power. His tactics became more and more violent. His private army of Storm Troopers, originally recruited as bodyguards and bouncers to protect him and his companions at their meetings, was now known as the Sturmabteilung (SA). The Storm Troopers, growing rapidly in numbers, were difficult even for Hitler to control. They engaged in blackmail, fought in the streets, often sacked public buildings during riots they themselves instigated. Once, angry over Goebbels' remarks, the SA even attacked the Berlin headquarters of the Nazi party and sent Goebbels scurrying for police protection.

Hitler wanted a tough, violent SA, but he wanted the organization under his strict control so that he could use the pent-up violence of the paramilitary force for his own purposes. He asked Ernst Röhm, his friend of the 1923 putsch in Munich, to return from La Paz, Bolivia, to head the SA. Röhm quickly agreed when Hitler promised him complete freedom in his new assignment. It was a decision that would cost Röhm his life in 1934, when Hitler decided that the SA commander was more of a hindrance than a help. But in 1932, when Hitler was still struggling for power, Röhm built the SA and the Schutzstaffel (SS), an elite group of about 15,000 men formed from a nucleus of Hitler's personal bodyguards, into a powerful and much-feared part of the Nazi organization.

Hitler recognized that the economic situation and the unrest in Germany provided him with a favorable opportunity to assume power. Nearly 21 million Germans were hungry and the unemployment figures rose out of sight. Hitler promised time and time again during this period that if he were given power in Germany he would make certain everyone had enough to eat, increase employment, and ensure Germany's rise from the degradation of defeat in World War I to a position of world power. Many of the country's citizens, desperate for help, desperate for change, believed him. Nazi party membership doubled in 1931 to over three-quarters of a million. Many of those who joined were also convinced that Hitler was right when he said that the Jews in Germany were the cause of much of the hunger, despair, and misery.

In 1932, the year that Riefenstahl's film *Das blaue Licht* was released, Hitler faced a decision critical to his political future. Should he run for the presidency of Germany? The odds against him were great. President von Hindenburg, though an old man presiding over a country in deep economic trouble, still had a large following and a sturdy, honest image. Hitler appealed to voters of lower status. He knew that if he opposed Hindenburg in the March 1932 election and received a small number of votes, his political future would be destroyed. Hitler delayed announcing his candidacy until February 22, when Goebbels spoke at the Sportpalast in Berlin. Goebbels noted in his diary:

Sportpalast packed. General meeting of the members of the northern, eastern and western districts. Immense ovations at the very outset. When after about an hour's preparation I publicly proclaim that the Leader will come forward as candidate for the Presidency, a storm of deafening applause rages for nearly ten minutes. Wild ovation for the Leader. The audience rises with shouts of joy. They nearly raise the roof. An overwhelming spectacle.[1]

The vote on March 13, 1932, was:

| Hindenburg | 18,651,497 | 49.6% |
| Hitler | 11,339,446 | 30.1% |

Hitler received enough votes to look far from ridiculous. In fact, since Hindenburg missed obtaining an absolute majority by 0.4 percent, the law required a new election. Before that election, scheduled for April 10, 1932, Goebbels organized campaign air trips for Hitler, a highly unusual election tactic at the time. Using the slogan "Hitler over Germany," Hitler flew from one city to another to speak to gatherings of his followers, sometimes visiting four large cities in one day. At one time he spoke in twenty-six cities in a week. Riefenstahl used air travel and the "Hitler over Germany" slogan to good advantage two years later when she made the film *Triumph des Willens*. The very dramatic opening of this film, Hitler's plane on its way to Nuremberg, is considered one of the most impressive scenes of the entire production.

While Hitler garnered more votes in the April election than he had in March, he actually lost political ground, because this time Hindenburg won an absolute majority:

| Hindenburg | 19,359,983 | 53.0% |
| Hitler | 13,418,547 | 36.8% |

The additional two million votes that Hitler gained were of no use to him because the presidency remained intact. Even during the Reichstag elections in July the Nazi party made only a small improvement in its standing, ending up with 230 seats out of a total of 608. While Hitler was discouraged, he still considered his party the strongest in Germany and himself the prime candidate for the chancellorship when the time was right. As he sat in a car the night after the July elections, Ernst (Putzi) Hanfstaengl, the party foreign press chief, heard Hitler say: *"Wir werden schon sehen"* ("We shall see").[2]

Not all of Hitler's time was spent on politics during this period. He enjoyed the attention of women, both romantic and platonic, and he spent many hours away from the political campaign in the company of adoring beauties. In December 1931 Goebbels had married Magda Quant, an attractive and wealthy divorcee who ranked high in the social circles of Berlin. Magda was an impulsive, emotional woman, fascinated not only by her new husband but by Hitler and the power politics of the Nazi party. Hitler soon became devoted to her too, admiring her beauty, her femininity, her quick wit, and the excellent care she gave her children by her former marriage. She was an experienced hostess and Hitler began visiting the Goebbels' luxurious apartment on the Reichskanzlerplatz, where Magda mothered him and listened to him talk for hours. Both Magda and her husband had an unending enthusiasm for finding female companionship for Hitler. One of the young women who appeared at the Goebbels' apartment was Leni Riefenstahl.[3]

Just when Riefenstahl first met Hitler is not known; she has given various versions of the initial meeting. Many are convinced that she wrote to Hitler after hearing him announce his candidacy in the Berlin Sportpalast in February 1932, and that their first meeting was arranged shortly afterward.[4] Luis Trenker thinks they probably met at a tiny Baltic resort they both frequented before 1933. He tells of an incident that occurred during the filming of *S.O.S. Eisberg* in 1932:

> At that time she was employed by Universal. She was expected in Hamburg—a whole company was to sail for the Balearic Islands to shoot a film on location. Udet and Fanck, the producer, were getting nervous, afraid to miss the boat—and Leni Riefenstahl was still absent. For days she had been missing and no one knew where she was. At last there came a telephone message. Hitler's private plane had just landed. Leni had been the Führer's guest in a place near Nuremberg. She walked into the hotel lobby with a tremendous bouquet of flowers; her eyes seemed to gaze into the distance, her whole being was transformed. She wanted everyone to know that she had just passed through a wonderful experience.[5]

It is certain that Riefenstahl knew Hitler in 1932. Hanfstaengl visited the Goebbels' apartment one night that year when both Riefenstahl and Hitler were present.

Riefenstahl was a very vital and attractive woman and had little difficulty in persuading the Goebbels and Hitler to go to her studio after dinner. I was taken along and found it full of mirrors and trick interior decorating effects but better than one would expect. There was a piano there, so that got rid of me, and the Goebbels, who wanted to leave the field free, leaned on it chatting. Out of the corner of my eye I could see Hitler ostentatiously studying the titles in the bookcases. Riefenstahl, I must say, was giving him the works. Every time he straightened up or looked around, there she was dancing to my music at his elbow, a real summer sale of feminine charm. I had to grin to myself. I caught the Goebbels' eyes, as if to say, "If Riefenstahl can't manage him no one can so we might as well leave." So we made our excuses, leaving them alone.[6]

Throughout his entire career Hitler insisted on keeping his personal life secret from the public. Consequently, when he first became acquainted with Riefenstahl, only his inner circle of friends was aware of it. These close associates were also the only ones who were aware that since 1929 he had been very close to a young girl named Eva Braun. She was the daughter of a schoolteacher, and twenty-three years his junior. During the summer of 1932, when Hitler neglected Eva Braun because of political matters and because of his association with Riefenstahl and other women, she became very depressed. On the night of November 1, 1932, she tried to kill herself with her father's 6.35-mm. pistol. The bullet lodged near the neck artery and only quick action by a doctor saved her life.[7] After this incident Hitler was more attentive to Eva Braun, but he certainly did not neglect Riefenstahl.

Hitler would not permit any woman to interfere with his ultimate goal of assuming power in Germany, however. After the July elections for the Reichstag, when his party won only 37 percent of the seats but more than any other party, he demanded that President von Hindenburg name him chancellor. The President replied that he could not do so because he would not be able to answer for such an act to God, his conscience, or the Fatherland. Hindenburg made his rebuke publicly, and Hitler retired to his Bavarian mountain retreat to lick his wounds. It was there that three American journalists interviewed him. One of them, H. V. Kaltenborn, asked him a significant question, and in his answer Hitler clearly outlined what he intended to do if and when he assumed power in Germany. Kaltenborn asked him why he was so antagonistic toward the Jews. Hitler shouted:

> You have a Monroe Doctrine for America. We believe in a Monroe Doctrine for Germany. You exclude any would-be immigrants you do not care to admit. You regulate their number. You demand that they come up to a certain physical standard. You insist that they bring in a certain amount of money. You examine them as to their political opinions. We demand the same right. We have no concern with the Jews of other lands. But we are concerned about any anti-German elements in our own country. And we demand the right to deal with them as we see fit. Jews have been the proponents of subversive anti-German movements and as such must be dealt with.[8]

Many of the great artists, screenwriters, actors and actresses, sculptors, writers, and stage and film producers were Jewish. Some of these people recognized the danger ahead and were prepared to leave Germany if the Nazi party came to power. Riefenstahl, not a Jew, realized that the German cinema would offer her greater opportunities than ever if Hitler became chancellor.

Hitler's drive for power met another setback in November. By adept maneuvering he had forced another election in the hope that his party would gain more seats in the Reichstag. But when the votes were counted on November 6, 1932, the Nazi party had lost two million votes and thirty-four seats. Instead of winning a majority, the Hitler forces received the support of only 34 percent of the electorate, down from 37 percent in April. It became obvious that he was not going to gain power by the vote, so he decided to get the chancellorship by behind-the-scenes maneuvering, if possible.

He soon discovered that if he was an expert in political intrigue, others were, too. Especially Kurt von Schleicher, the new chancellor appointed by President von Hindenburg. A general who had helped others form governments, Schleicher now wanted a chance to rule Germany himself. Unfortunately, Schleicher had few qualifications for the chancellorship. He had no firm plans, no strong supporting political party, and no real understanding of his responsibilities. He did have courage, however, and he immediately moved to divide the Nazi party and further weaken Hitler's chances of assuming power. Schleicher approached Gregor Strasser, who had helped organize the Nazi party but who from the beginning had often disagreed with Hitler, and asked him to become vice-chancellor. Schleicher knew that if he formed a coalition with Strasser, and if Strasser's followers broke from Hitler to support the Schleicher government, he would be unbeatable.

Hitler was shocked to discover that he might be deserted by Strasser, the man who had kept the party alive and extended its scope while Hitler was in prison. Even though Strasser declined the Chancellor's offer, Hitler was still furious. He knew the offer would not have been made unless Strasser had indicated he might support Schleicher. Before Strasser resigned all his posts in the Nazi party on December 8, 1932, he went to see Hitler for one last time. Hitler went into one of the rages that would later become famous and accused Strasser of wanting to displace him as head of the party. Strasser denied the charge, but Hitler continued to scream at him. Strasser turned and left the room. Neither he nor Schleicher had long to live.

In the latter months of 1932, while Riefenstahl's *Das blaue Licht* was reaping a rich harvest at the box office, Hitler and the Nazi party were facing bankruptcy. Several wealthy industrialists, such as Fritz Thyssen, who had backed the party for years, refused further funds. There was no money for payrolls, no money for the printers, no money for campaigning. Goebbels wrote in his diary on November 11: "The financial position of the Berlin organization is beyond hope. Nothing but debts and bills." [9] It appeared that Hitler had met a solid wall on the way to the chancellorship and power. In addition, many of the party members, especially those who held office in the cities throughout Germany, were greatly depressed when Gregor Strasser bolted the party. The people who had read with fear Hitler's assertion that "the Jews must be dealt with," recorded by H. V.

Kaltenborn, felt more at ease as Hitler's political star seemed to dim.

Those who counted him out of the fight made a serious error. The determined Hitler secretly met with Franz von Papen, the former chancellor who had been ousted by Schleicher, at the home of Baron Kurt von Schroeder, a Cologne banker. During this meeting the two men came to an understanding that each thought was to his own advantage: They would join forces and replace Schleicher with a Hitler-Papen government. Hitler would be head of the government and Papen's supporters would be cabinet ministers. The Papen supporters had to agree with the policy changes Hitler proposed before he would appoint them as ministers. One of the changes Hitler insisted upon was the elimination of Jews from leading positions in Germany. Hitler was convinced that he would run the government once he became chancellor, and Papen was equally convinced that once his ministers were in the cabinet, he could easily overrule Hitler and become the real ruler of Germany.

Schleicher, who had ousted Papen as chancellor, soon found their roles reversed. He admitted to Hindenburg his inability to find a majority in the Reichstag, just as Papen had done earlier. And just as Papen had done, Schleicher suggested that the Reichstag be dissolved and that he be permitted to rule as a military dictator. Papen, with the secret knowledge that he now had Hitler and the Nazi votes on his side, objected to the dissolution of the Reichstag, just as Schleicher had done when Papen had wanted such an action. Hindenburg, old, sick, and frustrated by the political intrigue going on all around him, ordered Schleicher to continue his efforts to obtain a majority in the Reichstag, emphasizing that as president he had sworn to uphold the present constitution and he intended to do so. He would not agree to a military dictatorship. The aged president did not realize that it was only a matter of days before he would appoint a man who would ignore the Constitution and rule Germany much more brutally than Schleicher could have dreamed.

As expected, Schleicher could not obtain a majority in the Reichstag, and in order to avoid having his archenemy Papen reappointed chancellor, Schleicher sent word to Hindenburg that he would support Hitler as the new chancellor. Shocked and surprised, Hindenburg sent back word that he had no intention of ever appointing "that Austrian corporal." This was on January 28, 1933. When Hitler heard that Schleicher was now supporting him, he ignored the General, confident that he and Papen would shortly assume control of the country regardless of Hindenburg's or Schleicher's wishes. Hitler and his intimate circle were at the Goebbels' home celebrating what they thought was his imminent appointment to the chancellorship when word reached them that Schleicher, as a last resort, had alerted the Potsdam garrison for action. It appeared that he was going to try to establish his military dictatorship by force.

Hermann Göring, the ace flier of World War I and party stalwart, was at the celebration, too. Göring hurried to warn Hindenburg of the pending action. Later, Hitler was to describe his own actions at this time:

> My immediate counteraction to this planned revolt was to send for the Commander of the Berlin SA, Count von Helldorf, and have him alert the whole SA in Berlin. At the same time I ordered Major Wecke of the Police, whom I knew I could trust, to prepare for an attack on the Wilhelmstrasse and to try and control the Wilhelmstrasse with six of his police battalions. I also instructed General von Blomberg to proceed at once, on arrival in Berlin at 8:00 A.M. on January 30, direct to the Old Gentleman to be sworn in [Blomberg had been selected as Reichswehr minister-elect] and thus be in position, as Commander-in-Chief of the Reichswehr, to suppress any possible attempts at a *coup d'état*. [10]

Actually, Papen had asked Blomberg to come to Berlin because Hindenburg, his options narrowed now to the Papen-Hitler government—or, as Hitler demanded, the Hitler-Papen government—wanted a man he could trust over the German military forces. When Blomberg arrived in Berlin he went directly to the President and was sworn in as defense minister. He was now ready to defend the President against any attempt at a coup d'état. He was also sworn to defend any new government appointed by Hindenburg.

A few hours later Hindenburg, with no other choice, appointed Adolf Hitler chancellor. That evening, thousands cheered the 30,000 SA and SS men who marched through the Brandenburg Gate and past the President's palace and the Chancellery to be reviewed by Hindenburg and Hitler. Thousands of others, among them many Jewish members of the film industry, shuddered with fear. They had a right to shudder, as later events proved.

One film star did not shudder that evening when she heard the news that Hitler had been appointed chancellor. The star was Leni Riefenstahl. As she admitted many times: "Hitler fascinated me." [11]

5

Time of Decision

When Hitler assumed the chancellorship on January 30, 1933, it was evident to many German citizens, especially the Jews, that the time of decision had arrived. Many important figures of the film industry left Germany as soon as possible. Josef von Sternberg, whose film *Der blaue Engel* (*The Blue Angel*), starring Marlene Dietrich, had won international success; Erich Pommer, who had worked with Fritz Lang and organized a successful film company of his own in Berlin; G. W. Pabst, who had been in charge of *Die weisse Hölle vom Piz Palü*, starring Leni Riefenstahl; and Max Reinhardt, who had started Riefenstahl on the road to fame in his stage productions—all of them left the country.

Many stars, not all of them Jewish, also went into exile: Marlene Dietrich; Elisabeth Bergner and her husband, Paul Czinner; Peter Lorre, Oskar Homolka, and Conrad Veidt, all of whom, like Marlene Dietrich, would later become well known in Hollywood; Joe and Mia May, a husband-and-wife team who were very popular in pre-Nazi Germany; Wilhelm Thiele, who later specialized in Tarzan films in the United States; and Vladimir Sokoloff, a stage and film actor.

Many other leading exponents of German culture also took up residence outside the country. Among them were Thomas Mann, Kurt Tucholsky, Erich Maria Remarque, George Groz, Fritz von Unruh, Arnold Zweig, Lion Feuchtwanger, Carl Sternheim, Herwarth Walden, and Georg Lukacs. Hitler began a systematic dismantling of the former Weimar culture shortly after he took over the chancellorship. The members of Hitler's intimate circle competed for the top cultural position within the Nazi hierarchy after the cultural housecleaning, but there was one principle that they all kept foremost in their minds: Jews had to be removed from the cultural scene as soon as possible.

Leni Riefenstahl was one prominent figure on the German cultural scene who did not leave. Why not?

"I have never denied that the personality of Hitler fascinated me to an extraordinary degree," she admitted.[1] "At that time all diplomats agreed that the world needed a Hitler. No one knew what he would be like years later."[2]

She was correct in saying that no one knew what he would be like in later years, because in 1933, even those who hated and feared him did not really believe he was the monster he later proved to be. It was impossible then to conceive of his later barbarities. Shortly after Hitler became chancellor, however, even Riefenstahl, if she had wanted to think about it, could have forecast the dominant characteristics of the new Third Reich.

"It was impossible for the young girl that I was to foresee what was going to come about."[3]

At thirty-one years of age, Riefenstahl was old enough to understand the ominous portent in the slogan "Jew perish" scrawled on the walls of synagogues across Germany, and in the widely publicized photograph of a Jewish lawyer in Munich who, having appealed to the police for protection from the SA, had his head shaven and a sign hung from his neck stating: "I shall never complain to the police again." If these incidents went unnoticed, others were too prominent to be overlooked even by a young film director. The decree "for the Protection of the People and the State," which Hitler issued on February 28, 1933, announced:

> Restrictions on personal liberty; on the right of free expression of opinion, including freedom of the press; on the rights of assembly and association; and violations of the privacy of postal, telegraphic and telephonic communications; and warrants for house searches, orders for confiscations, as well as restrictions on property, are also permissible beyond the legal limits otherwise prescribed.

This decree was supposedly required as a "defensive measure against Communist acts of violence endangering the state." On the evening before, the Reichstag, the parliament building in the center of Berlin, burned down. Marinus van der Lubbe, a three-quarters blind, mentally deficient Dutchman, twenty-four years old, who was found wandering in Bismarck Hall behind the Reichstag, was accused of setting the fire. Van der Lubbe was a Communist with a passion for arson. Hitler called the fire evidence of a Communist conspiracy in Germany and ordered his SA and SS to take forceful and immediate action against the Communists. At Van der Lubbe's trial it was established that he had indeed threatened to set fire to the Reichstag and had been picked up by the SA a few days before the fire for questioning; that he could not possibly have set so large a building on fire so quickly; that the most he could have done was strike a few matches and toss them in the general direction of large and well-deployed stockpiles of chemicals and gasoline to which he did not have access and which he could not have carried into the building. He was convicted and executed. The Communist leaders who were tried for conspiracy were acquitted. The trial cast a great deal of suspicion on Göring and the SA, but by that time the fire had served its purpose: The dictatorship was established.

Riefenstahl saw it all differently. "At that time, one believed in something beautiful. In construction. In peace." [4]

Another "constructive" act was the Goebbels-inspired book burning on the Unter den Linden opposite the University of Berlin. Load after load of books was piled in front of the university buildings, books that were "unacceptable to the Nazi party." The works of Thomas Mann, H. G. Wells, Marcel Proust, Albert Einstein, Emile Zola, and Erich Maria Remarque went up in flames. So did the books of Heinrich Heine, one of which included a prophetic sentence: "Wherever they burn books, sooner or later they will burn humans also."

The so-called Enabling Act—the "Law for Removing the Distress of People and Reich"—was forced through the Reichstag in March 1933. With this one measure Hitler took the power of legislation, including approval of treaties, approval of the budget, and the initiation of constitutional amendments, into his own hands. The act even stipulated that the laws would be drafted by the Chancellor and "might deviate from the Constitution." The Enabling Act formed the legal basis for Hitler's dictatorship and freed him from any restraint by the Reichstag. Those who had been in doubt about Hitler, and understood the language of the Enabling Act, now knew they were entirely at his mercy. For those who feared the new Führer, it was time to run, hide, or join forces with the small group of underground units that vowed to oppose Hitler to the last breath. For those who admired Hitler, as Riefenstahl did, it was a time to rejoice . . . to maneuver for the most favorable position in the new regime.

Of all the important people in the German film industry, Riefenstahl was in a most enviable position in 1933. Not only was she adored by a large proportion of movie audiences and considered an exceptionally talented director by her peers; she also enjoyed the admiration of the Führer, the all-powerful dictator of the country. She had impressed him with the film she had directed before he became chancellor, *Das blaue Licht;* and once he met her, Hitler saw more in her than her talent. Her beauty captivated him, as it captivated all men who knew her. Not only was she a gorgeous, sensual woman; Riefenstahl was always enthusiastic about her work and about the "idealistic future of Germany," applying her fantasy as a creative artist to the vision of the country as she wanted it to be. Hitler loved her praise and her talk about the wonderful things she knew he would do for Germany.

"I believed that he would create employment and prosperity for the country," she said. "And I was flattered by his praise for *Das blaue Licht.*" [5]

Riefenstahl saw an opportunity to further her ambitions through her friendship with Hitler. She had used others as steppingstones for her ambitions—Max Reinhardt, Arnold Fanck, Luis Trenker, Hans Schneeberger. Now, as a confidant of the most powerful man in Germany, she recognized the opportunity to take a giant step in the film industry through his influence. She was correct. One man, however, was not enthusiastic about Riefenstahl's favored position with Hitler, and that was Joseph Goebbels.

As the celebrated campaign manager for the elections that brought Hitler to power, Goebbels was an expert in the use of the communications media for propaganda purposes. Before 1933 Goebbels had exercised whatever influence he could over the press, films, and radio, but without Hitler's influence as chancellor it had been a difficult battle. He had learned one important thing, however: the potentialities of film for propaganda. He had arranged for party rallies to be covered by newsreel crews, had made several documentaries for Nazi party meetings, and had made a film to be shown on the campaign trail by means of mobile projection equipment. Looking into the future when Hitler would be chancellor, Goebbels formed a film section in the Nazi party propaganda office not only to produce and distribute films but to prepare to take control of the German film industry once the party came to power.

By 1932, Riefenstahl and all others involved in the film industry had become aware of the new Nazi party magazine published by the film section. The magazine *Der Deutsch Film* immediately launched an attack against the Jews in the industry, a forewarning of what would happen once the Nazi party assumed control of the country. *Der Deutsche Film* lamented the fact that 40 percent of the films released in 1932 were made from scripts written by Jews, that 86 percent of production was accomplished by Jewish-owned companies, and that these companies represented 70 percent of the production companies in existence. The inference was that once the Nazi party controlled the film industry, this Jewish influence would be eliminated. Later, the film section used acts of violence to interrupt screenings of films of which Goebbels did not approve.

If the acts of violence or the attacks against Jews in *Der Deutsche Film* had any effect on Riefenstahl, it was not obvious. She continued to cultivate her friendship with Hitler, spending considerable time with him at his apartment and at his Obersalzberg retreat.

"They say I was Hitler's mistress," Riefenstahl said later. "I deny this." [6]

It is true that during this period Hitler already had a mistress—Eva Braun—but he also delighted in the company of beautiful actresses, and none drew more attention from him than Riefenstahl. Hitler's intimate associates were aware of the close relationship between the Führer and Riefenstahl, and most of them were happy about it. They felt that Hitler should be married, that a wife would restrain him in his relations with others and help him control the irritation that so often turned to violent anger.

Goebbels had initially tried to interest Hitler in Riefenstahl, but as the friendship became more serious, he began to have second thoughts. He feared that Riefenstahl might convince Hitler that she should control the German cinema industry instead of Goebbels. At length, Goebbels decided it was time to act.

Thirteen days after the Reichstag fire, on March 13, 1933, Goebbels persuaded Hitler to give him cabinet status. He was appointed minister for "People's Enlightenment and Propaganda." On March 25 he moved into the building formerly occupied by the press liaison office of the Prussian State at the Wilhelmplatz, directly opposite the Chancellery. He had the entire building renovated and refurnished by Albert Speer, Hitler's favorite architect, making certain that the minister's room was three times bigger than that of any minister of the former republic. Goebbels was determined that he alone would control state propaganda, and he wanted everyone, including Riefenstahl, to know it. One way to make his power plain was to have ostentatious offices. Another was to use propaganda to further Hitler's influence and reap the benefits of the Führer's praise. Goebbels was aware of Hitler's belief in the power of propaganda. As Hitler stated in *Mein Kampf:*

The art of propaganda consists precisely in being able to awaken the imagination of the public through an appeal to their feelings, in finding the appropriate psychological form that will arrest the attention and appeal to the hearts of the national masses. . . .

Propaganda must not investigate the truth objectively and, in so far as it is favorable to the other side, present it according to the theoretical rules of justice; but it must present only that aspect of the truth which is favorable to its own side.

As soon as our own propaganda makes the slightest suggestion that the enemy has a certain amount of justice on his side, then we lay down the basis on which the justice of our own cause could be questioned.

Goebbels knew that Hitler was interested in the use of films for propaganda as well as for entertainment. He also knew that Hitler was interested in Riefenstahl and in several other actresses and actors. Goebbels was irritated to learn that Hitler liked not only the mountain films in which Riefenstahl appeared, but also the ones that starred Luis Trenker. Trenker, a close friend of Riefenstahl's, would probably praise the ambitious actress and director when he talked with Hitler. Even though he had obtained his desired cabinet post, Goebbels still was worried that Riefenstahl might gain control of a large part of the German cinema. He himself had slept with enough actresses in return for making them stars to be well acquainted with the unique advantage a beautiful woman had when seeking favors.

Goebbels was further upset when he learned that Riefenstahl had the title, at least unofficially, of "Film Expert to the National Socialist Party," [7] and was recognized as such by many Nazi party officials, especially those who did not like Goebbels. An additional insult was the article in an American newspaper which stated that Riefenstahl had been named "Film Director of the National Pomp and Pageantry" and called her "the woman behind Hitler." [8] The writer's description of her was entirely complimentary:

> She is a striking, dark-haired, determined woman, dressed in the simple but effective fashion of Nazi Germany. Her eyes—dark brown and glowing with life and spirit—are heavy-lidded. At times they display a decided squint, as the movie camera has revealed again and again.
>
> Her appearance—brunettish, extremely athletic, rather tall—distinguishes her in any gathering. She moves along with a swagger and haughtiness that betrays her assertiveness. Self-confidence and a knowledge of capabilities are plainly expressed in her carriage.

Her beauty is of a type that has a distinctive appeal in Germany. Lithe, spare, and boyish is her figure. Her mouth is wide and suggestive. Collectively, her features radiate youth and verve; taken singly, one is apt to be critical of her looks.[9]

Goebbels moved quickly to counteract such worldwide praise for Riefenstahl. As minister for people's enlightenment and propaganda, he began organizing his own sphere of power, and he did an excellent job of it. He was an indefatigable worker, interested in all details of his responsibility, and a hard taskmaster who could be brutal when angry, charming when pleased. Werner Stephan, who held various positions in the ministry under Goebbels for more than a decade, said, "Goebbels was regarded with a mixture of amazement and instinctive dislike." [10] But no one underestimated his intelligence . . . or his cleverness. He gathered an efficient staff of older party members who were always loyal, naive enthusiasts who believed in him, ruthless career men who could handle his dirty work, and intellectuals who were well acquainted with the nuances of culture.

Goebbels set up separate divisions in his ministry so that he could control all art, culture, and propaganda in the Third Reich. These were the main divisions:

Division I	Legislation and Legal Problems; Budget, Finances, and Accounting; Personnel Administration; Council of Commercial Advertising
Division II	Propaganda
Division III	Department of Broadcasting
Division IV	Press Department
Division V	Film Department
Division VI	Department of Theater
Division VII	Department of Counterpropaganda

Later he organized the Bureau of Culture, of which one important section was the Film Bureau (*Filmkammer*). The official purpose of the Film Bureau was "the task of furthering the realm of German films, of regulating economic and social affairs of the occupations concerned and of effecting a just balance between their members." Goebbels divided the Film Bureau into various sections, an indication of his attention to detail:

Section I   Administration, Legal Matters, and Finance
Section II   Political and Cultural Aspects of Films
Section III Artistic Advice on Creative Films, Scenarios, Casting, and Methods of Presentation
Section IV   Liaison with Film Credit Bank
Section V   Technical Aspects of Film Production
Section VI   Advice to Film Producers
Section VII Film Distribution Inside Germany
Section VIII Price Setting, Taxes, and Related Matters
Section IX   Film, Photography, Raw Materials
Section X   Propaganda for Cultural and Educational Films

This thorough, well-operated organization gave Goebbels complete control of all filmmaking activities. A representative of the president of the Film Bureau in each district (*Gaufilmstellenleiter*) reported to the regional representative of the Bureau of Culture. No action, however minor, slipped unnoticed past Goebbels. The Film Bureau worked closely with the Film Credit Bank, which provided financing for approved scripts, directors, and artists. Naturally, Goebbels had the power of final approval. Both the district representatives of the Film Bureau and the money provided to approve directors and artists benefited Riefenstahl later, although she and Goebbels did not always agree on film projects and each was jealous of the other's close association with Hitler.

If those involved in the German cinema had any doubts about Goebbels' intention to control the industry or his hatred of the Jews, they were eliminated in April 1933, one month after he received his cabinet post. On the first day of the month he ordered an organized boycott of German Jews, in retaliation, he said, for their spreading of false reports around the world and sending of photographs to Jews exiled in other countries purporting to show scenes of oppression and violence in Nazi Germany.

"Generosity does not impress the Jews," he wrote. "One has to show them one is equal to everything." [11]

Storm Troopers were ordered to stand in front of all Jewish shops and signs were posted:

> Jews are given until 10 A.M. on Saturday to reflect. Then the fight begins! The Jews of the world want to destroy Germany! German people! Defend yourselves! Do not buy from Jews!

Goebbels thought that by these measures he could stop the Jews who had left Germany from talking about the terrorist measures the Nazis were using against German Jews. On April 3, 1933, the party-controlled newspaper *Völkischer Beobachter* reported:

> Saturday's boycott is to be regarded merely as a dress rehearsal for a series of measures that will be carried out unless world opinion, which at the moment is against us, definitely changes.

Riefenstahl, secure in her favored position with Hitler, did not allow the boycott of the Jews or the threat of further violence against them to interrupt her own career. Others did. Fritz Lang, one of the most important filmmakers in Germany, a scriptwriter, director, and producer, made his decision quickly. Summoning Lang to his office, Goebbels told him that years earlier he had seen Lang's film *Metropolis* and he and Hitler had both liked it very much. He asked Lang to make films under the protective wing of the Nazis, promising the necessary financing, facilities, and equipment. When Lang mentioned that his mother was a Jew, Goebbels shrugged and said he was prepared to overlook the matter because of Lang's talents as a filmmaker.

"I asked for twenty-four hours to think the matter over," Lang explained later. "I then returned home, booked a sleeper on a night train to Paris, and fled the country." [12]

He lost his beautiful home and his valuable art collection to the Nazis and never returned to Germany while Hitler was in power. He could not compromise his principles or ignore his moral responsibility just because Goebbels promised him a bright future in the Nazi cinema. Other Jewish artists, writers, and intellectuals left Germany after the boycott, taking as much of their property with them as possible and abandoning the rest.

Many artists who were not Jewish but who were opposed to Hitler's brutal doctrines also departed at this time, certain that personal liberties in Germany were a thing of the past.

Riefenstahl, however, was not deterred from her goal to become an important figure in the Nazi cinema, and neither the boycott nor any of the other decrees of Hitler and the Nazi hierarchy changed her mind about the Führer. In a newspaper interview some time later she said:

> To me Hitler is the greatest man who ever lived. He is really faultless, so simple and yet so filled with manly power. He wants nothing, nothing for himself. He is really beautiful, he is wise. Radiance streams from him. All the great men of Germany—Friedrich, Nietzsche, Bismarck—have all had faults. Hitler's followers are not spotless. Only he is pure. [13]

As the autumn of 1933 approached and plans were readied for the party congress, scheduled to be held as usual at Nuremberg, the beautiful actress and the crippled minister vied for Hitler's patronage.

6

The Hitler Image

As Dietrich Bonhoeffer, the young German pastor later executed by the Nazis, said: "The power of some needs the folly of others." [1] Bonhoeffer was convinced that folly was a moral rather than an intellectual defect, that there are people who are mentally agile but foolish. In his cell he wrote:

> It is not that certain human capacities, intellectual capacities, for example, become stunted or destroyed, but rather that the upsurge of power makes such an overwhelming impression that men are deprived of their independent judgment and—more or less unconsciously—give up trying to assess the new state of affairs for themselves. [2]

When Hitler took power in 1933, many Germans, including German Jews, were extremely slow to understand the altered situation in the country. They convinced themselves that after the initial flurry of boycotts, assaults, and authoritarian decrees, German intelligence and love of order would reassert themselves. Gerhart Hauptmann, the popular playwright, was one of these. When Hitler first began attacking the Jews, Hauptmann said, "Ah, those few Polish Jews! Good God, it's not all that important—every revolution starts off by bringing the dregs to the top." [3]

Five years later he had a different opinion. "This wretched Austrian decorator's mate has ruined Germany. This dog's muck will cover the world with war; this miserable brown ham actor, this Nazi hangman is pushing us into a world conflagration, into catastrophe." [4]

Hitler was selective in his weeding out of the Jews at the beginning of his regime. Some professionals, such as Jewish civil servants, lawyers, and intellectuals, were immediately harassed and forced to flee, while doctors, economists, and technicians needed by the regime were given a grace period. A Jewish employer who hired many non-Jews was not forced to close his business because of the effect such a closing would have on the Nazi goal of full employment, but Jewish employees were quickly dismissed. Thus Hitler fooled some Germans into thinking that the rumors they heard about his brutal treatment of the Jews were not correct, that they were started by his enemies, probably the Communists.

Leni Riefenstahl, however, certainly was aware of the Führer's determination to strip the Jews of their power and wealth and even deny them the opportunity to earn a living. She knew that many of her associates in the film industry had been banished from the German production companies and that many of them had gone into exile. Yet in August 1933 she sent the following memo to the Reich Film Association:

From: Leni Riefenstahl
To: Reich Film Association
Date: August 8, 1933
Herewith I register as a member of the Reich Film Association and request the forwarding of the appropriate application and regulations.

Respectfully,
LENI RIEFENSTAHL [5]

Her close association with Hitler would seem to make the approval of the application automatic, but it wasn't. Twenty days later the following letter was received at Goebbels' ministry:

Confidential!

August 28, 1933

To Herr von Allwörden:
In a conversation the previous Saturday with Herr von

Reith, the name Riefenstahl came up. In addition, Herr von Reith related the following with the request for verification:

Herr Podehl, the producer for Ufa, met with the film writer Katscher, a Jew. Herr Katscher is married to an Aryan. Frau Katscher related that Leni Riefenstahl was her lawful cousin and that, indeed, Leni Riefenstahl was the only Jew of her blood relations. Leni Riefenstahl is said to have a Jewish mother who was considered to be the only Jew in her family.

LANGE [6]

Investigators in the special department for research into racial purity and genetics immediately began tracing Riefenstahl's ancestry, with particular attention to her mother's family. Within a short time a completed *Abstammungs-Nachweis* (proof of family) form was completed and sent to the Film Bureau. In an accompanying letter the investigators cleared Riefenstahl of the accusation of having Jewish blood.

From: Film Agency (Kontingent)
To: N.S.B.O. Film Group, Attn. Herr Auen
Date: September 6, 1933
Re: Leni Riefenstahl

According to the evidence known to me, the above-mentioned is registered in the documents of the Central Registration Office as Evangelical on her father's side to the great-grandparents and on the mother's side to the grandparents, so that her Aryan descent is without doubt.[7]

The required forms were sent to her at last and Riefenstahl returned the completed questionnaire on October 2, 1933. Within a short time she received the *Reichsfachschaft Film* identification card, with the proper Nazi swastika stamp on it. The card was numbered 1352 and identified her as a member in good standing.[8]

Even though the Nazi investigating team cleared Riefenstahl of the charge of having Jewish blood, not everyone was satisfied. Padraic King, in an article published in the United States, stated: "Although her mother was *Jewish*, her political influence is established."[9] Henry Jaworsky, the cameraman who worked with Riefenstahl, admitted after World War II that there was a persistent rumor that Riefenstahl was partly Jewish. While he knew of no proof that the rumor was true, he said that when he visited her apartment in Berlin during the war he noticed that she had a candelabrum with seven candles, normally a Jewish custom.[10] Riefenstahl, of course, vehemently denied the rumor, and clearly Hitler was satisfied. He asked her to film the 1933 Nazi party congress to be held at Nuremberg that fall.

Riefenstahl directed the film of the NSDAP congress of 1933 but she had considerable difficulty and ended up with much less footage than she wanted. Goebbels, jealous of her favored position with Hitler and afraid that she was using her influence to invade what he considered his own area of control, made certain that his staff did not cooperate with Riefenstahl or her film crew. Indeed, all possible obstacles were placed in her path. Riefenstahl protested to Hitler that she did not have the film footage she needed to edit into a satisfactory final print. He wanted to know the reason. Riefenstahl explained:

> I met with Hitler at lunchtime. The place was crowded so he, Dr. Goebbels and I went into a small room by ourselves and had coffee. I told him what had happened. Naturally, I was excited, but I noticed that as I talked to Hitler Dr. Goebbels' face was very white.[11]

Riefenstahl insists that she didn't understand the situation at that time. She had received the order to film the party congress of 1933 directly from Hitler and she expected Goebbels to obey the Führer's orders. According to her, she was interested only in artistic considerations and had no intention of trying to use her influence with Hitler to reduce Goebbels' power.

> I told Hitler that filming the party congress was too difficult for a girl. I told him the men are jealous and that the problems I encountered affected my nerves. Hitler became very angry. He told Goebbels that when he gave an order, Goebbels was supposed to obey it. Hitler then told me that I must make a film of the congress in 1934 but I protested, saying that the same thing would happen. He said that he wanted me to make the film in 1934 and assured me that there would be no interference.[12]

Five minutes after Riefenstahl arrived home after the meeting, she received a call from Goebbels' office requesting that she come to the ministry immediately.

> When I walked into the office Goebbels was furious. He wanted to know why I spoke bad of him and his staff to Hitler. "Why did you not come to me?" he asked. I was shocked. I told him he was in the Chancellor's office when I received the order from Hitler to make the film so why did he treat me the way he did? I also told him that I did not talk behind his back, that I told Hitler about my problems when Goebbels was present at lunch. From that moment Goebbels hated me.[13]

The film of the 1933 party congress, although short, was excellent. Titled *Sieg des Glaubens (Victory of Faith)*, it was premiered on the night of December 2, 1933, and revealed masterful editing of the sparse footage. The *London Observer* reported the next day that the film

> was one long apotheosis of the Caesar spirit, in which Hitler played the role of Caesar while the troops played the role of Roman slaves. It is certainly hoped that this film will be shown in all cinemas outside Germany, if one wishes to understand the intoxicating spirit which is moving Germany these days. Hitler handed Leni Riefenstahl a bouquet at the end of the performance.

No copy of *Sieg des Glaubens* has been found since the end of World War II. It is possible that Hitler had ordered the film destroyed, since a violent purge in 1934 changed the Nazi hierarchy and *Sieg des Glaubens* was a reminder of those who were executed, a reminder that Hitler may not have wanted the public to see.

Even before the 1934 purge and the 1934 party congress at Nuremberg, where Riefenstahl was expected to make another film, she was busy establishing herself as a staunch supporter of Hitler and ingratiating herself with the leaders of the party who could help her the most. One member of the Nazi hierarchy with whom she became friendly in this period was Julius Streicher, one of Hitler's staunchest adherents. Streicher was *Gauleiter* (regional party leader) of Franconia, which included Nuremberg, where the party congresses were held each year. Bald, paunchy, and fiery-tempered, Streicher fanatically hated Jews. His associates found it impossible to speak with him for more than a few minutes before he started to discuss the "Jewish problem." Twenty-four hours a day he was concerned about "the Jew conspiracy." His newspaper, *Der Stürmer,* provided him with an excellent means of spreading his propaganda. A representative headline of the paper in 1933 was: "The Dead Jew: Fritz Rosenfelder Sees Reason and Hangs Himself." [14]

Streicher became famous for his huge collection of pornographic literature; his boasts of being a prodigious fornicator; the sexual gratification he stated he received from horse-whipping prisoners; his affairs with an assortment of young actresses to whom he provided retainers and jobs; and his financing of a country house with a special love chamber for his mistress, Anni Seitz, with money obtained by melting down wedding rings confiscated from men in his district. He was considered so loathsome that most Nazi leaders ignored him . . . except Hitler, who read *Der Stürmer* from front to back and considered it an excellent sounding board for Nazi policies. Riefenstahl didn't consider him loathsome, either, and depended upon him to help her in her film activities. When she became involved in legal problems with Béla Balázs, the author-director who had helped her in the filming of *Das blaue Licht*, she got in touch with Streicher. On stationery of the Hotel Kaiserhof in Berlin, she sent this handwritten letter to the *Gauleiter* of Franconia:

> 11 December 1933
> I grant to Herr Gauleiter Julius Streicher of Nuremberg—publisher of *Der Stürmer*—power of attorney in matters of the claims of the Jew Béla Balázs on me.
>
> Leni Riefenstahl [15]

Who could be a better choice to handle "matters of the claims of the Jew Béla Balázs" than a *Gauleiter* who was experienced in what he always termed "the Jew conspiracy"? It was another example of her wise selection of men who could further her goals and aid her with her problems.

The year 1934 was extremely important for both Leni Riefenstahl and the Nazi regime. Hitler had seized more power in one year than any other chancellor in German history. He had destroyed all other political parties, established a dictatorship, eliminated labor unions, harassed Jews out of public and professional careers, abolished freedom of speech, and destroyed all the democratic organizations that had existed in Germany when he took office. As 1934 began, Hitler started consolidating his power so that he would have absolute control of all political, economic, social, and cultural matters. He made the plans and his ministers carried them out.

Goebbels didn't need any motivation along these lines other than his own desire to create an empire for himself. His first decree was published in the party newspaper, *Völkischer Beobachter*, on January 19, 1934:

> The Kulturfilmstelle of the Reichsfilmkammer reports the following: The authorization to produce films, either professionally or for the common good, under public or private management, is by legal definition only permitted to members of the Reichsfilmkammer. With the exception of local movie houses, all moving picture enterprises, and therefore itinerant producers, firms which produce publicity films, associations or corporations privately or publicly directed, must, by February 1, 1934, at the latest, become members of the appropriate branch of the Reichsfilmkammer, the "Reich Union of German Moving Picture Departments." After the specified date, a general control will be established.[16]

Riefenstahl had, of course, already received her membership card in the Reich Film Association; in addition, Hitler himself had requested her to film the party congress to be held at Nuremberg. There was no need for her to be concerned with the new decree. It did, however, affect all Jews still active in the German film industry, because membership "in the appropriate branch of the Reichsfilmkammer" was refused to them. A letter from Goebbels to the Berlin offices of six American film companies was quite explicit:

> As the commissar at the head of this cell, and by the authority given to me, I call on you to give notice of the dismissal of all your representatives, rental agents and branch managers of Jewish extraction and give them leave of absence immediately. No more employment contracts may be entered into and so far as such have been effectuated lately from transparent causes, they shall be canceled immediately. I emphasize that it is not religion but race that is decisive. Christianized Jews are thus equally affected. In place of these gentlemen, only members of the National Socialist Party shall be employed.[17]

Since two of Riefenstahl's pictures, *Die weisse Hölle vom Piz Palü* and *S.O.S. Eisberg*, were backed by the American film company Universal, Goebbels' letter affected people who had helped her reach stardom. Men such as Carl Laemmle, Harry Sokal, and Paul Kohner, well-known producers, were forced to leave the country.

Goebbels was just getting started on his program to control the German film industry with these two orders early in the year. In February he created a censorship committee under the chairmanship of Willi Krause, an old friend who had been film reviewer for *Der Angriff*, Goebbels' newspaper. This committee was ordered to review every film produced in Germany. The full scope of Krause's power was revealed in the February 3 issue of *Lichtbild-Bühne:*

> The Filmdramaturg of the Reich is charged with advising the movie industry in all important problems concerning production. He is to examine all manuscripts and scenarios to see that topics which run counter to the spirit of the time are suppressed.[18]

Goebbels had six rating levels for films: (*a*) very valuable politically and artistically, (*b*) valuable politically and artistically, (*c*) valuable politically, (*d*) valuable artistically, (*e*) valuable culturally, and (*f*) of educational value. An annual award for the best

German film was to be presented. Within a few months Riefenstahl was to make the film that would win this award in 1935.

After the censorship decree became law in February, the Nazi party rigidly controlled all production in the film industry. Before a movie could be started, the producer was required to submit the scenario and treatment for Willi Krause's approval. If the movie was approved and permitted to be made, the completed film had to be sent to the censor, who made certain that the approved scenario and treatment had been followed. Approved movies were subsidized by the Reich Film Credit Bank or other party financing facilities. Consequently the only films that were made were those that Hitler wanted produced, and those producers, writers, actors, and actresses whom he admired were treated very well. Those willing to cooperate with the regime received scripts, financing, excellent distribution of their films, and reams of publicity. Those who refused to abide by the strict decrees were subjected to violent harassment.

Such harassment had already occurred at the premiere of the film *Catherine the Great* on March 8, 1933, in Berlin. Elisabeth Bergner, who played the title role in this English movie, was Jewish. She had been very popular in Germany before the Third Reich, but in 1932, realizing Hitler's plans for Jews, she had left the country and was living in London when Hitler became chancellor. When news of his repression of the Jews reached England, Bergner was very outspoken in her denunciation of him, and her remarks were published in many foreign newspapers. *Catherine the Great* therefore presented a censorship problem for Goebbels and Willi Krause. The subject was harmless; the actress, in their eyes, was not. Since Goebbels was aware that the foreign press was watching closely to see whether or not this film would be permitted to be shown in Germany, he decided it would be wiser not to ban it.

At the premiere a crowd massed outside the theater, shouting anti-Semitic slogans and threatening physical harm to the invited guests. Hitler ordered the demonstration broken up, but two days later Goebbels suppressed the film. That same day, March 10, 1933, the *Völkischer Beobachter* published an article by Alfred Rosenberg, the Nazi party philosopher, which said: "The attempt to present in Berlin émigré Jews, especially the warped Elisabeth Bergner, and to make money from them in Germany, represents an inartistic attempt against which we turn, especially because it is not an isolated case."

At the film's second performance, on the previous evening, a mass demonstration against Bergner had been stopped by the SA under the leadership of Ernst Röhm. Röhm strode onto the stage and announced that his troops would arrest anyone who interrupted the showing of the film. This squat, craggy-faced homosexual had only a little more than a year to live. His death was to have an important effect on the film Riefenstahl was to make at the Nuremberg party congress in the fall of 1934.

Röhm was in a very influential position in 1934. His SA consisted of between two and three million men, a restive group that had tasted blood while aiding Hitler to become chancellor and now wanted to share in the spoils. The SA leader felt that his troops should have the dominant role in the Third Reich military plans, not the Reichswehr, the regular German Army, and he wanted to be appointed minister of defense. Hitler knew that he still needed the support of the German Army high command to consolidate his position. He also was aware that Hindenburg was dying, and he wanted to assume the presidency himself after the old man's death. He could do this only with the agreement of the German Army high command if he wanted to avoid a bloody confrontation between the regular troops and his SA troops. During naval maneuvers off Kiel in April, Hitler met with General Werner von Blomberg, the minister of defense, and the German Army high command and the agreement was made. Röhm and the SA would play a secondary role to the Reichswehr in the military.

Röhm, however, was tough-minded and courageous. Hitler knew he would not concur with such an agreement, so once again the Führer contrived to rid himself of an obstacle. The fact that Röhm had been his close associate for years and was one of the few Nazi leaders who could address him with the intimate *du* made no difference. Hitler decided that in one fast action he would rid himself of Röhm, appoint a leader to the SA whom he could control completely, and eliminate other men standing in his path to absolute power. The purge, which occurred on Saturday and Sunday, June 29 and 30, 1934, became known as the "Night of the Long Knives." It was one of the worst blood baths in German history.

Hitler, Hermann Göring, Heinrich Himmler, who led the SS and was loyal to Hitler, and Reichswehr leaders spread a false rumor that Röhm was conspiring to take over the government in a putsch scheduled for the latter part of June. After the details of the purge were set, Hitler traveled to Essen to attend the wedding of Gauleiter Josef Terboven. It was undoubtedly one of the most spectacular weddings to take place during the Third Reich, a show that even Riefenstahl would have been proud to direct and film. Essen became the stage for parades, fireworks, floodlights, and 20,000 marching soldiers carrying torches. Hitler appeared to enjoy every minute of the spectacle, but early the next morning, grim-faced, he flew south to take charge of the blood bath.

While Riefenstahl was in Spain arranging to make the film *Tiefland*, the events that were indirectly to change her life unfolded. Hitler arrived at the Munich-Oberwiesenfeld airfield shortly after 4 A.M. on June 30, stepped into his armored car, and with an escort of six cars filled with soldiers headed for Wiessee, where Röhm was still sound asleep in the Pension Hanslbauer. Hitler confronted the surprised SA leader, still half asleep, and screamed accusations at him about the putsch he was supposedly planning, of which Röhm knew nothing. When Röhm became angry and began screaming at Hitler, he was overpowered by soldiers and taken to the Stadelheim Prison in Munich. Hitler, in what he presumably considered a heroic gesture, ordered that Röhm be given a gun so he could die as a "good soldier." Röhm spat on the gun.

"If Adolf wants me dead, let him do it." [19]

Hitler didn't do it personally, but Sepp Dietrich, leader of the SS *Obergruppe Ost* and commander of Hitler's *Leibstandarte*, did shoot him. Hundreds of other "enemies" died that weekend, including Kurt von Schleicher, the former chancellor; Gregor Strasser, whom Hitler felt had deserted him; Gustav von

Kahr, the Bavarian politician who had helped stop the abortive Beer Hall Putsch; Edgar Jung, an adviser of Papen; and Edmund Heines, Röhm's SA lieutenant. Many were shot in their homes; others were taken to swamps or woods, where they were executed and their bodies hidden.

Goebbels prohibited the press from reporting anything about the purge and had all official documents pertaining to it destroyed. But the disappearance of so many people who had played prominent roles in the political and military life of the country could not be kept secret long. Hitler knew that. In the film to be made at the party congress in September, he would show the public the changes in the Nazi party leadership and at the same time the image of himself he wished projected. He wanted to show that the party was united despite the purge and the changes in leadership, and that he was the new savior of the country. He wanted the violence of his regime concealed. He wanted the Germans and the world in general to believe that he was a benevolent dictator, a great humanitarian who held the welfare of his people foremost in his mind. Hitler wanted his true characteristics camouflaged in a film fantasy that would conceal his actual plans for Germany, the Jews, and the world.

To create this film he chose his favorite filmmaker, Leni Riefenstahl. He was confident she would handle the assignment to his satisfaction.

part two

The Glory Years

7

The Führer's Choice

Hitler distrusted everyone. Like most dictators, he knew that his position was insecure. He wanted prestige, fame, the image of savior of his country. One of the means by which he decided to imprint this image on the minds of the masses was the medium of film. He had expressed his views about the usefulness of films earlier:

> I want to exploit the film as an instrument of propaganda in such a way that the audience will be clearly aware that on such an occasion they are going to see a political film. It nauseates me when I find political propaganda hiding under the cloak of art. Let it be either art or politics.[1]

There was no question in Hitler's mind what type of film he wanted when he asked Riefenstahl to shoot the events at the 1934 Nazi party congress at Nuremberg. He wanted a political film, a propaganda film that would convince audiences across Germany and around the world that he was in complete control of a united Nazi party. He wanted the German citizens to know that their new Führer would lead them from World War I defeat to world power.

Until she decided to film the 1934 party congress, Riefenstahl had not allied herself with Hitler professionally except for the short film of the 1933 congress. She had been seen with him many times, had praised him in her conversations with others, and had become a member of the Reich Film Association. By maintaining her relationship with Hitler after the initial violence against Jews and the exclusion of Jews, many former associates, from the film industry, Riefenstahl indirectly expressed her support for him and his policies. Yet it was not until she decided to make the film of the 1934 congress that she really committed herself to the Third Reich.

Hitler had requested that she film the 1934 activities shortly after she made *Sieg des Glaubens* in 1933. At that time she was reluctant to take the assignment for two reasons: She had never before made a full-length documentary film, and she had plans to shoot a film titled *Tiefland* in Spain, based on the popular operetta by Eugen D'Albert. Hitler insisted. She enlisted the aid of a friend, Walter Ruttmann, who had directed the famous documentary *Berlin: Die Symphonie einer Grosstadt*, to create an opening sequence that would show the Nazi rise to power. Ruttmann was a Communist but a close friend of Riefenstahl's, and she considered him an expert producer of documentaries. He was enthusiastic about the assignment, so Riefenstahl left for Spain, confident that Ruttmann would take care of the production.

While in Spain in 1934, Riefenstahl became ill and spent several weeks in a Madrid hospital. The plans for *Tiefland* were temporarily abandoned and in August she returned to Germany. She didn't resume work on this film until after the end of World War II and finally completed it in 1954. As soon as she reached Berlin, Rudolf Hess, Hitler's deputy, contacted her. Hess reminded her that the Führer had asked her, not Ruttmann, to make the film, and said she was expected to fulfill the assignment.

"I went to speak with Hitler," Riefenstahl said later in an interview granted to the British Broadcasting Corporation. "He was not in Berlin so I went to Nuremberg in my car. I found him there with Speer and other people." [2]

According to Riefenstahl, she tried to persuade Hitler to change his mind, to permit Ruttmann to make the film, but Hitler refused.

"I told Hitler that I don't know what is SS and what is SA,"

Riefenstahl explained. "I don't know what is important, what is not important." [3]

When this argument failed, Riefenstahl said, she tried another approach.

"I say Dr. Goebbels don't like me and Dr. Goebbels is the head of the cinema." [4]

Hitler just smiled and assured her that Goebbels would cooperate because the Führer had ordered him to do so. Whatever she needed to make the film successful, he said, she would have. Just ask and he would see that she got it. When she demanded that the film be made by her own company and not by the Goebbels-headed Ministry for People's Enlightenment and Propaganda, Hitler quickly agreed. He also agreed that he would not interfere with the filming, that she would have complete freedom to make the film as she desired.

It was Riefenstahl's time of decision. The lure of artistic freedom and the unlimited resources Hitler dangled before her were great enough to make her ignore the moral consequences of supporting him and his regime. She has said many times since the end of World War II, "Since *Das blaue Licht* I have always done what I want or I don't work." [5] In August 1934 Riefenstahl decided she wanted to make the film about the Nazi party congress, the film that was to identify her forever with Adolf Hitler.

She committed herself to making the film, to supporting Hitler with all her talent and skill. Now her determination to succeed was as important to Hitler and the Nazi party as it was to herself. Perhaps a true indication of her feelings toward Hitler at this time can be drawn from a series of letters about a cinematographer she wanted to hire. When he refused to work with her, she wrote to Karl Auen, an official of the Reich Film Bureau.

From: Leni Riefenstahl
To: Karl Auen
Date: August 17, 1934
Dear Herr Auen:

As you have perhaps already heard, I am again making a film by commission of the Führer for the Reich Party Day, 1934.

Since I need many cinematographers for the Nuremberg days, I have asked the association to give me names and addresses of cinematographers. Among the names submitted to me was that of Herr Schünemann. When my secretary telephoned Herr Schünemann, he said he was busy, but for which film was he being considered? My secretary replied that it was the Reich Party Day film, at which point she was asked if this was the film Leni Riefenstahl was making. When this was affirmed, Herr Schünemann said he would not make this film as a matter of principle, that it was beneath his dignity.

Since I feel that this statement is a degradation of a task that will be undertaken at the commission of the Führer, I feel that it is my duty to communicate this information to you and to suggest that you act upon it.

> With the German greeting,
> Heil Hitler!
> LENI RIEFENSTAHL [6]

At a time when the Nazi party leaders encouraged people to spy on each other, urged children to inform on parents, and detailed SS and SA troops to watch German citizens for actions or talk that indicated opposition to Hitler, Riefenstahl's letter posed a direct threat to the cinematographer. The Nazi official of the Reich Film Association immediately checked with Schünemann.

From: Reich Film Association
To: Emil Schünemann
Date: August 21, 1934

Fräulein Leni Riefenstahl, who is commissioned by the Führer to produce the new Reich Party Day film, complains that when her secretary spoke with you, explaining that she was calling in regard to the Reich Party Day film that Fräulein Riefenstahl is making, you said to her, "I would not make that film as a matter of principle, it is beneath my dignity."

We request your point of view concerning this matter.

> Heil Hitler! [7]

Schünemann was caught in a serious situation. If he gave the wrong answer, concentration camp—and at this time it was estimated that 100,000 Jews and dissident Germans were incarcerated—or even death could result. Although he knew that Riefenstahl was a favorite of the Führer, the stubborn cinematographer did not relent.

From: Emil Schünemann
To: Reich Film Association
Date: August 23, 1934
    In reply to your letter of the 21st, I take the following position:
    The complaint of Frl. Riefenstahl is completely unjustified. I have, of course, the greatest interest in assisting on the Reich Party Day film and would view it as a matter of honor to place myself at your disposal to this end without fee.
    I have merely refused to work under the artistic direction of Frl. Riefenstahl. My statement refers to this alone.
    I must firmly protest the insinuation in the complaint of Frl. Riefenstahl in respect to her secretary.
Heil Hitler! [8]

This letter evaded giving the reason for his refusal to work with Riefenstahl, and Schünemann hoped that the matter would be dropped. It wasn't. The same day the Reich Film Association demanded a more detailed answer to the charge.

From: Head of the Reich Film Association
To: Emil Schünemann
Date: August 23, 1934
    In reference to your letter of the 23rd of this month, I request that you tell me the reasons that prompt you to decline to work under the artistic direction of Fräulein Leni Riefenstahl.
Heil Hitler! [9]

The harassed cinematographer answered the letter two days later. He wrote that because of certain past experiences during his thirty years in the film industry, he would not work under the artistic direction of a woman. Years later he was to reveal the true reason for his refusal, but in 1934 he relied on the fact that she was one of the very few female directors in a male-dominated field. He hoped his reason would be accepted on this basis. Auen did accept this explanation, and explained to Riefenstahl Schünemann's reluctance to work under a woman. She wasn't happy. She referred to Hitler five times in her answering letter.

> From   Leni Riefenstahl
> To: Karl Auen
> Date: August 29, 1934
> Dear Herr Auen:
>   I have received your letter concerning Herr Schünemann, and I would like to tell you that I, too, have not taken his remark any other way than Herr Schünemann expressed it to you, but that does not alter the fact that this remark of Herr Schünemann's is a boycott against the Führer and therefore it is my duty to engage cameramen and coworkers who support me artistically.
>   If the Führer does not find it beneath his dignity to entrust me with the artistic direction, then it is unusual, to say the least, if Herr Schünemann finds it beneath his dignity to acknowledge this. The commission of the Führer would be impossible to carry out if even more coworkers were of Herr Schünemann's view. For this reason, I have found it necessary to communicate this to you.
>
> >   Heil Hitler,
> >   LENI RIEFENSTAHL [10]

It wasn't until 1949, fifteen years after the controversy, that the true reason for Schünemann's refusal to work on the film became known. Schünemann wrote to a newspaper that had reported the details of Riefenstahl's denazification hearing, during which the correspondence was reviewed:

> It was with great satisfaction that I read in your paper the article "Leni Riefenstahl Not Affected." . . . I said at the time that it was beneath my dignity to make propaganda films of that kind.

Since that remark put me in great danger, I put a different construction on my words at the suggestion of Herr Alberti, who was then head of the Culture Section and superior to Herr Auen, and said that it was beneath my dignity to work under Leni Riefenstahl. Riefenstahl received a villa in Dahlem from her Führer. She also admitted that her Führer would receive her at any time without an appointment. At that time she would gladly have handed me over to the Gestapo if Herr Alberti had not protected me. [11]

It was obvious from her actions at this time that she was devoted to Hitler and that those who opposed her would be accused of indirectly opposing Hitler and the Nazi party.

One of the most controversial issues about the Nuremberg Reich Party Day film was the financing of it. In a postwar interview in England, Riefenstahl said that she had no difficulty obtaining financing; she simply went to Ufa and Ufa signed a contract with her for distribution. [12]

Ufa (Universum Film A.G.) was founded December 18, 1917, with capital of 25 million marks from the German government and 7 million from two private banks. In addition to producing films, by 1932 Ufa owned a large number of movie theaters and was a major distributor, employing more than five thousand workers in all branches of the film industry. The majority of shares in the company at that time was held by Alfred Hugenberg, a press lord who was a firm supporter of Hitler. With his large interest in Ufa, Hugenberg was able to bring pressure on studio executives to produce films supporting Hitler and the party, although some of the other stockholders opposed the new Führer. Thus Riefenstahl's claim that Ufa provided the money for her private production company, Riefenstahl-Film GmbH, seems logical.

Later investigation, however, indicated that Riefenstahl did not receive the money merely because she requested it. In a postwar court action involving the Nuremberg film, the decision stated in part:

The court views *Triumph des Willens* as a protected work under law but is not convinced that Leni Riefenstahl is, in the meaning of the law, the producer of the film and entitled to rights. The reason for this is: although Leni Riefenstahl did not receive money from the Reich Treasury for the film, Ufa recognized her as the "agent of the Reich leadership" in the contract "in the name of the Führer." Therefore Ufa intended to make a contract with the NSDAP, not Leni Riefenstahl solely. [13]

The decision is self-explanatory. Ufa, convinced that any money loaned to Riefenstahl was guaranteed by Hitler and the Nazi party, gladly financed the film. The Ufa executives not only expected to have the loan repaid, but to make a profit from distributing the film.

The Reich Party Day film, however, was definitely Riefenstahl's work. During the planning, the actual filming, and the later editing of the footage, Riefenstahl showed why she was considered one of the most skilled filmmakers in history. Her ability as a director must be admired. She planned her moves and those of her crew in minute detail.

"She would assign you to a position, every single cameraman," explained Jaworsky, "and she would tell you what lens to use, what focal length, how many frames to run, what filter to use. She knew what she was talking about." [14]

Riefenstahl had pits dug before the speakers' platform, tracks laid so her cameramen could make traveling shots, elevators built so that filming could be done above the million and a half people expected to attend, and she even arranged to have a cameraman aboard a dirigible for some aerial shots. Riefenstahl provided many of the cameramen with SA uniforms so that they would not be interfered with during filming. Twenty-two chauffeur-driven cars were provided for the crew's transportation. Rudolf Hess made certain that the lifts were constructed, the track put in place, the pits dug, and any other of Riefenstahl's demands fulfilled during the planning stage. Heinrich Himmler provided the SA uniforms, knowing that the film would establish him as one of the top Nazi leaders in the minds of the German audiences. And when Goebbels—or anyone else—caused problems, Riefenstahl notified the Führer, who quickly took care of them.

Her claim that "my film is composed of what stemmed from the event," [15] that nothing was staged for her cameras, and that she did not suggest any activities to enhance the film ignores the fact that Hitler himself did a great deal of planning for the gathering. He knew the importance of producing an interesting film that would tell the story about himself and the party that he wanted told. Like Riefenstahl, he did not overlook any details.

Early in 1934, Hitler assigned Albert Speer to remodel Zeppelin Field at Nuremberg, one of the sites to be used for the rally. Speer wanted to replace the temporary bleachers with a huge flight of steps topped and enclosed by a long colonnade. The overall dimensions were estimated at 1,300 feet by 80 feet, almost twice the length of the famous Baths of Caracalla in Rome. Hitler agreed to the plan, but the grand reconstruction project was not completed in time for the rally. However, Speer made certain that the buildings and grounds in Nuremberg were in excellent condition by September. He was the one who suggested the famous "pillars of light" used at the rally. While the military units and the SA and SS troops marched in impressive ranks, the middle and minor party officials (*Amtswalter*) lacked both bearing and discipline when they assembled. Speer wanted the *Amtswalter* to appear more impressive when they approached Hitler, so he decided he would have them march to the reviewing stand in darkness. Behind the fence surrounding Zeppelin Field, Speer arranged for thousands of flags belonging to local groups to be displayed in groups of ten and spotlighted by 130 antiaircraft searchlights. The beams of the searchlights penetrated the darkness to a height of 26,000 feet, giving those assembled the feeling that they were in a vast room, a "cathedral of light."

"I imagine this 'cathedral of light' was the first luminescent architecture of this type," Speer said, "but, after its fashion, the only one that has survived the passage of time. For me, it remains my most beautiful architectural concept." [16]

Speer first met Riefenstahl during his preparations for the Nuremberg rally. He had admired her ever since her famous mountain films and was delighted when Hitler appointed her to film the rally. Many others were not. Speer explained:

As the only woman officially involved in the proceedings, she had frequent conflicts with the party organization, which was soon up in arms against her. The Nazis were by tradition antifeminist and could hardly brook this self-assured woman, the more so since she knew how to bend this men's world to her purposes. Intrigues were launched and slanderous stories carried to Hess in order to have her ousted.[17]

Speer, a tall, handsome man, was surprised to discover that Riefenstahl carried a newspaper clipping with a photograph of him. Three years before, Riefenstahl had seen his picture in the newspaper and decided he would be ideal for one of her movies, so she saved the clipping for future reference.

Speer's use of flags at Zeppelin Field during the assembly of the *Amtswalter* fitted in nicely with Riefenstahl's plans to use motifs to transfigure the events of the Reich Party Day. Some of the motifs and images she used in the footage were shots of the swastika from all angles; ancient buildings, statues, and icons to contrast with the "new order" in Germany; fire, to support the theme that Hitler had come from the sky to kindle a new movement that would liberate the spirit of the German people; clouds, to represent his coming; and various groups of people— students, workers, soldiers—paying their homage to the new Führer as an indication that he was supported by the masses.

Riefenstahl planned the camerawork with her customary talent and creativity. Basically, she decided on fundamental effects that resulted in disoriented and animated frames. In the first camera setup she intended to film people and objects in unreal situations. She would show the upper parts of buildings and the sky, but not the earth, to give the effect of floating buildings; she would shoot human bodies from angles that made them appear to be apparitions from the sky. Closeups of the marchers, the flags, Hitler, and his lieutenants all provided the raw material for animated footage. If the subject was not moving, she ordered the cameraman to move his camera. She wanted no static newsreel shots. She wanted animation, action, life.

In addition to help from Hess, Himmler, Speer, and Hitler,

Riefenstahl received from Julius Streicher, the *Gauleiter* whose domain included the city of Nuremberg, an empty building next to the beautiful Adolf Hitler Platz as a dormitory for her staff. Leopold Gutterer, head of the important Department II (Propaganda) of the Ministry for People's Enlightenment and Propaganda, and later undersecretary to Goebbels, massed a work force that transformed the building into an ideal place for Riefenstahl and her crew to stay. As she said later in a book she wrote about the film:

> In Nuremberg, Frankenführer Streicher helped us over many difficulties. Through the cooperation of the city of Nuremberg, the totally novel exploitation of all technical means for the film was especially furthered. All the resources we needed, down to streetcars and fire ladders, were placed at our disposal.[18]

By early September 1934 Riefenstahl was in Nuremberg with a production staff of more than 170 persons. This staff included:

- 9 aerial cameramen to take photographs from dirigible D/PN 50, piloted by Captain Rolf Hanasch, and from a Klemmer plane flown by Anton Riediger
- 36 cameramen and assistants under the overall direction of Sepp Allgeier
- 18 newsreel cameramen
- 12 newsreel cameramen from Tobis Film Company
- 26 drivers
- 37 security men
- 17 lighting technicians
- 2 business managers, Walter Traut and Walter Groskopf

She was ready to shoot the film that would make her a legend and a cause célèbre.

8
Masterpiece at Nuremberg

Is *Triumph des Willens* a great film? Critics differ, often because of their feelings toward Riefenstahl rather than because of the artistic and propaganda content of the film itself. A calm appraisal results in the conviction that it is one of the technical and artistic masterpieces of film history, a truly great film. The fact that *Triumph des Willens* projected a false image of Hitler and the Nazi party does not alter this conclusion. Let us consider the film in detail.

Triumph des Willens [1]

Commissioned by:	National Socialist German Workers' Party (NSDAP)
Producer:	NSDAP, bureau for the National Party Congress Film
Overall Direction and Artistic Production:	Leni Riefenstahl
Photography, Overall Direction:	Sepp Allgeier
Musical Direction:	Herbert Windt
Cameramen:	Karl Attenberger, Werner Bohne, Walter Frentz, Hans Gottschalk, Werner Hundhausen, Herbert Kebelmann, Albert Kling, Franz Koch, Herbert Kutschbach, Paul

	Lieberenz, Richard Nickel, Walter Riml, Arthur von Schwerführer, Karl Vass, Franz Weihmayr, Siefried Weinmann, Karl Wellert
Assistant Cameramen:	Sepp Ketterer, Wolf Hart, Peter Haller, Kurt Schulz, Eugen O. Bernhard, Richard Kandler, Hans Bühring, Richard Böhm, Erich Stoll, Josef Koch, Otto Jäger, August Beis, Hans Wittmann, Wolfgang Müller, Heinz Linke, Erich Küchler, Wilhelm Schmidt, Ernst Kunstmann, Erich Grohmann, Unit of Svend Noldan, Hans Noack, and Fritz Brunsch
Aerial Photographs:	From the airship D/PN 50 (captain, Rolf Hanasch) and from a Klemmer plane (pilot, Anton Riediger; cameraman, Albert Kling)
Sound:	Siefried Schulz and Ernst Schütz
March Music Dubbing:	Band of the SS Bodyguard of Adolf Hitler directed by Bandmaster Müller-John
Business Managers:	Walter Traut and Walter Groskopf
Assistants:	Erna Peters, Guzzi and Otto Lantschner, Walter Prager, Arthur Kiekebusch
Architectural Planning:	Albert Speer
Nuremberg Movie Set Plans:	City Councilor Brugmann, Architect Seegy
Newsreels:	Ufa, Tobis-Melo, Paramount, Deulig, and Fox
Distributor:	Ufa-Filmverlein GmbH

Lighting:	Bernhard Delschaft, Jr., of Koerting and Mathiesen A. G., working with Bernhard Delschaft, Sr., Felix Koziolek, Han Kubisch, Otto Schroeder, R. Bude, H. Compart, E. Erdmann, W. Fried, K. H. Grohwald, O. Hilbert, R. Rusch, K. Schreiber, R. Radtke, R. Reinke, W. Stangenberg
NSDAP Propaganda Consultant:	Herbert Seehofer
Still Photography:	Rolf Lantin

Triumph des Willens titles, flashed on the screen at the opening of the film to the sounds of Wagnerian marching music, include, in addition to the information that the film was produced at the Führer's order and created by Leni Riefenstahl, the following explanation:

> September 5, 1934, twenty years after the outbreak of the World War, sixteen years after Germany's crucifixion, nineteen months after the commencement of the German renaissance, Adolf Hitler flew to Nuremberg again to review the columns of his faithful adherents.

Scene I begins with Hitler's aircraft approaching Nuremberg through the clouds, turning and banking gently over the old city. The clouds, dark at first, gradually become lighter as the sun breaks through and the shadow of the wing encompasses a long line of marching Nazi Storm Troopers on the ground. This gives the impression that the Führer is reaching out to them. Hitler is not visible in the plane. Frame by frame, while the "Horst Wessel Song," the Nazi anthem, is played in the background, the camera descends to the streets of Nuremberg, showing the city crowded with marching columns. The German eagle and the swastika are often visible in this opening scene.

Finally the aircraft lands at the airport and taxis into the parking area, where a huge throng of supporters, arms extended in the Nazi salute, await the Führer. The door of the plane opens, but no one appears. After what seems an interminable wait, Hitler emerges. Behind him is Goebbels, wearing a raincoat and smiling. As the Führer walks to his waiting car, the throng surges forward, excited, trying to touch him.

On the screen we now see Hitler's car moving between lines of cheering Germans, interspersed with shots of the famous buildings of Nuremberg. Riefenstahl has often said that she planned nothing for this film but camera placement, but one incident on the screen indicates very clearly that *someone* did some planning. Hitler's car stops so that he can accept a bouquet of flowers offered him by a small girl held up by her mother. Both the girl and the mother then salute the Führer while those standing around smile.

At the Hotel Deutscher Hof, SS troops and Hitler's personal orderlies surround the car, standing at attention and saluting while they hold back the crowd. There are closeup shots of the soldiers' faces, belts, boots, insignia, and their hands linked together as they protect Hitler. The Führer walks into the hotel to the cries of those gathered around his car. "We want to see our leader! Heil Hitler!" Later Hitler is seen at the window of his room saluting the crowd below, and the scene ends in a darkened screen.

Riefenstahl used these opening scenes to establish the impression that Hitler was revered by the masses and that their reverence gave him power. She also emphasized that his power derived not only from his popular support but from the well-disciplined, loyal troops so much in evidence during these first scenes.

It is quite evident that much planning was involved in the dramatic spectacle that took place at Nuremberg that year. It would have been impossible to have so many people perform in such a disciplined manner without a script. Storm Troopers, Hitler Youth, Labor Service, Nazi officials, bands, German citizens—all of these and hundreds of others took part in the giant gathering. There would have been bedlam if no precise plan had been made before their arrival. Hitler and his aides outlined the events very carefully. Riefenstahl states that she had no voice in any planning of the events, that she filmed only what happened in front of her cameras. If this is true, then more credit is due Hitler and his staff than is usually given. The entire rally was a natural show for a film director. All the elements necessary to produce a propaganda movie were included; all the scenes needed to make the film a success were available for her cameras.

Once Riefenstahl has established Hitler as immensely popular with the massed throng and as strongly supported by the uniformed soldiers gathered around him, she reverts to the calm of dawn over the old city. She goes from night to day, from cheering masses to a sleeping city. Slowly the city comes to life—windows are opened, curtains are drawn, people appear—and always, as the camera pans across the rooftops, we see banners and flags bearing the swastika. Gradually the tempo quickens as the camera centers on the huge tent city erected to house the visiting troops, workers, and Hitler Youth. The background music, from Wagner's *Die Meistersinger von Nürnberg*, is the hymn "Awake, the Dawn Draws Near." At the tent city, youths beating drums signal a transition to trumpet calls. As usual, Riefenstahl devotes much footage to the bodies of the muscular young men; she has always celebrated the well-formed, developed, controlled human body. Her shots during this scene give the impression that everyone is having fun, that the tent city inhabitants are enjoying every moment of their visit with the Führer, playing games, wrestling, laughing. Part of this sequence was filmed in a studio, although this fact is not discernible in the movie.

She then switches her lens to a group of men, women, and children dressed in regional costumes walking into Nuremberg. The music now is provided by a costumed man playing a concertina. As in the previous sequence, everyone is happy, excited, eager to see the Führer. Suddenly Hitler walks from the Hotel Deutscher Hof and greets the peasant group, shaking hands, touching children, smiling. Yet he never appears overly friendly, never "one of the boys." He maintains an aloofness that Riefenstahl's cameras clearly catch.

After the peasants comes a marching unit of young flag-bearers. Hitler shakes the hand of each of them. He is now serious, demonstrating his interest in the group and at the same time showing that he is their leader.

Riefenstahl has shown Hitler's popularity with the inhabitants of the tent city, the peasants, and the young flag-bearers. It is time now for her to convert this evident popularity and power into a show of political authority. Once again she changes the background from day to night, the setting from an informal gathering to the huge congress hall and the official opening of the rally. Her cameras focus on the eagle banners and swastikas inside the building and then slowly move to Rudolf Hess, who is the first speaker. They stay on the deputy leader of the Nazi party as he says:

> I open this, our sixth party congress, in respectful remembrance of Field Marshal and President von Hindenburg, who has passed on into eternity. We remember the Field Marshal as the first soldier of the great war, and thus also remember our dead comrades.
>
> I welcome the esteemed representatives of foreign countries who honor the party by their presence, and the party, in sincere friendship, welcomes especially the representatives of the military forces, now under the leadership of our Führer. My Führer! Around you are gathered the flags and banners of this National Socialism. Only when their cloth has worn thin will people, looking back, be able to understand fully the greatness of this time and conceive what you, my Führer, mean to Germany.
>
> You are Germany. When you act, the nation acts; when you judge, the people judge. Our gratitude to you will be our pledge to stand by you for better and for worse, come what may! Thanks to your leadership, Germany will attain her aim to be the homeland of all the Germans of the world. You have guaranteed our victory, and you are now guaranteeing our peace. Heil Hitler! *Sieg Heil! Sieg Heil! Sieg Heil!*

Hitler beams at the audience during Hess's speech, and at the end he shakes hands with his deputy while the crowd cheers. Ten speakers follow, each introduced by a fade-in to his name and then a medium or closeup shot of the man himself. By careful editing and splicing, Riefenstahl transfigures reality completely here. The speeches were *not* all made at this opening session, but were compiled for the film from many meetings. In addition, she excerpted only those parts of the speeches that fitted the occasion and projected the desired image of unity and optimism. Adolf Wagner, *Gauleiter* of Bavaria, sets the stage for the ten speakers by reading a statement excerpted from Hitler's proclamation:

> No revolution could last forever that would not lead up to anarchy. Just as the world does not exist on wars, nations cannot exist on revolution. Nothing great on this earth that has lasted for millenniums was created in decades. The higher the tree, the older its age. Things that have withstood centuries grow strong only during centuries.

Wagner is followed by Alfred Rosenberg, whose official title was Reich Leader of the Foreign Policy Office and Commissioner for Supervision of Ideological Education of the NSDAP. He stresses the regime's confidence in the younger generation: "It is our belief that our young generation will march on and, as destined, continue the efforts started during the stormy years of the Munich revolt, an event of historical importance which today is embodied by the entire nation."

As the speakers appear on the screen it becomes more and more evident that Riefenstahl selected only those parts of each speech that fitted the circumstances and blended with the excerpts of the previous and succeeding speeches. We hear vows throbbing with sincerity, vows of progressive leaders, leaders responsive to the needs of the citizens, leaders who believe in justice for all, and, of course, leaders concerned about racial purity. Otto Dietrich, later named press chief of the Third Reich, who dealt in lies much more often than truth, says: "Truth is the foundation on which the power of the press stands and falls, and our only demand of the press, and the foreign press as well, is that they tell the truth about Germany."

In 1938 this man announced that it was the responsibility of the German press to inform and enlighten the people about events and developments in a way that would support the party movement and "give impulses to the political thinking of the people." [2] He warned that "it was never the task of the press to lecture the party or the state and to give advice to them or to criticize public institutions or personalities." [3] Truth was a long way down the list of Otto Dietrich's objectives.

Fritz Todt, engineering expert, gives a short talk on the progress of the construction of the *Autobahn* system. Then Fritz Reinhardt speaks briefly about various construction projects other than highways. Walter Darré, farm spokesman and head of the Ministry of Agriculture, vows: "The continued welfare of our farmers is the first condition for the success of our prosperity in our country and abroad."

Next comes the Jew-baiter Julius Streicher. As usual, he speaks on his favorite subject: "A nation that does not attribute high value to its racial purity will perish."

It is interesting that Riefenstahl excerpted this line for the film, and did not edit it out in the final print. She has always insisted that she had complete freedom in the filming and editing of *Triumph des Willens*, that neither Hitler nor any other Nazi official saw the completed film until it was premiered in Berlin on March 28, 1935. Consequently the responsibility for this line must be hers and in view of the treatment of the Jews in the later years of the Third Reich, it is a line that condemns all who agree with it. This includes the director.

After Robert Ley, labor leader, asserts he is going to make the German worker "a proud, upright, and equal member of the nation," Minister of Justice Hans Frank speaks: "As minister of German justice, I want to say that our supreme leader is also our supreme judge. We know that the principles of justice are sacred to our Führer. Therefore, fellow citizens, your life and freedom in this Nationalist Socialist state is assured."

Hans Frank was speaking several months after the Röhm purge, when hundreds of Hitler's enemies were executed without benefit of trial. When Hitler tried to explain the purge to the Reichstag he said:

> If anyone reproaches me and asks why I did not resort to the regular courts of justice, then all I can say is this: In this hour I was

responsible for the fate of the German people and thereby I became the supreme justice of the German people. . . . And everyone must know for all future time that if he raises his hand to strike the state, then certain death is his lot.[4]

Hitler's speech was made before the filming of *Triumph des Willens*. And Frank, who promised so much at Nuremberg, sent millions of people to their doom in Poland without trial. He did more than anyone but Hitler himself to establish the fact that German law existed not to protect the individual but exclusively to benefit the state—that is, Hitler and the Nazi party.

Goebbels was not reluctant to appear in the film, although he and Riefenstahl did not get along. He is the next speaker on the rostrum:

> May the glowing flame of our enthusiasm never go out. This flame alone gives light and warmth to the creative art of modern political propaganda. This art rises from the depths of the people and must always descend back to the people because its power is there. Power based on guns can be a fine thing; however, it's better to win the heart of a nation and keep it, and also more gratifying.

Konstantin Hierl, head of the Labor Front, is the final speaker: "The German people today are ready, spiritually and mentally, for the introduction of general labor-service conscription. We are waiting for the order of our Führer."

Since conscription turned into slave labor during World War II, Hierl's words were indeed prophetic.

Riefenstahl has explained that she believes two things are important to a film. "The first is the skeleton, the construction, the architecture. The second is a sense of rhythm." [5] She maintains the rhythm in the Nuremberg film as she shifts from the night meeting in the congress hall to the daylight rally at Zeppelin Field, where 160,000 members of the Labor Service are massed, armed with shining shovels. This scene must have been carefully planned and rehearsed; the entire event moves too smoothly to be spontaneous. The workers handle their shovels in unison, like soldiers presenting arms. Discipline is perfect, actions are precise. After a verbal ritual between Hierl and the workers, and a mournful selection by the band titled "I Had a Comrade," Hitler addresses the men of the Labor Service.

While he talked, Riefenstahl filmed him from a variety of angles, in closeups, in distance shots. Other cameras concentrated on the listening men, the swastikas, the imperial eagle.

Men of the Labor Service! It is the first time for you standing here for my inspection and the inspection of the German people. You represent a great ideal. We know that to millions of our citizens work is a uniting concept, not a dividing one, and that manual labor is no less highly regarded than other types of labor. The entire nation will have to be trained as you have been trained. The time will come when no German will be able to unite with the community of this nation unless he has been united with your community first. Not only the hundreds of thousands at Nuremberg are watching you, but all of Germany is looking at you. And I know that just as you are serving this nation with devotion, Germany, in proud joy, will see you, her sons, marching.

After Hitler's words, the Labor Service formations march toward the cameras, as though the Führer has inspired them to go to work immediately.

The following scene is a solemn night rally of the Storm Troopers. We see profiles of the Storm Troopers against a background of burning torches. There is a sense of excitement and mystery to the scene. Riefenstahl runs the film of the firework explosion backward so that the initial burst directs the attention of the audience toward the center of the frame, then runs the film forward again.

Viktor Lutze, Röhm's successor as head of the SA, makes a short address. Clearly he is the leader of the SA and Röhm is out of the picture. Riefenstahl, who professed ignorance about the Röhm purge when she made *Triumph des Willens,* nevertheless made certain that Lutze's speech was included.

"Comrades!" Lutze shouted. "Many here tonight remember me from the first years of the movement when I marched in ranks with you of the SA. I am still a Storm Trooper. You and I of the SA know only one thing, fighting for the Führer."

This is a short scene, but Lutze's words express clearly why the SA was formed, what it did in the past, what it is doing in 1934, and what it will do in the future: serve Adolf Hitler. Before the end of the Third Reich, the SA performed some of the most brutal actions in the history of humanity.

This scene is in sharp contrast with the next. Riefenstahl moves from the dark, smoky, mystic gathering of the uniformed SA troops to the bright sunlight of the Youth Stadium, where members of the Hitler Youth are gathered. Fresh, innocent young faces fill the screen. When Hitler arrives the boys and girls cheer wildly. There was doubtless no need to stage this scene; members of the Hitler Youth worshiped the new Führer. Baldur von Schirach, the Hitler Youth leader, explains the feelings of the youngsters very well.

My Führer. My comrades. The hour that will make us very proud and happy has arrived. At your order, my Führer, a young generation that is not aware of caste or class is facing you. Because you express unselfishness to the nation, this young generation wants to be unselfish, too. You are the incarnation of faith so we want to be faithful. Adolf Hitler, the leader of the German youth, will speak.

For the first time in *Triumph des Willens,* Riefenstahl's footage reveals the deep emotions Hitler could express when he was moved to do so.

My German Youth! After one year I welcome you here again. You in this stadium are only a small segment of what is outside of it, all over Germany. We wish you German boys and girls to absorb in your minds all that we expect of Germany in times to come. We want to be one nation, and my German youth will be this nation. In the future we do not want to see classes and castes and you must not allow them to develop among you. We want only one nation and you must prepare for this time. You must be obedient, must practice obedience. You must be peace-loving but also brave . . . and you will have to be peace-loving. It will be necessary to be peace-loving and courageous at the same time. There must be no weaklings and you must harden yourselves while you are young. You must face danger without retreating. Our creations and acts will not last, we shall pass on, but in you Germany will continue and you will carry the banner we have lifted high. You are the flesh of our flesh, blood of our blood, and in your mind is the same spirit that dominates us. At our side you can exist. And when the great formations will march victoriously through Germany, you will be among those formations. Germany is before us, within us, and behind us.

Several times during this speech Riefenstahl's cameras show in closeups the deep emotion on Hitler's face when he pauses to receive the applause, cheers, and salutes of his young audience. The speech is remarkable for the principles that Hitler expounds, the principles that he enforced during his regime. Obedience, for example. He demanded absolute obedience; disobedience often ended in death for the rebellious. He would not put up with weaklings and eliminated them from his ranks. "Weakling," however, was often defined as anyone who opposed him. When he said, "You must face danger," he was obviously referring to the military actions that he was already planning. His statement that German youth must be "peace-loving" was, of course, the most misleading of all. Hitler's career was based on violence and most of his personal life involved violence of one type or another. He wanted the Germans, not yet mentally or physically prepared to fight again so soon after the defeat of World War I, to think that war was far from his mind; the rest of the world, too, must believe he wanted peace. Actually, his conquest of Europe and the world was already planned.

So was his conquest of the younger generation, as this scene in *Triumph des Willens* indicates. Schirach's views are stated clearly when he says: "The rearing of young people is the inalienable sovereign right of the state. The aim of state youth education is the systematic development of the unmindful youngster into a mindful citizen of the state and an upholder of its principles." In the Third Reich, a German child was to be under the direction of the Nazis from infancy to adulthood and the parents' role was to be little more than biological. The boys and girls had no choice. They were forced to join the Hitler Youth, where they were indoctrinated with Hitler's policies. This indoctrination often caused a split with their parents, and many parents were afraid to speak openly in front of their children. Even the bodies of the Hitler Youth, especially those of the girls, belonged to the Nazis. Sex was rampant—and encouraged—among Hitler Youth members. The first commandment of ten listed by the official physician to the Hitler Youth in 1939 stated:

1. Your body belongs to your nation, to which you owe your existence and are responsible for your body.[6]

This, then, was the future that Hitler offered to the younger generation. Riefenstahl's footage of this impressive scene did much to convince young people all over Germany that the new Führer planned great things for them. It wasn't until they were dying in defense of their country without the proper weapons, clothing, or food that the irony of this scene was appreciated.

Now Riefenstahl moves from the hopes of the younger generation to the reality of the present strength of the German army. The scene is brief, mainly because filming was restricted by weather conditions. Later Riefenstahl was to have problems with the army high command, who complained that the army had been slighted. In the span of one minute and twenty-eight seconds, however, her cameras are able to show that the Nazis are rebuilding their military forces. They also show Hitler smiling and laughing as he, Göring, and several military officers review the marching troops.

The footage of the following outdoor rally, a huge affair involving 185,000 party members, a quarter of a million spectators, and more than 21,000 party flags, is often referred to as the scene in which Riefenstahl deifies Adolf Hitler. The rally was held at a large outdoor stadium in the early evening and gave the film crews an ideal setting. The rostrum from which Hitler spoke was constructed at a distance from the gathered throng and from his own entourage, and was high above the spectators. The setting was very impressive, giving him an image of great strength, individuality, power, of leadership to which the masses looked up. Everyone else is faceless; Hitler is in sharp closeup. As he speaks, he appears like a god. His people, far below, wait with bated breath for his commandments.

> A year ago, the initial meeting of the National Socialist Party political leaders took place on this field. Now, two hundred thousand men have assembled here, summoned by nothing but the orders of their hearts, nothing but the commands of their faith. Our people's great misery seized us, united us in battle, made us fight and become strong. Those who have not suffered so cannot understand us. They can't believe that this meeting would bring together hundreds of thousands and make them bear misery, suffering, and privation. They think such a thing is possible only by order of the state. They are not correct. The state has not created us. We have created the state.
>
> Our movement is built on sound foundations, and until we can breathe no more, we will devote our entire strength to the movement, just as we have in years past. Drum to drum, banner to banner, group to group, district to district. Then our people will be led by the gigantic column of our united nation. It would be a crime if we ever gave up what was attained by so much hard work, sorrow, and sacrifice. You cannot be disloyal to something that has given your life purpose and meaning. All this would be worthless were it not directed by a great command. This command was not given us by a human master but by the hand of the Lord who created us. Therefore, let us take a vow this evening, namely, at every hour, on each day, to think only of Germany, of the nation, of the regime, of our German people. To our German people—*Sieg Heil! Sieg Heil! Sieg Heil!*

Riefenstahl's camera direction is superb. There are shots of Hitler from behind, in front, below, above, and the side, long shots, medium shots, closeups. These are intermingled with footage of the listening audience and the banners bearing swastikas and eagles. Mostly, however, the cameras concentrate on Hitler. They flatter him, give the audience a physical impression of him that is misleading. Actually Hitler was of medium height and unimpressive stature. Riefenstahl, a celebrant of the human body all her life, tried to avoid showing his full figure. Behind the rostrum, sitting in a car, standing in a crowd—in all these settings his physical deficiencies were concealed. Most of her shots were from in front and below, giving the impression that the audience was looking up to him, as indeed it was. There is little wonder that Adolf Hitler was pleased with *Triumph des Willens*.

The closing three scenes of the film are the most solemn and should have been taken more seriously by other world leaders than they were. The first of the three is a filmed sequence of Hitler, Lutze, and Himmler paying tribute to the war dead and Hitler once again reviewing a parade of Storm Troopers. The setting is the huge Luitpold Arena. The awesome size of the Nazi military might should have been enough to alert other nations of the world to Hitler's future intentions. Riefenstahl's opening shot shows this gathered throng standing in formations across the entire Luitpold Arena. Cutting through the throng is an opening resembling a wide roadway, at one end a speaker's platform and at the other a war memorial. With a camera mounted in an elevator attached to one of the high masts behind the speakers' platform and others placed strategically along the roadway between the platform and the war memorial, Riefenstahl made some of her most memorable footage. The three solitary figures march along the roadway while the formations remain completely silent. As they lay the wreath at the war memorial in honor of Germans fallen in battle, smoke from braziers drifting over them adds a somberness to the scene. Then, through the same tense silence, they walk back along that long roadway between the Storm Troopers to the speakers' platform. The precision of the massed troops and the solemnity of the three Nazi officials are so effectively timed and projected that some critics have believed that the entire scene was staged for the benefit of Riefenstahl's cameras. She denies this allegation.

In his speech to the SA and SS, Hitler referred obliquely to the Röhm purge and the party unity that had resulted from it. "A few months ago," he said, "a black shadow covered our movement." Clearly he expected his listeners to know what the "black shadow" was; otherwise there was no need to mention it at all. Did Riefenstahl, his close associate, remain unaware of what he meant, as she has claimed, when the audiences for her film were assumed to understand perfectly well? This is what he said:

> Men of the SA and SS! A few months ago a black shadow covered our movement. Neither the SA nor any other institution of the party has anything to do with the shadow. They are mistaken who believe that one split has occurred in our movement. And if anyone sins against the Storm Troopers, it will not break the spirit of the Storm Troopers but of those who dare to sin against them. Only a lunatic or a deliberate liar would decide that I or any one of us would dissolve that which we have built up during so many long years. No, comrades, we are firmly standing by our Germany, and we have to stand firmly by her. I give you new flags, convinced that I am giving them to the most faithful hands in Germany. In past days you have proven your faith a thousand times, and it cannot and will not be different in the future. And so I greet you, my old and faithful Storm Troopers. *Sieg Heil! Sieg Heil! Sieg Heil!*

Riefenstahl then shows Hitler walking past a long line of flag-bearing Storm Troopers, holding his own banner in his left hand while touching each of the formation flags with his right. He appears to be consecrating each flag and its bearer. Meanwhile cannons are fired in the background. There is no doubt that Riefenstahl wanted to show both his spiritual nature and his great military force in this scene, but the military might far overshadows any quality of spiritual leadership.

In the next-to-the-last scene, Hitler reviews the departure of his Storm Troopers, and soldiers of the Wehrmacht from Nuremberg as the rally draws to a close. With her cameras placed on buildings and bridges, in moving vehicles on the ground and planes in the air, Riefenstahl covers this long show of military might in an interesting manner. March music accompanies the sound of the marching feet. The parade provides for her cameras goose-stepping elite troops, SA and SS formations, the Black Corps, bands, and various other military organizations that show the world the growing strength of the Nazis . . . which is what Hitler wanted the world to see. He wanted to give other nations the impression that he was supported not only by his private military force, the SA and SS, but also by the highly respected German high command with all its resources.

The final scene of *Triumph des Willens* takes place in the jammed Luitpold Hall, where Hitler takes the opportunity to proclaim his own greatness and that of his Nazi party and to tell the gathered audience of the glorious future in store for them. The film gave him an ideal way to present his political propaganda to a larger audience than he had ever before been able to reach. Realizing this, Hitler took full advantage of the occasion.

The sixth party congress of the movement is coming to its close. What to millions outside our party has appeared but an impressive spectacle has meant a great deal more to our old fighters: the meeting of old comrades-in-arms and supporters. And perhaps one or another among you, in spite of the compelling excitement of the review of our troops and of our party, may have wistfully remembered those days when it was dangerous to be a National Socialist.

Even when there were only seven in the party, it voiced two principles: first, that it be a party of the people, and second, that it be the only power in Germany. As a party we had to remain a minority, because at most times the most valuable elements of fighting and sacrifice have been the minority, not the majority. And because these men, the finest of the German nation, laid claim to the leadership of the country with pride and self-confidence, people in large numbers have supported this leadership.

The German people are content to know that the changes in leadership have finally ended and been replaced by a strong force, a man of the best blood, who has assumed the leadership and is determined to keep it, to use it to the best advantage of all, and never to relinquish it. Only a part of the nation will be made up of active fighters and the demands on them will be much greater than the demands on millions of other countrymen. Their motto will be: "I will fight."

The party will always represent the elite of the political leadership of the German people. Its doctrine will be unchangeable, its organization as hard as steel. Its tactics will be supple and adaptable but in its entity will be a great strength. All upstanding

Germans will join the National Socialists. Only the best will be National Socialists.

In the past our opponents have sifted the chaff from our party by persecution and repression. Today we must do the sorting and eliminating of what is not good for us. It is our wish and our will that this Reich may last in the millenniums to come. We can be joyous because the future belongs to us. While the older generation could still have doubts, the younger generation is ours body and soul. After we have made the thought and spirit of the National Socialist party its highest embodiment, it will be an eternal and indestructible pillar of the German people and our Reich. Then our great army will join in the service of the party, and the tradition-minded warriors and party members will educate the German people and support on their shoulders the German state, the German Reich.

At this hour, a large number of our party members are already leaving the city. And while some of them will still be reveling in recollections of these days, others are already planning the next meeting. Once again people will arrive and depart, and once again they will be moved and inspired, for our idea and the movement are a living expression of our people and a symbol for all time. *Heil* to the National Socialist movement! *Heil* to Germany!

This is the longest speech in the film. Hitler once again emphasizes the unity of the party and promises the German citizens a glorious future. This scene ends the rally and the filming of it. Riefenstahl's next task on the road to triumph in the Nazi cinema was to edit the footage and produce the final print for Hitler to review.

9

Triumph!

"In my cutting room, it was the most difficult work of my life," Riefenstahl said when interviewed in 1972 by the British Broadcasting Corporation. "I was eighteen hours day and night in the cutting room thinking how I can make the film interesting." [1]

Riefenstahl used none of the footage that Walter Ruttmann had shot for the opening sequence because it did not appear suitable to her. Her aim, according to the book she later wrote about her experience at Nuremberg, was to bring to Germany and the world the word of the Führer and of his faithful, his word for the present and for the future. Ruttmann's newsreel-type montage did not contribute toward this aim, so she discarded it and opened with her famous scene of Hitler's plane flying over the city, bringing him to the huge rally.

One of her most difficult tasks was to make an interesting film out of numerous events that were similar in content—speeches, throngs, marching. Without skillful editing, the film would have been dull and repetitive. Riefenstahl made certain there was movement at all times, so that the events were dramatized. She changed the chronological order of events to enhance viewer interest.

"It didn't matter about chronological accuracy on the screen," she explained. "The architectural line demanded that I instinctively find a unifying way to edit so that the film takes the viewer from act to act and impression to impression most progressively." [2] At another time she said: "The ensemble must be arranged so that the strong points may be brought out." [3]

By rearranging the speeches, she managed to give the impression that all the Nazi leaders at Nuremberg were of one mind about Germany's future, that they were all devoted to Hitler, their god. She selected those parts of each speech that contributed best to the impression she wanted audiences to receive and discarded the rest. It has been reported that when a scene did not please her for any reason, she filmed it again.

Albert Speer tells about one scene she did not like and wanted to reshoot in a studio. Hitler agreed and issued the necessary orders, including one for Speer to construct a realistic backdrop so that the audience would think the scene had taken place in the Congress Hall at Nuremberg. He even had to build a platform and lectern to duplicate the ones in the Congress Hall.

> The production staff scurried around while Streicher, Rosenberg, and Frank walked back and forth memorizing their parts. Hess posed for the first shot and, exactly as he had done at the rally in front of 35,000 people, he raised his hand in salute, turned to where Hitler would have been sitting, and gave his welcoming speech. The others were just as convincing. In fact, Riefenstahl thought the reconstructed scene was better than the original. [4]

Riefenstahl says Speer is wrong; she denies that anything at Nuremberg was staged or that any part of the film was reshot in a studio. According to her, only some sound effects were made in the studio.

She did not complete her editing and have the final cut of the film to her liking until early in 1935. According to her, neither Hitler nor any other Nazi official saw any of the footage before the premiere on March 28, 1935. One of the last—and most difficult—problems she faced in editing was synchronizing the action with the musical score, which was composed by Herbert Windt. The cameras she used at Nuremberg were not motor-driven, and consequently the footage was of various speeds. This presented difficulties when Windt attempted to conduct his music at the same speed as the marching men, because the cadence of the marchers changed from shot to shot. Every time Windt established a proper beat to match the feet of the marchers, footage shot by another camera changed the speed of the foot movement. Finally Riefenstahl, who knew every frame of the film, conducted the score herself and perfectly synchronized the music with the marching men.

Hitler saw the film at the Ufa-Palast-am-Zoo in Berlin the night of the premiere, and was delighted. He immediately saw the value of the production for himself and his party. He recognized, too, that Leni Riefenstahl had been an excellent choice as director. Not all of his associates shared his enthusiasm. Some thought the film was too "artistic," others thought they or their organizations had been slighted. The Wehrmacht was one important segment of the power structure that complained.

Riefenstahl had shot the footage of the German Army's participation in the rally on a rainy day and was not satisfied with the quality of the developed film. She discarded most of it. When General von Blomberg learned that his forces would be seen for less than a minute and a half, he was furious. He went to Hitler and demanded that additional footage be shot and included in the film. Blomberg recognized the propaganda value of the film and wanted the German Army publicized equally with the Nazi party and the SS and SA. This presented a delicate problem for Hitler. He needed the full support of the German Army at this time, yet he had promised Riefenstahl he would not interfere with her film. He suggested that Blomberg and other officers of high rank assemble and be filmed as background for the title of the film. Riefenstahl refused.

"I told him no," she explained. "I can't do it. And for the first time he looked shocked. He told me that if I acted like a donkey I would have enemies." [5]

Relating her conversation with him that day, she said that Hitler told her he was only trying to help, but she was so angry about the efforts to alter her film that she refused to compromise.

"He looked at me and said that I had forgotten to whom I was speaking," Riefenstahl said. "That was the first time I was really scared of him." [6]

Thinking better of her stubbornness, Riefenstahl agreed to make a short film about the Wehrmacht. She shot the footage in a single day with six cameramen and titled it *Tag der Freiheit* (*Day of Freedom*). She used a montage technique, both pictorially and aurally, and the experiment resulted in an excellent movie. Blomberg was very happy. The only known copy of this film is one seized by the Soviet Union after the war.

Riefenstahl blamed Ufa, the distributor of *Triumph des Willens,* for giving the world the impression that the film was produced by the Nazi party and not by her own production company. The credit for *Triumph des Willens* states: "Producer: NSDAP, Bureau for the National Party Congress Film."

"The reason some people think that the film was made by the party is because Ufa did the dedication, not me," she said. "I gave the completed film to Ufa and started other projects. But Ufa brought a man in from the Propaganda Ministry and he wrote the credit: 'This is a film of the party.' Yes?" [7]

After the war, when she brought suit to have herself named as producer, the court refused to find in her favor, but did agree that she had been in charge of "overall artistic production." And, of course, over the years she has insisted that it is a documentary, not a propaganda film. But Hitler definitely used it as propaganda, and Riefenstahl did not protest its use as such, nor did she refuse awards for the film long after it was the most famous of all Nazi party propaganda presentations. Goebbels presented her with the National Film Prize of 1935 and she gratefully accepted, while well aware that the Minister for People's Enlightenment and Propaganda was interested in only one aim: furthering the goals of the Nazi party.

In June 1936 Riefenstahl was invited to the Italian embassy in Berlin, where Mussolini's daughter, Countess Ciano, was present to watch her receive the Italian Film Prize, consisting of an engraved gold-bronze bowl resting on a marble base. Bernardo Attolico, the Italian ambassador, read her note of acknowledgment to the guests and congratulated her on her success. Countess Ciano handed her a bouquet of flowers bound with the Italian national colors.

Among the guests were Reichsminister Goebbels and his wife, and if Goebbels had opposed the film, he certainly showed no ill feelings at the reception. Also present were Joachim von Ribbentrop, the German ambassador to England; Ulrich von Hassel, the German ambassador to Rome; State Secretaries Otto von Meissner and Walther Funk and their wives; Viktor Lutze, chief of staff of the SA; the president of the Reich Film Board, State Minister (Retired) Lehnich; Jenny Jugo, the actress; Luis Trenker; almost all of the staff of the Italian embassy; and a representative of the Italian Film Institute. Riefenstahl was the star of the evening as she received the plaudits of the Nazi and Fascist leaders.

In the world beyond Germany and Italy, however, the praise was mingled with protest. In 1937 she was delighted to accept the gold medal at the Paris International Exposition; however, many French citizens protested because of the propaganda aspects of the film.

Paul Rotha, well-known film critic, is convinced that *Triumph des Willens* can be classified only as propaganda. He says:

> *Triumph des Willens* was unique in film history as a dramatized account of a fictional spectacle organized for propaganda. No effort was spared in staging the conference at Nuremberg, 5–10 September 1934, so that a film should be made of an event that for a mass-parade surpassed any Hollywood super-film. Hitler in person supervised the production. Thirty-six cameras shot it. Millions of feet of negative were exposed.[8]

It is obvious that no director or producer could have made a film such as *Triumph des Willens* without having an avid interest in the subject: Hitler and the Nazi party. The viewer senses this intense interest all through the film, as though the cameras were revealing the inner thoughts of the director. Comparing a newsreel shot of Hitler to a Riefenstahl shot of Hitler is like comparing the painting of a street-corner artist to a Picasso. Her cameras captured him as a leader of compassion and inspiration because that was the way she saw him. This makes the film a great film—and at the same time reveals Riefenstahl's devotion to Hitler and his plans for Germany.

Triumph des Willens could not have been made into the outstanding film it is if the person in charge had not also been an artist. Riefenstahl's skill as a filmmaker is as evident in the production as her homage to Hitler. Her talent enabled her to turn the overblown display at Nuremberg into an exciting spectacle and the most successful propaganda film ever made. By treating the rally at Nuremberg as a pageant of new leaders who intended to better the world and everyone in it through their daring, discipline, and ability, she overcame the complex problems inherent in filming such an event and established Hitler as the "savior" Germany needed.

Goebbels continued to tighten his grip on the film industry, gradually plugging the loopholes in the censorship regulations. Early in April he demanded that all members of the Film Bureau inform the government of any films in their possession made by banned associations or organizations hostile to the Nazi regime. On June 8 he established an office to control distribution of all films made in Germany, especially those intended for export abroad. Only films that he approved could be sent abroad—and *Triumph des Willens* had his complete approval. On that same day he banned all films made before Hitler took power in which Jewish actors or actresses appeared.

At the same time, Julius Streicher stepped up his harassment of the Jews. The *Westdeutscher Beobachter* reported in August 1935:

Yesterday the leader of Franconia, *Gauleiter* Julius Streicher, spoke to an audience of about 16,000 in the Berlin Sports Palace. A further 5,000 Berliners gathered in the Tennis Hall, the second largest hall in the capital, where Streicher's speech was relayed over loudspeakers. Days before, tickets for both meetings were completely sold out. "What business is it of anybody else," asked

Streicher, "if we are cleaning our house? Nobody should trouble himself if we in Germany lead the defilers of our race through the streets to deter others. The Jewish question has not, as many people assume, been solved with the assumption of power by the National Socialists. On the contrary, the hardest work is only beginning." [9]

This was the man whom Riefenstahl had credited with providing technical help and with putting the facilities of Nuremberg at her disposal. This was the man with whom she remained friendly for many years, whom she publicized in her film, and with whom she corresponded long after he became known as a sadist who reveled in the title "Jew Baiter No. 1."

Hitler issued new orders that vitally affected the Jews. On September 15, 1935, he proclaimed the Nuremberg Laws at a special session of the Reichstag held in that city. Among them were the "Reich Citizenry Law" and the "Law for the Protection of German Blood and German Honor." Deprived of the voting privilege and the right to hold public office, German Jews became second-class citizens. Marriages and extramarital sexual relations between Aryans and Jews were forbidden. These new laws prohibited any physical contact between Jews and the so-called master race. In addition, Hitler introduced his new definition of Jewishness: A Jew was any person three of whose great-grandparents had been Jews. Also, a new category called "fractional Jew" was established, covering people of Jewish ancestry who could not be categorized as Jews. By the end of 1935, while Riefenstahl was planning her next film, 8,000 German Jews had committed suicide and 75,000 had emigrated. Thousands more were besieging the foreign consulates for visas. [10]

Goebbels, meanwhile, had his staff search for foreign anti-Semitic films that could be imported for showing in Germany. He found only one such film, a Swedish melodrama entitled *Petterson and Bendel,* and it was a poor production. When the dialogue was dubbed in German it was hopelessly garbled, and the audiences laughed instead of taking the film seriously. A full-scale investigation into the incident produced no results. This was only one more failure in Goebbels' attempt to produce successful films for domestic viewing. He also had difficulty establishing the Nazi cinema in the world film markets. Except for Riefenstahl's *Triumph des Willens*, the German films of this period were nondescript and boring. Production costs rose and many films lost money. Goebbels' one desperate effort to produce an outstanding film was a dismal failure. Willi Krause, the friend he had appointed to the post of *Dramaturg*, had written a novel called *Nur nicht weich werden, Susanne! (Don't Lose Heart, Suzanne!)*. It was made into a film at Goebbels' order, with Arzen von Cserepy, a Hungarian director, in charge, and a fine cast of actors and actresses headed by Veit Harlan. Unfortunately, the finished film was so bad that the premiere audience booed it, a rare occurrence in Nazi Germany. Goebbels was so angry that he sent Cserepy back to Hungary and ordered the newspapers not to report the disturbance at the premiere.

With each failure, Goebbels saw more and more value in the production Riefenstahl had made at Nuremberg. Even though he was unhappy that she worked directly through Hitler and not through his ministry, he still exploited her skill and talent as much as possible. Consequently, when he finally scheduled his long-planned International Film Conference on April 25, 1935, at the Kroll Opera in Berlin, Riefenstahl was one of the prominent guests. More than two thousand delegates from thirty-eight countries accepted invitations, although the British contingent stayed away from Berlin at the last minute. The official explanation indicated that not only those directors and producers working in Germany were aware of Goebbels' domination of the German cinema; so was the outside world.

> The entire German film business is today so much under the thumb of the government that a strong London representation would have to listen to the opinions of official Nazi Germany instead of cooperating in a free conference. Frankly, we don't regard this Berlin conference as in any way important.[11]

Riefenstahl and the other guests, German and foreign, were entertained lavishly as Goebbels tried to show Nazi Germany in the most favorable light. In a speech at the final session of the conference, Goebbels tried to explain his approach to filmmaking. He said that art had to bridge the gap between politics and emotions, that even the greatest artists are children of their nation and draw their material from their native soil. He considered a number of principles the foundation for successful filmmaking. He listed a few:

1. The film has its own laws, and these laws differ from those of the stage. Things that are acceptable in the dim lights of the stage are unmasked in the harsh klieg lights of the film. The film must establish its own character and break away from the condescending sponsorship of the stage.

2. The taste of the audience does not always have to be accepted, although the film must not lose touch with the people. The artistic quality of the film depends upon the decision to educate the audience in a practical manner even at the cost of financial sacrifices.

3. This does not mean that movies have to cater to the beautiful things of life at all times. On the contrary, because of its wide popularity, the film, more than any other form of art, must be an art of the people. It cannot evade the realities of our time and escape into a dreamland of fantasy that exists only in the heads of ivory-tower directors and scenarists.

4. Like every other art form, the movies must be closely related to the present and its problems. Film subjects have to express the spirit of our time in order to speak of our time.

5. Movies have the task of creating with honesty and naturalness evidence for their being.

Germany has the honest intention to erect bridges that will connect nations. Let us start with the determination to be natural the way life is natural. Let us remain truthful so as to accomplish the effect of truth. [12]

Shortly after the end of the International Film Conference, Goebbels awarded the best-film prize to Riefenstahl for *Triumph des Willens*, thus rejecting all but point 2 of his principles.

As the end of 1935 approached, it was clear to everyone in the film industry that past freedoms were gone. Goebbels had made himself the dictator of the German film industry and controlled every detail of filmmaking. He approved all new productions, directors, and casts, and once his approval was given, he exercised further control by arranging financing through the Film Credit Bank. His staff advertised and publicized the films, handled their distribution, and controlled the critics who reviewed them.

Goebbels maintained this tight rein on the film industry through complex channels of control that worked through three different departments: the Ministry of People's Enlightenment and Propaganda, the Central Propaganda Office of the Party, and the Bureau of Culture. In the ministry he had Section V, the Film Department; he had two Central Propaganda Office headquarters, in Munich and Berlin, where the execution and ideological aspects of propaganda were handled; and in the Bureau of Culture there was the Film Bureau. Filmmakers who had the support of the Nazi regime had the services of these three vital departments, which meant unlimited resources, financial and physical. Riefenstahl had one added advantage: She had the complete cooperation and support of the Führer himself.

Basking in the success of *Triumph des Willens,* and secure in the knowledge that she had made one of the few successful films of the two-year-old Third Reich, Riefenstahl knew her future was assured—if she could continue to cooperate with Hitler and the Nazi party. Once again Riefenstahl and all Germans faced a critical decision as Hitler's policies became more obvious and his actions hinted more broadly at his future plans for the country and the world.

The situation in the film industry—the tight controls; the elimination of Jewish producers, cast members, and directors; the censorship; the subject restrictions; the flight of film artists who would not work under these conditions—all this was known to Riefenstahl in 1935. Much of the cream of the pre-Nazi cinema industry was already gone. Leni Riefenstahl stayed.

After the war, asked why she decided to stay, Riefenstahl said, "Whoever defends himself accuses himself. A commission was proposed to me and I accepted. I filmed the truth as it was then. Nothing more." [13]

The truth in *Triumph des Willens* was obviously much more

acceptable to Hitler than the images produced by another artist of the period. August Sander, one of the greatest portrait photographers of the twentieth century, was recording and documenting the social and professional types of his country with his camera. From bricklayers to waitresses, field marshals to industrial executives, Sander carefully posed his subjects at ease in their natural surroundings. Yet Hitler was so incensed by the portrait of Germany that emerged from Sander's photographs that Sander's book was ordered destroyed and he was forced to photograph landscapes instead of German citizens.[14] Why was Hitler outraged? Because the portraits of the Germans Sander photographed revealed the truth, did not transform reality into a glamorous image. Sander portrayed the Germans as ordinary people, not a master race. Hitler wanted the truth as he, the Führer, saw it . . . and, more important, as he wanted viewers to see it. Hitler was convinced that his favorite film goddess, Riefenstahl, would produce the image of Germany that he wanted.

She did.

10
Leni, Athletes, and Nazis

Hitler was determined to make a great national spectacle of the Olympic Games of 1936, to be held in Berlin. The XI Olympiad was to be a project of major cultural importance. He appointed Dr. Carl Diem, for twenty years secretary of the German government's Commission for Sport and Recreation, to handle the details of the festivities. Diem had attended the lavish production of the previous Olympic Games at Los Angeles. He planned to make the German games even more lavish. The Nazis were masters of mass pageantry. In fact, Hitler relied on large rallies and pageants, such as his party rally of 1934 at Nuremberg, to establish and maintain his hold over the nation's citizens.

For the Summer Olympic Games of 1936 Diem had his technicians devise many new solutions to the complex problems that usually plagued such large festivals. Since more than 100,000 visitors would be crowded into the new stadium, a strong loudspeaker that would not echo was needed. One was devised from the speakers that had been used at Nuremberg two years earlier. New scoring devices, equipment to provide improved pictures of close finishes in the athletic events, an electrical touch device to determine winners of the fencing contests, and a computer to show the judges' decisions in the diving contests were all produced by Diem's staff in time for the games. In addition he issued the invitations, scheduled many of the events, assigned artists to design the medals and award certificates, and devised promotional advertising.

With the help of Captain Wolfgang Fürstner, Diem also supervised the building of the Olympic Village, which was situated in a forest near small lakes on the west side of Berlin. The village consisted of meeting halls and 160 houses built of brick, stone, and concrete. The entire area was landscaped after the buildings were constructed, making the Olympic Village appear as though it had been standing there for years. Diem catered to the athletes of the various nations. He provided the Japanese with their customary mats so they could sleep on the floor if they wished, the Americans with American mattresses for their beds, and the Swiss with feathered comforters. He even provided a sauna for the Finns. The steward's department of the North German Lloyd shipping line was assigned to prepare and serve the food for the estimated four thousand athletes expected.

Diem also edited a monthly newsletter that reported on the progress of his preparations and touted the coming festival. In one issue he explained some of his concerns:

> How many telephones should be furnished for the Reich Sports Field; which should be local and which should be connected to the central exchange; how many lights; where should the microphones and loudspeakers be installed; how high should the flagpoles be; how many steps; with what should the seats be covered; should there be flooring on the galleries; how should the temperature of the water in the swimming pools be regulated. . . ? [1]

Besides Diem's promotional material, general domestic and international advertising and publicity were arranged by Goebbels' Ministry for People's Enlightenment and Propaganda. At the urging of Hitler, who wanted the festival of the games to reach as many people as possible, both inside and outside Germany, Goebbels granted Riefenstahl permission to organize a film company that would have exclusive rights to film the 1936 Olympic Games in Berlin.

According to Luis Trenker, the project of filming the Olympic Games of 1936 was first offered to him by the president of the Reich Film Board, but he declined in order to make his movie *Der Kaiser von Kalifornien (The Emperor of California)*.

It was then, he says, that Riefenstahl hurried to Hitler, who gave her the production rights to the event with all necessary authority and informed Goebbels of his decision.[2]

A press release issued on May 18, 1936, by Goebbels' office stated:

> The Reich Minister for People's Enlightenment and Propaganda, Herr Dr. Goebbels, has given total filming rights of the Olympic Games of Summer, 1936, to the Olympic Film GmbH under the management of Leni Riefenstahl. The Olympic Film GmbH will work in cooperation with the German newsreels. Pictures of the Olympic Games on normal film from other sources are not permitted.[3]

Another news release explained further:

> Leni Riefenstahl has turned over the production of the shots of the Olympic battles on the regatta course in Grünau to the well-known sportsman and film amateur Ottomar Krupski. These shots, which will be recorded on 8-mm. film, are to be copied on normal film and added to the great Olympic film that the Führer has commissioned Leni Riefenstahl to do.[4]

One of the many controversial statements that Riefenstahl has made over the years is her assertion that Goebbels opposed her filming of the Olympic Games.

> I ask Ufa one year before I want to make *Olympia* if they want to make an agreement with me. They are not interested. So I asked Tobis and the director Mainz agreed immediately. I told him I will make two films. He knows that the government is against. Yet he guarantees 1.5 million RM. After he makes this agreement with me, he got a lot of trouble with Goebbels and the Ministerium.[5]

The official records of the Ministry for People's Enlightenment and Propaganda do not support her statement. They show that rather than opposing Riefenstahl's project, Goebbels supported it; that the film was actually financed by the Nazi government; that the Olympic Film Company, which Riefenstahl claimed was her personal production company, was founded by the Nazi government; and that the Nazi government made considerable profit by distributing the film through the Tobis company.

An agreement dated October 15, 1935, is among the records:

AGREEMENT

#1

Fräulein Leni Riefenstahl of Berlin-Wilmersdorf, Hindenburgstrasse 97, will carry out the production of the Summer Olympics film. Said individual heads the total management and production of this film.

#2

The costs of production, estimated at 1.5 million RM, are to be handed over to Frl. Riefenstahl at the following rate for disbursement:

November 15, 1935	300,000 RM
April 1, 1936	700,000 RM
November 1, 1936	200,000 RM
January 1, 1937	300,000 RM

#3

Of the amount of 1.5 million RM (#2), Frl. Riefenstahl is to receive for her activities, including expenses for travel, expenditures, transportation, etc., a personal compensation of 250,000 RM.

#4

Frl. Riefenstahl is obligated to render to the Reich Ministry for People's Enlightenment and Propaganda an accounting of the utilization of the 1.5 million RM by submission of vouchers.

#5

Frl. Riefenstahl alone is responsible for the artistic form and the organizational management of the Olympic film.

#6

The Reich Ministry for People's Enlightenment and Propaganda undertakes to place the German newreels Ufa, Tobis-Melo, and Fox under the authority of Frl. Riefenstahl, as was done in the case of the production of the Reich Party Day film, *Triumph des Willens*, and to cause them to place material filmed by them at the disposal of the Olympics film in the following manner:

(a) Archive material already on hand, for a license fee not higher than 3,000 RM.
(b) Newly taken and remaining material, free of charge.
(c) A copy of every newsreel to appear in theaters which is produced at Frl. Riefenstahl's expense.

#7

Frl. Riefenstahl is to assume the cost of the official stamps affixed to this contract.[6]

This document was issued by the Minister for People's Enlightenment and Propaganda. The contract specifically refutes many of the statements that Riefenstahl has made since the end of World War II. She wrote in 1958, for example: "On higher orders [Dr. Goebbels'] the German newsreel cameramen who were very important to my film were removed from the control of Leni Riefenstahl." [7] Section 6 of the contract reveals that far from "removing" them from her control, Goebbels assigned them to her. Further, an itemized list presented to Goebbels in April 1937 shows that newreel footage was delivered to Riefenstahl. Item 11 of the list reads: "Raw film and newsreel material—220,003.41 RM." [8]

Other memos reveal that Goebbels definitely arranged for the Nazi government to finance the Olympic Games film for her—that she did not finance it by her own efforts through Mainz at Tobis. The budget expert of the Ministry for People's Enlightenment and Propaganda, Dr. Karl Ott, wrote a short note to his section chief:

Re yesterday's proposal concerning the filming of the Summer Olympics by Frl. Riefenstahl, for which 1.5 million RM will be needed, Dr. Ott of the Propaganda Ministry declares that the financing of this project is not possible through the Film Bank because the resources of the Film Bank are only for entertainment films of private undertaking and do not stand at the disposal of a film commissioned by the Reich.[9]

With his views on record, Dr. Ott and Goebbels arranged other financing, as an October 17, 1935, memo from a section chief in the Finance Ministry reveals:

> The Ministry of Propaganda submits the draft of a contract according to which Frl. Leni Riefenstahl is commissioned to produce a film of the Summer Olympics. The cost is budgeted at 1.5 million RM.
>
> I have pointed out that since this film is certain to bring in revenue, there would be no difficulty in financing the costs by private enterprise. This method would avoid government financing. But Ministerial Counselor Ott replied that Herr Minister Goebbels requests the prefinancing with government funds.
>
> According to information from Ministerial Counselor Ott, Herr Minister Goebbels will request the proposed funds in the cabinet meeting of October 18, 1935.[10]

The contract and the memos leave no doubt that the Riefenstahl film was financed by Third Reich funds and that Goebbels provided those funds.

If any further proof is needed that the organization that filmed the Olympic Games of 1936 was not her own company, as she so often said, the records on file at Koblenz relating to the Ministry for People's Enlightenment and Propaganda are available. All newly established film companies were required to post 50,000 RM with a court as security bond. Dr. Ott, however, knowing that the Nazi government was funding the company, felt that there was no necessity for such a bond to be deposited. On January 30, 1936, he informed the Berlin-Charlottenburg court:

> The Olympic Film GmbH is being established at the request of the government and is financed by government funds. All re-

sources required by the company to produce the film are also being supplied exclusively by the government. The company has had to be established because the government does not wish to appear publicly as the producer of this film. It is planned to liquidate the company when the production of the film is concluded.[11]

The Nazi officials had to be very careful, even secretive, about their financing of the film. If the International Olympic Committee learned that Hitler intended to make such a film and use it for propaganda purposes, it might cancel the games or move them to another location. Already the Nazi harassment of Jewish athletes in Germany, many of whom had fled the country, had brought criticism from around the world. Hitler intended to use Leni Riefenstahl as a front for the Nazi party and give the IOC and the world the impression that the famous actress-director was filming the Olympic Games as a private project, using private funds and her own film company.

The Berlin-Charlottenburg court was not altogether satisfied with Dr. Ott's communication about the formation of the film company, however, and asked for additional information. This time the Film Bureau answered the inquiry. The letter was dated February 12, 1936:

We are not communicating in regard to a private company or a company with ordinary commercial aims, but about a firm established exclusively for the purpose of external organization and production of the named film. It would be unwise for the government itself to be listed as producer.[12]

After this exchange of communications, the Berlin-Charlottenburg court agreed that a security bond of only 20,000 RM would be sufficient. However, this reduced bond was not paid, either.

One of the clauses in the contract that perturbed the determined, independent Riefenstahl the most was the one requiring her to submit vouchers to verify her expenses. Money and time meant nothing to her when she was producing a film. She was interested only in the results, in making a film as near perfect as she could. She would go to any lengths to get one small detail just right and expenses never entered her mind. David Stewart Hull tells about the time she was working on the film *Tiefland* and asked the set designer to create a forest on the stage. After the simulated forest was completed, Riefenstahl rode on a crane high above it and had it moved to a new position, tree by tree. One entire day's shooting was lost because of her perfectionism.

Goebbels and the Film Bureau officials did not share Riefenstahl's attitude, and the General Accounting Office auditors working out of Goebbels' ministry hounded her throughout the making of the film. To them she was not so much an artist as a manager, an employee of the government, and they expected her to keep accurate accounts and strict control of the disbursements of the government's money. The auditors complained that her spending practices "contradicted the order concerning government economies to administer official funds economically and carefully." [13] They stated that the vouchers she submitted for such general expenses as per diem payments, meals, drinks, tips, charges, and gifts indicated that she was not conservative when it came to spending money. Riefenstahl, of course, was not conservative in much of anything—spending, dressing, or life style. She enjoyed eating and drinking in the best restaurants, wore expensive one-of-a-kind dresses and specially designed sports clothes, and rode only in limousines. Since she was accustomed to associating with Hitler and other high-ranking Nazi officials who had the luxurious fringe benefits that came with their positions, she did not understand why the auditors expected her to be parsimonious when she was producing a film for government use.

The auditors continued to harass her about her expenses. They wanted to know why she always paid the lunch or dinner bill when she met with other members of the film company; why she paid 202.40 reichsmarks for a business course for her secretary; why she spent funds for a "Reich Race Research Office" without specifying what the funds were used for; why she expected the government to reimburse her and her staff for lost fountain pens; and why, by September 1936, she had already requested and received 1.2 million of the budgeted 1.5 million reichsmarks when actually only 1 million was due.

When Karl Hanke, head of the ministerial secretariat, submitted this report, Goebbels, far from flying into a rage and trying to discredit Riefenstahl as she has so often claimed he did, wrote across it in green pencil, "Let's not be petty." [14] Goebbels did refuse to give her an additional 500,000 reichsmarks when it became obvious that she was going to exceed her budget and instructed Hanke to talk with her. Later, however, he even relented on this point and authorized an additional payment of 300,000 reichsmarks. At this point, Dr. Ott once again suggested using funds from the Film Credit Bank, since it could check much more closely on her expenditures, although he admitted there were problems connected with such a move. "Undoubtedly Frl. Riefenstahl will resist such an order with all means at her disposal. It would also permit a private firm to have intimate details about a company entirely set up by the government, and this is undesirable." [15]

Shortly afterward the Film Bureau auditors discovered that Riefenstahl's business manager, Walter Grosskopf, was in the habit of taking the company's working capital home with him at night, and during an October audit "had produced 14,000 to 16,000 RM from different pockets of his clothing." Goebbels decided to appoint an adviser to the Olympic Film GmbH to "ensure the purposeful and economic use of the means of this company." [16] In an order bearing his signature, Goebbels appointed Judge Pfennig, legal counselor of the Film Bureau, to handle the assignment. There is no evidence that he was able to halt Riefenstahl's free-spending ways, although he managed to irritate her when he appeared on the scene as an "official observer" of her activities.

Riefenstahl's claim that Tobis and the company's director, Friedrich Mainz, financed the Olympic Games film and "recouped the money because of the film's immense success, a total of 4,210,290 RM within several weeks after the premiere of the film," [17] is explained much more clearly in the official documents at Koblenz. Even a government-owned company such as Olympic Film GmbH needed someone to distribute the completed film, just as a private film company did. Consequently, on December 4, 1936, long after the government contracts had been signed to set up Olympic Film GmbH and to finance the project, Olympic Film contracted with Tobis to distribute the film. Riefenstahl represented Olympic Film at the signing and Mainz represented Tobis. Tobis agreed to a guarantee of 1 million reichsmarks for the distribution rights. While the contract did not state that accounting records of the film's distribution had to be submitted to Goebbels' ministry, since Goebbels and Hitler did not want the public to know that the Nazi government had financed the film company, these reports were required. Tobis periodically sent one copy of an accounting report to Olympic Film and two copies to Goebbels' ministry, one of which was forwarded to Dr. Ott. By late September 1938, approximately five months after the film's premiere, Dr. Ott reported to the Ministry of Finance: "A million reichsmarks of unplanned revenue have flowed into the coffers of the Reich Treasury." [18]

Not only did Hitler gain the publicity he wanted for his new Germany through the film; his treasury also benefited substantially.

Once the secret plans for setting up the government-sponsored film company were completed and the financial resources were assured by Goebbels, Riefenstahl prepared for the actual shooting. This was one assignment that the Nazi government could not help her with; there was no precedent for her to follow. Until 1936 sporting events were recorded on film only by newreel cameramen. No accomplished filmmaker had ever considered sports worthy of his talents or time. So when Riefenstahl accepted the assignment, she faced a multitude of problems that no film director had ever faced before. Film at that time did not have much range of light sensitivity, for example, so the depth of field was limited. Participants were always moving, disappearing underwater, leaping high in the air, throwing a javelin that was nearly impossible for a camera to follow. In addition, the International Amateur Athletic Federation restricted her actions to ensure that neither she nor her cameramen would interfere with the contests. Riefenstahl could film only the first trials of some events, and even then her cameramen were required to stay a certain distance from the field. Many film directors of the period were convinced that she could not produce a successful film because of these restrictions and others, and because they felt movie audiences would find the subject uninteresting.

Riefenstahl, however, with her usual organizing skill and innovative techniques, prepared for the assignment with all her usual verve and enthusiasm. Henry Jaworsky, the cameraman who had refused to work with her on *Triumph des Willens*, joined her staff for the filming of the Olympic Games, and has stated that she worked extremely hard during this time. "She would work a sixteen-hour day herself and then gather the whole staff around a big table later to discuss the shooting. We were all falling asleep but she was full of energy. And she knew what she was talking about." [19]

The final film proved that she certainly *did* know what she was talking about. She developed new camera techniques that amazed other filmmakers. When she studied the requirements for filming the 100-yard dash, she decided that she wanted a camera on a catapult that would ride rails alongside the track. She wanted the catapult to have a variable speed so that the camera could always be kept just a few steps ahead of the runner. Of course the noise of the camera and the wheels of the catapult on the rails had to be muffled so they would not distract the runners. The engineers devised a camera whose whirring could scarcely be heard. This was very important, since in 1936 there were no zoom lenses. For a closeup, the camera had to be close to the subject or the difficult-to-handle telescopic lens had to be used.

To reproduce the motion of a horse and rider in competition, Riefenstahl obtained an automatic camera that could be fitted on the saddle of another horse and turned on before the event. To lessen the vibration caused by the horse's movement, the camera was placed on a rubber bag filled with feathers. The method she used to take shots from high overhead were also unique. She put small automatic cameras in baskets, attached the baskets to balloons, and released them to drift over the stadium. Riefenstahl advertised in all Berlin newspapers, explaining how people who found the cameras after the balloons landed could return the equipment to her studios. The auditors probably shuddered when they studied the cost of this operation, since for every ten meters of good film she obtained, she exposed one thousand. For an overhead shot of the opening ceremonies she summoned Jaworsky from Greece, where he had been filming historical footage for inclusion in the film, and had him board the airship *Hindenburg* at Frankfurt. He was over the stadium in Berlin at precisely the right minute, but unfortunately it was raining. The exposed film was not good.

For the diving events Riefenstahl had a special camera adapted for use underwater. Her cameraman would climb to a high board, focus his lens, then dive with the Olympic diver, filming him as they dropped. The cameraman would continue shooting as he hit the water and often change lenses at the bottom of the pool. This maneuver required much practice and rehearsal as well as an expert cameraman. Underwater shots were expensive, too, because for every hundred meters of film shot, only five were good. For shots above the water Riefenstahl attached a camera to a frame on the side of a small rubber raft. She was not permitted to propel the boat with oars because they would cause waves in the pool. She solved this problem by having the boat pushed along with a pole. In this manner she obtained many fine shots of the swimmers.

> The problems I started with were not resolved so easily. I knew that the film could be interesting only on one condition. I knew that the restraints imposed by the events, while serving as a guide, had to be violated at times. Otherwise I would have just a newsreel film. I started to think about things in order to find out why the camera should be placed in various spots, various angles. I wanted to show the complete domination of the body and the will by the individual and the camaraderie and loyalty of the competitors. From this results an extraordinary atmosphere that is lifted well above ordinary life. This is what I wanted to show.[20]

According to Albert Speer, Hitler wanted to show something else. He gave orders that everything possible should be done to convey the impression of a peace-loving Germany to the many foreign guests and to Riefenstahl's audiences. Yet when Albert Speer pointed out to him that the athletic field in Berlin did not have the prescribed Olympic proportions, he said, "No matter. In 1940 the Olympic Games will take place in Tokyo. But thereafter they will take place in Germany for all time to come. And then *we* will determine the measurements of the athletic field." [21]

So much for peace.

While Riefenstahl was organizing her film crew and resolving her technical problems, Hitler was having problems of his own. By 1936 his racial policy had permeated all aspects of German life, including sports. Three years earlier, shortly after the Nazis had come to power, Jews were forbidden to belong to youth, welfare, and gymnastic organizations, and the club facilities were not available to them. Streicher, as could be expected, supported the move wholeheartedly: "We need waste no words here, Jews are Jews and there is no place for them in German sports. Germany is the Fatherland of Germans and not Jews, and the Germans have the right to do what they want in their own country." [22]

Gradually the restrictions against Jews in sports were tightened. Swimming resorts were closed to them; Jewish Boy Scout units were dispersed and their funds confiscated; Jewish war veterans' athletic organizations were ordered disbanded; and all private and public practice fields were closed to Jews. A sign posted in the center of the famous Bavarian ski resort of Garmisch-Partenkirchen stated the policy very clearly: "Jews, your entry is forbidden!" Bruno Malitz, sports director for the Storm Troopers, expressed the Nazi view on athletics in Germany in a treatise that Goebbels declared should be read by every German. In part, Malitz stated:

> Frenchmen, Belgians, Polacks, Jew-Niggers have all run on German tracks, competed on German football fields, and swum in German swimming pools. Many foreigners have been having a marvelous time at our expense. The sports promoters have spent great sums of money so that the international connections of Germany with her enemies shall be made yet closer.
>
> Jewish sports leaders, like the Jewish plague, pacifists, and other reconcilers have absolutely no place in German sport. They are worse than rampaging hordes of Kalmucks, worse than a

burning conflagration, famine, floods, drought, locusts, and poison gas—worse than all these horrors.[23]

If the exclusion of Jewish athletes perturbed Riefenstahl, there is no evidence of it. She continued with her preparations despite the statements of Streicher, Malitz, Goebbels and others and the obvious racial policy of Hitler. Other countries that were scheduled to participate in the Olympic Games of 1936 were troubled, however. When it was learned that Hitler was going to oust Dr. Theodor Lewald, the president of the German Olympic Committee, because his paternal grandmother had been a Jew, the IOC threatened to remove the games from Berlin. Hitler quickly changed his mind and retained Lewald as an "adviser" for the event. The United States was not satisfied. American Olympic officials advocated removing the Olympic Games from Germany if Hitler did not halt his discrimination against German Jewish athletes. They pointed out that many distinguished Jewish athletes had already been forced to leave Germany because of Hitler's discrimination policy: Alex Nathan, a sprinter on a German team that had equaled the world record for the 400-meter relay in 1929; Rudi Ball, Germany's finest hockey player; Dr. Daniel Press, the country's best tennis player; and Helene Mayer, a world-renowned fencer.

Finally Leward announced from Berlin that Germany would abide by all Olympic resolutions and that "as a principle" Jews would not be excluded from the German teams. The protests in the United States continued, however. The National Council of the Methodist Church, the American Federation of Labor, Governor Al Smith of New York, and most American newspapers were strongly against United States participation in the Berlin games. In December 1935, after Rudi Ball and Helene Mayer had been assured consideration for places on the German Olympic teams, the Amateur Athletic Union voted by a narrow margin to send the American Olympic teams to Berlin. Still the protests continued. A letter written to the IOC by the president of the Maccabi World Union, an international organization of Jewish sporting clubs, spoke for many:

We cannot as Jews accept lightly the situation created by the Olympic Games being held in Berlin. I, in common with all other Jews and many non-Jews, look upon the state of affairs in Germany from the point of view of general humanity and social decency. We certainly do urge all Jewish sportsmen, for their own self-respect, to refrain from competing in a country where they are discriminated against as a race and our Jewish brethren are treated with unexampled brutality.[24]

Judith Deutsch, Austrian swimmer; Philippe de Rothschild, French bobsled champion; and Jean Rheims and Albert Wolff, two other French athletes, refused to participate in the events. Although Hitler and the German Olympic Committee vowed that there would be no discrimination against Jews at the Olympic Games of 1936, certain incidents were too obvious to conceal. The death of Captain Wolfgang Fürstner was one such incident. Fürstner, director of the German army's athletic program, had designed and helped supervise the construction and operation of the Olympic Village. He did an excellent job, but a short time before the opening he was suddenly replaced as director of the Olympic Village and dismissed from the army. No reason was given, but foreign correspondents were aware that he had Jewish blood. After a banquet honoring his successor, Fürstner returned to his barracks and killed himself. German newspapers announced that he had died in an automobile accident, but the world press corps knew how and why he had died.

The Jewish question came up again during the Winter Olympics at Garmisch-Partenkirchen, which preceded the summer event at Berlin. While driving to the Winter Olympics, Count Henri Baillet-Latour, president of the IOC, was amazed to see a large number of obscene anti-Semitic signs along the highway. He immediately demanded an appointment with Hitler and told the Führer bluntly that unless the signs were removed, he would cancel both the Winter and Summer Olympic Games. Hitler replied, "I cannot alter a question of the highest importance within Germany for a small point of Olympic protocol." [25]

When Baillet-Latour did not withdraw his demand and instead repeated his threat, Hitler became very angry and excited and talked for several minutes about a number of unrelated subjects while staring at the ceiling. Finally he became silent, and when Baillet-Latour also remained silent, the Führer muttered, "You will be satisfied; the orders shall be given." [26]

The signs were taken down . . . until the Olympic Games of 1936 ended.

Hitler's attempts to mislead the world about the Nazi brutality against Jews were matched by his attempts to conceal the fact that he was preparing for war. On March 7, 1936, Hitler ordered his troops into the Rhineland, a German territory from thirty to seventy miles wide that bordered France, Luxembourg, Belgium, and Holland. The Versailles Treaty had required that this territory be demilitarized so that it could serve as a buffer zone between Germany and the other countries. The Locarno Pact stated that a remilitarization of the strip would be a cause for war. But while Hitler was ostensibly watching the Winter Olympics at Garmisch-Partenkirchen, he was preparing to seize this vital territory, to test the will of France and the other nations involved. As he said later:

> The forty-eight hours after the march into the Rhineland were very nerve-racking. If the French had marched into the Rhineland we would have had to withdraw with our tails between our legs, for the military resources at our disposal would have been wholly inadequate for even moderate resistance. [27]

France did not resist and Hitler managed to project to the world a false image of a powerful Germany, just as he was preparing to project a false picture of a unified, strong, and egalitarian Germany at the Summer Olympics.

He had selected the most skilled filmmaker in Germany to create that image, and Riefenstahl was well prepared when the games opened in August. The threat of war, the Jewish problem, the brutal policies of Hitler—all were ignored. Art, not moral responsibility, was her goal.

11

Olympia

Olympia was a radical departure from previous sports films. It broke new ground for the cinema and has been unequaled since. Riefenstahl gathered an excellent staff to make the film. The official credits list many of the best cameramen, musical directors, and technical personnel of German cinema.

Olympia [1]

Part I	*Fest der Völker*
Part II	*Fest der Schönheit*
Production Company:	Olympic Film GmbH
Production Leader:	Walter Traut, Walter Grosskopf
Director:	Leni Riefenstahl
Camera:	Hans Ertl, Walter Frentz, Guzzi Lantschner, Heinz von Jaworsky, Andor V. Barsy, Wilfried Basse, Josef Dietze, Edmund Epkens, Franz von Friedl, Hans Gottschalk, Richard Groschopp, Willi Hameister, Wolf Hart, Hasso Hartnagel, Prof. Walter Hege, Eberhard van der Heyden, Albert Höcht, Paul Holzki, Werner Hundhausen, Sepp Ketterer, Hugo von Kaweczynski, Herbert Kebelmann, Albert Kling, Ernst

	Kunstmann, Leo de Laforgue, A. Lagorio, E. Lambertini, Otto Lantschner, Waldemar Lemke, Georg Lemki, C. Linke, E. Nitzschemann, Albert Schattmann, Wilhelm Schmidt, Hugo Schulze, L. Schvedler, Alfred Siegert, W. Siehm, Ernst Sorge, H. von Stwolinski, Karl Vass
Music:	Herbert Windt, Walter Gronostay
German Narration:	Paul Laven, Rolf Wernicke
Cameraman for Prologue:	Willy Zielke
Directors of Cameramen:	A. Kiekebusch, K. Boenisch, R. Fichtner
Sound:	Siegfried Schulze, M. Michel, Hermann Storr, Otto Lantschner, Guzzi Lantschner, J. Lüdke, Arnfried Heyne, W. Brüning
Film Sets:	Robert Herlth
Sports Consultant:	J. Schmücker
Newsreels:	Tobis, Ufa, Fox, Paramount, Melo

Riefenstahl had immense resources for the film, although she has often protested, "We had less than people said." [2] The Weimar Republic had insisted that the German Olympic Committee obtain its financing for the 1936 games from sources other than the government, but when Hitler took over he gave the committee a blank check. He wanted a showcase as lavish as could be arranged, and money was no object. Riefenstahl obtained the money she needed through Goebbels' ministry and used it to great advantage.

Well before the games began in August, Riefenstahl knew the order of events that were to take place as well as Diem, who was in charge of the games. Events were to take place not only in the new Berlin stadium, but at many other sites in the area as well, and it was necessary for her to schedule her cameramen well ahead of time. She also had to make certain that they had the correct equipment, knew the restrictions placed upon them by the IOC, and knew when these restrictions could be ignored.

"I had the whole thing in my head," Riefenstahl said later. "I treated the whole thing like a vision. I was like an architect building a house." [3]

Not all the footage, of course, could be filmed in Berlin. The opening sequence, which in the finished film consists of approximately 950 feet of 35-mm. film, was shot on location. As music surges, the viewer sees a montage of the Acropolis at Athens; the temple of Zeus at Olympia; nude men and women, hazily backlighted, who seem to represent the Greek spirit of athletics; and then a solitary runner carrying the Olympic torch on his way to Berlin. Through a series of such runners she brings the viewer from the ancient games to the modern games of 1936, finally showing the torch being carried into the stadium in Berlin. Swastika banners wave among the spectators.

Willy Zielke, a skilled cameraman who later feigned mental illness to avoid working in the Nazi cinema industry, was in charge of photographing the prologue. Not even all of it was filmed in Greece; the nudes were photographed at a beach on the Baltic. They were an afterthought. Riefenstahl thought the footage shot in Greece lacked interest, so she made the nude scenes and added them to the prologue. One of them shows a woman on a bench shot full-figure from the rear, her arms extended toward the heavens; it is Riefenstahl herself. [4]

The footage obtained in Greece was shot before the games began. Two cameramen, one of whom was Jaworsky, went to Greece with Riefenstahl. The two men traveled to Olympia by car through Czechoslovakia, Austria, Hungary, and the other countries as a goodwill gesture and to promote the upcoming games. Riefenstahl met them in Athens and rode with them from Athens to Olympia. When they arrived at Olympia she learned that the arrangements made by the Olympic committee for lighting the holy fire with a parabolic mirror were much too dull. Riefenstahl swore—and she was very good at it—and ignored the official plans.

"We will arrange our own," she said, disgusted and angry. [5]

Using her experience in mountain films, Riefenstahl staged and filmed a prologue that blended the ancient rites and beautiful bodies. In all her films she showed a keen appreciation of muscular male bodies, and included many closeups of them in *Olympia*. In fact, she was so appreciative of one of the runners who carried the Olympic torch in Greece that she refused to leave him behind.

The first few runners were chosen for their past deeds or positions. A former Olympic medal winner, now sixty years old, covered the first two kilometers, and when he was picked up by a bus, the son of the prime minister of Greece took over for the next two kilometers. Riefenstahl and Jaworsky followed in her big Mercedes convertible, shooting footage of the runners as they moved along.

"She kept telling me to shoot this and that and was very excited, as usual," Jaworsky said. "But when a certain young runner took over, one of the first twenty, she suddenly wanted me to shoot his every move." [6]

Riefenstahl was so taken with this extremely handsome, muscular, tanned young runner that when it came time for the bus to pick him up after he had run the prescribed two kilometers, she insisted he get into her car instead and travel with her to Berlin. His name, she learned, was Anatole. He couldn't speak German but she took him anyway. She stopped in Athens long enough to buy him some new clothes and arrange for a passport and then continued her trip, Anatole at her side. At the ancient stadium in Delphi, runners were waiting to be photographed in the white leggings, flared skirts, and tight vests, the same costume Spiridon Loues had worn when he won the marathon in 1896. Riefenstahl ignored them and shot more footage of Anatole.

"As usual, she had a perfect instinct for what was good for the film," Jaworsky said. "Of course, being a woman, a sexy woman, the rumors were flying right away that she was having a love affair. I don't know. I didn't see her having an affair with him but most people thought she was." [7]

After following the runners from Greece to the German border, Jaworsky left Riefenstahl and boarded the airship *Hindenburg* for the overhead shots of the opening ceremonies at the Olympic Stadium in Berlin.

Riefenstahl had many subjects and actions to focus her cameras on during these opening festivities and she shot a great deal of footage, although only a small amount of it finally appeared in *Olympia*. The new Olympic Stadium was the largest built up to that time, yet whenever Hitler visited it during its construction he told Werner March, the architect, that it was still too small. In addition to the stadium there was a vast complex of arenas, athletic fields, and parking lots where contests took place and celebrities gathered. The area, called the *Reichssportfeld*, covered hundreds of acres. The equestrian events and rowing contests took place in yet other locations in or near Berlin. Although Riefenstahl had a large number of cameramen, more than she admits and more than the official credits list, she still had to schedule them with extreme care so that she could get all the footage she wanted. She never knew when or where an important incident might occur that could be the highlight of the movie.

The opening ceremonies, on August 1, 1936, were impressive, and even those who opposed the Nazi regime agreed that the Führer and his staff had planned it well. A crowd of 110,000 filled the new stadium, eager to see the athletes, eager to see Hitler. For Riefenstahl's cameras on the ground and in the *Hindenburg* overhead, the long string of black Mercedes-Benz convertibles that heralded the Führer's arrival signaled the start of the festivities. Hitler, wearing high leather boots and the brown uniform of the SA, led the parade of officials into the stadium. Behind him came the king of Bulgaria, several crown princes of European countries, and Mussolini's sons. Hitler made certain that his close associates were available for Riefenstahl's cameras, yet not so obviously that the IOC officials would object. Göring in his colorful blue uniform of a Luftwaffe marshal, Field Marshal August von Mackensen in his army uniform, Goebbels in a pure white suit that accented his tanned face, and others were scattered throughout the crowd, all targets for Riefenstahl's cameras.

The traditional march of the athletes of the world into the stadium and past the Tribune of Honor was, as always, a stirring scene. The varied uniforms, flags, and modes of acknowledgment of Hitler's salute were watched with interest by the crowd in the stadium. In the editing room, Riefenstahl was very selective of the footage she used on these opening ceremonies. The Olympic salute, unfortunately, was similar to the Nazi salute—arm outstretched, hand open, palm down—except that the arm was extended to the side. The Austrians, Bulgarians, Germans, most of the French team, and the Italians gave Hitler the Nazi salute. Other contingents dipped their national flags as they passed the Tribune of Honor. As the United States team passed Hitler, they gave him eyes right, but the Stars and Stripes remained high. Alfred Joachim, the flag-bearer, had vowed that the American flag would dip for no earthly king. The German audience was not pleased.

Lewald, in a long-winded, pompous speech, claimed to see in the Olympic flame "a real and spiritual bond between our German fatherland and the sacred places of Greece founded nearly four thousand years ago by Nordic immigrants." [8] He, who had been a near-victim of Hitler's Jewish policies, also proclaimed Hitler "the protector of these Olympic Games to be held in this stadium, built according to your will and purpose." [9] After Lewald's lengthy remarks, the restless crowd was uneasy when Hitler rose to speak, but he had gauged the temper of the audience well and was brief.

"I announce that the Games of Berlin are opened, celebrating the eleventh Olympiad of the modern era." [10]

The last runner, a slender, Nordic-looking young German named Schilgen, entered the stadium then, heralded by a fanfare of trumpets. He ran to the marble dais and dipped his torch into the brazier. The Olympic flame flared to life. Riefenstahl's footage of the lighting of the flame, with the sun in the background, is pure artistry.

"Our crew was composed of six cameramen who formed the principal crew," Riefenstahl explained. "Sixteen other cameramen and assistants took care of the trials at other places. Our main crew were the only ones permitted to go into the stadium. In addition, I had ten nonprofessionals whom I asked to mingle with the crowd with small cameras to get reaction shots." [11]

Riefenstahl tried to place her cameramen so that the skill of each was put to best use. Hans Ertl was in charge of diving and the field and track events; Walter Frentz, the sailing regatta, the marathon, and the balloon cameras; Guzzi Lantschner, the swimming events, riding, gymnastics, and rowing; and Willy Zielke shot the prologue. All were excellent cameramen. Zielke, who suspended his career by pretending mental illness during the war, went on to become a film director after the end of the Third Reich. He produced *Der Stahltier* (*The Steel Beast*), a film about the German railroads that was highly acclaimed. Walter Frentz became the photographer at Hitler's headquarters, while Ernst Sorge became one of the top Soviet spies during World War II. Eberhard van der Heyden joined the German paratroopers and was killed when he landed on a bridge that was blown up seconds later. Jaworsky was later demoted and forced into the army because his grandmother was Jewish. Hans Scheib, who was half Jewish, went into exile in Madrid.

Riefenstahl requested and received a building for technical and administrative purposes at the Geyer Works, not far from the *Reichssportfeld*. It was here at Haus Ruhwals that her crews lived, argued, and planned their work. Riefenstahl worked constantly and expected her crews to do the same. Her energy was incredible, and there was no indication that she used drugs, liquor, or any other such means to keep going at her fast pace.

After the prologue and the opening ceremonies, which took a combined footage of nearly 1,900 feet of 35-mm. film, Riefenstahl concentrated on the field and track events. The fact that the field and track events follow the opening ceremonies in the final cut, however, does not mean that they took place immediately after them. They did not. Riefenstahl determined the final sequence of events in the editing room. In order to keep the theme of "ancient Greece to modern Berlin" dominant, she cut to women's discus throwing immediately after the opening ceremonies, focusing on the beautiful and dignified Gisela Mauermayer, who won the event for Germany with ease. Some critics believe that since Mauermayer was expected to win, because she was so attractive, and because she was German, Riefenstahl's concentration upon her was a cleverly contrived blending of propaganda with art. After all, an excellent and beautiful German athlete following Hitler so closely on the screen gave the viewer a strong impression that Germany was dominating the Olympic Games of 1936. However, the fact must not be overlooked that Mauermayer's graceful spins, shown in slow motion, and her delicate smile made good footage. And Mauermayer did win the event by setting a new Olympic record of 47.63 meters, nearly two meters farther than her nearest competitor. She deserved recognition, and Riefenstahl would have been squandering her material if she had failed to spotlight her.

Hitler's glee when a German contestant won an event was intense. He would smile, hit his thigh with his open hand, and often stomp in joy like one of his Storm Troopers marching in place. It soon became obvious that while he was not a true sports fan, he was very much interested in the outcome of the games, in the final status of the German teams, and in the impression his new Germany would project to the world. He did everything he could to be a good host. He pleased the crowds by appearing at most of the major events, arriving in his long black Mercedes-Benz and waving to the gathered fans. In fact, he was so enthusiastic, especially when Germans won gold medals, that the Olympic officials had to remind him that the head of state was expected to keep a low profile and remain neutral toward the victors. After that, Hitler congratulated the German winners in private.

The discus sequence occupies 900 feet of the final version of *Olympia*, and is followed by the women's hurdles, the hammer throw, and the 100-meter race. In each of these events Riefenstahl displays her innovative techniques. She shows the hammer throwers in their preparatory spins, shows their perfect coordination and balance, and then immediately cuts to shots of their whirling shadows, accentuating these characteristics and at the same time giving an abstract quality to a rather brutal activity. The 6.80-kilogram head, steel chain, and triangular handle all blur into a single shadow of a whirling dervish of great strength and superb control. Karl Hein, a German carpenter, won the event by hurling the hammer 56.49 meters, also a new Olympic record.

There is no question that Riefenstahl was fascinated by the

American athlete Jesse Owens. Any charge that she discriminated in favor of German athletes can easily be refuted by pointing to the footage devoted to Owens. To her credit it must be remembered that Hitler greatly resented Owens' victories. She knew that Hitler had told Baldur von Schirach, "The Americans ought to be ashamed of themselves for letting their medals be won by Negroes. I myself would never even shake the hand of one." [12]

When Schirach wanted Hitler to be photographed with Owens, thinking that it would show the world that the Führer was amiable to all Olympic contestants, Hitler went into one of his famous rages and refused. Yet Riefenstahl considered Owens one of the outstanding film subjects of the Olympic Games of 1936 and shot a large amount of footage in which Owens appeared in a heroic role. Thus *Olympia* does give viewers the impression that Nazi Germany did not discriminate against blacks. Had Hitler concealed his own feelings, the deception might have succeeded completely. By his words and actions, however, Hitler dispelled much of the impression of good fellowship that Riefenstahl projected.

It is extremely unlikely that Riefenstahl had any idea ahead of time that Owens would be one of the heroes of the Olympic Games of 1936. She was not a sports fan, she did not keep track of participants' records, she did not try to predict who would win a medal. She did not care. She was interested in the grace and beauty of the human body, and it became evident to her early in the games that Owens' body was an ideal subject for her cameras. The fact that he was also a superb athlete who won three of the events was an added bonus.

Riefenstahl was not the only one interested in Owens. He had made it to the top in a field that at the time was generally hostile to blacks. There were, for instance, no blacks on any of the major-league baseball teams, few black college football players, no black swimmers. Until the 1932 Olympics at Los Angeles, the only black who had starred in the Olympics was DeHart Hubbard, who won a gold medal at Paris in 1924. Consequently, the fact that Owens was in Berlin at all was a real accomplishment.

Owens began developing as a track star at Ohio State University, and by 1935 his fame began to spread. He equaled the world record for the 100-yard dash and set new world records in the broad jump, 220-yard low hurdles, and 220-yard dash. In addition to this ability as a track competitor, Owens was handsome and had a body that was not only lean and hard but extremely photogenic, a quality that Riefenstahl recognized immediately. Much of the footage she shot of Owens concentrates on this body, the expansion and contraction of his muscles, the perspiration on his glistening skin, the grace and power of his movements. His face is very expressive in closeups. Riefenstahl caught his concentration, his determination, his weariness. Riefenstahl wasn't interested in the results of the races. She was interested in the man and his reactions to the effort required, to the other contestants, to the crowd. Her cameras followed him while he was warming up, during false starts, beyond the finish line. When he won the 100-meter dash in record time but the time was disallowed because the German officials said there had been a following wind, though photographs of the stadium flags hanging limp proved otherwise, Owens' expression was one of disappointment but not anger. He won not only the 100-meter dash but the running broad jump and the 200-meter dash as well, setting a new Olympic record in the 200-meter dash and a new Olympic running broad jump distance of 8.06 meters. And Riefenstahl, who had selected Owens as the prime target for her cameras before these events, had it all on film. Her choice was further evidence of her excellent artistic taste, regardless of whether she was making the film for herself or for the Nazi regime.

Riefenstahl became as well known to the stadium crowds as the athletes. Her white waterproof greatcoat, large hats, and sensual beauty were the focus of attention as she moved about the stadium directing her cameramen. With a flair for the dramatic, she was always surrounded by assistants in dark raincoats that contrasted with her white coat. When this group appeared, many of the spectators ignored the ongoing athletic contests and watched Riefenstahl and her companions. She loved every minute of it. Often she would rush up to a German victor and congratulate him profusely—while her cameramen recorded the scene, of course. And in direct contradiction to her statements that Goebbels did everything possible to impede her filming, her chauffeur-driven car had a high-priority clearance and moved about the sports complex without hindrance. It was the only way she could oversee the activities of her scattered cameramen and give the necessary orders. Giving these orders kept her very busy.

"Really, if I start a work I forget food, I forget that I am a woman, I forget my dress, I only see my work," she said. "I forget because I am fascinated by my work." [13]

While she never really forgot her appearance—she always dressed in a way that would attract attention—it is true that she exhibited a fanatical devotion toward her work. In seeking to have her cameras show the power of the human spirit over all physical obstacles, she was constantly on the move, searching, experimenting, cajoling. If, as she has claimed, Goebbels interrupted her as much as possible and tried to prevent her from accomplishing her aim with the film, there is no evidence of it in the final result.

In the remainder of the first part of the film, *Fest der Völker* or *Festival of Nations*, she included footage of many of the other track and field events, always careful to avoid straight reporting with her cameras, always determined to show the beauty of the human body, especially the male human body. When a winner lacked the physical beauty she desired for her film, either she eliminated the footage in the final cut or, if some other element of the contest was so interesting that she felt compelled to incorporate it into *Olympia*, she would use a long shot instead of a closeup. Sometimes it was the colorful or unique uniform of the contestant that she focused on.

In the long 42.195-kilometer marathon race Riefenstahl found her second hero of the Olympic Games of 1936. Kitei Son, a Korean whose real name was Sohn Kee Chung, was entered in the games under the flag of Japan, the conqueror of his country. He looked less like a marathon runner than any of the other competitors entered in the event: small, slender, thin, bowlegged. Why Riefenstahl decided to concentrate on the marathon, not the most exciting race to watch, and why she focused on Son, an Oriental who was so different in appearance from the tall Nordic type Hitler praised, can be explained only by her instinctive feeling for what is right in filmmaking. First Owens, now Son: superb athletes, superb camera subjects, living refutations of Hitler's racial ideology. As time proved, both selections were ideal.

The marathon, over a course extending more than twenty-six miles, is traditionally the most grueling test of the games, and the distance is an obstacle that the individual has to conquer in his own way. Riefenstahl shows the way Son won the race in his own *Triumph des Willens*. Fifty-six runners started the marathon, including entrants from Finland, Argentina, South Africa, Sweden, the United States, Japan, and England. The lead changed often during the race, and Riefenstahl's cameras recorded the changes, capturing the turn of the leader's head as he glances back to see how close his nearest competitor is, his desperation as he realizes he is being overtaken, the joy of the new leader. Her cameras follow Son as he takes over sole possession of first place, emphasizing his pace by showing the passing scenery in the background, relating the lone, slender runner to nature with shots of the sky and surrounding fields, at times dissolving his sharply focused body into a shadow. Once, during the most grueling part of the long race, when other runners are dropping out and the straining faces reveal near-exhaustion, she shows Son calmly brushing back his hair. Then, in a climactic scene that has never been equaled in a sports film, Son approaches the Marathon Gate of the stadium, where trumpeters on both sides announce his arrival. The small figure disappears into the dark tunnel and emerges a few seconds later inside the crowded stadium, where he sprints to the finish line while the fans cheer, the trumpeters play, and the Olympic flame burns brightly. Some of the best footage of the film was shot at this time . . . and Riefenstahl had an unexpected star for the movie to join Jesse Owens and, of course, Adolf Hitler.

The first part of *Olympia* ends in darkness as the pole vaulters run, leap, soar, and drop, their competition unexpectedly prolonged beyond the hours of daylight. When at last the event is over, Riefenstahl's cameras focus on the empty stadium, the rows of flags at its perimeter, the Olympic flame glowing against the night sky.

Fest der Schönheit (Festival of Beauty), the second part of *Olympia*, does not have the unity of the first part because of the wide variety of events covered by the cameras. To the background music of Herbert Windt, Riefenstahl shows the athletes at Olympic Village early in the morning. In a way, this sequence is much like the early-morning scenes of Nuremberg in *Triumph des Willens*. Showing the still-wet grass, the first rays of the rising sun, the birds and insects, Riefenstahl intersperses shots of the wonders of nature at this early hour with shots of the wonders of the human body. Athletes are seen loosening up, clowning, resting. The Americans engage in playful fighting to the accompaniment of jazz on the sound track; the Italians kick a soccer ball to Neapolitan tunes; Japanese and Filipinos limber up to Oriental music. Once again Riefenstahl concentrates on the male body. One scene shows the nude Finns in their sauna, their genitals in full view.

Much of *Fest der Schönheit* deals with mass gymnastics and team sports. Some of this footage depicts the Nazi love for festivities in which thousands participate, the regimentation of the crowds, the controlled actions of massed humanity. One outstanding sequence shows three German girls swinging exercise clubs in perfect unison. As music plays in the background these three grow to twenty and then to a hundred and finally to what appears to be approximately ten thousand girls moving in perfect unison. Riefenstahl accomplishes these dissolves skillfully and without a break in the unity of the action. By moving her cameras to higher and higher positions as the number of gymnasts increases, she brings to the viewer an acute sense of proportion that accentuates the beauty—and the regimentation—of the scene. Only a skilled filmmaker could have planned and executed such footage.

As in most of Riefenstahl's films, there is very little humor in *Olympia*. Nor does the film reflect an attitude of compassion for the athletes. Only in the marathon, where her cameras catch the sympathy and concern of German officials as they wrap blankets around the exhausted runners, give them cold drinks, pat their heaving shoulders, does Riefenstahl exhibit any emotional empathy with the athletes. She devotes no footage to attempts by other athletes to comfort Ilse Dörffeldt, the anchor runner of the German women's relay team, who dropped the baton when she tried to grab it from the third runner and lost a certain victory for her country. Perhaps Riefenstahl thought it best to skip lightly over this incident because Hitler was so angry about it.

One of the most famous sequences of *Olympia*, and one that is known to film viewers throughout the world, is the diving footage near the end of *Fest der Schönheit*. Not all of this footage was obtained during the actual contest; some was shot while the divers were practicing. The diving sequence undoubtedly required the cameraman's greatest technical skill as well as his ability to make an actual dive. The beginning of the sequence seems little more exciting than a newsreel as divers stand poised on the board, make their approach and spring, glide through the air and enter the water. But the pace steadily increases. Now the camera follows the diver down, enters the water with him, and shoots back up with him as he rises in a graceful arc and breaks again through the surface of the water.

The real art of the sequence comes after this opening scene, as Riefenstahl begins to show less of the diver's preparations on the board, less of his actions in the water, and more of his graceful moves in the air. Now the camera lingers longer on the diver's twists and turns and glides, slowing the motion until he appears to be flying under his own power, effortlessly rising, soaring, turning. The law of gravity seems suspended. They appear to have complete freedom from all earthly restrictions . . . even from the harsh reality of the Third Reich. In the background, the music of a full orchestra blends perfectly with the action on the screen. Music was very important, especially in these scenes. "The diving sequence was a simple idea," Riefenstahl has said modestly many times, "but the secret of *Olympia* is the sound." [14]

The "simple idea" becomes more innovative as the sequence continues. After showing the divers in slow motion, Riefenstahl deliberately underexposes the figures so that their features are indistinguishable. Against the background of a cloudy, ominous-looking sky, we see the silhouettes of the competitors cleaving the air in graceful, intricate patterns. To heighten the interest and speed the pace without cutting the scenes shorter, Riefenstahl shows two or more divers in the air at once, one image superimposed on another. Finally the diving sequence comes to an end and the viewer is jolted back to reality.

Olympia ends rather abruptly with some footage of the various flags in the stadium and the Olympic bell, a fadeout that is much less dramatic than the rest of the film.

It is very difficult to list the order of sequences in *Olympia* because there are numerous versions of the film in a multitude of languages, and during the years, others have reedited it to their own liking, changing it at times until it is only a reminder of the original, and much less effective.

Altogether Riefenstahl's cameramen shot approximately 400,000 meters of film, or 1 million feet. There was no doubt that the Olympic Games of 1936 were well preserved on film, and Riefenstahl brought all of her considerable artistry to its editing. But would the critics, for the first time in film history, review a sports film seriously? Would Hitler like it?

12

Olympic Film Queen

During the eighteen months that it took Riefenstahl to edit *Olympia*, many changes took place in Nazi Germany. The Rome-Berlin axis was established; the Enabling Act was extended for four years; General Werner von Blomberg, minister of defense, and General Werner von Fritsch, commander in chief of the army, were ousted and the Führer appointed General Walther von Brauchitsch to head the army, although in reality he assumed both posts himself. Ribbentrop became the new foreign minister, extending the influence of the Nazi party to the Foreign Office, and Germany annexed Austria without a fight.

Goebbels was also busy. He was dissatisfied with the progress of the film industry, and with good reason. Despite all his efforts, output had dropped and quality was getting worse each year. Late in 1936 Goebbels decided that the only solution to the problem was for the Nazi government to take complete control of all German film companies. At this time there were three major companies in the Third Reich: Ufa and Tobis in Berlin, and Bavaria in Munich. Using government funds and anonymous groups of Nazi party members, Goebbels took over Tobis in 1937. Ufa was a more difficult problem. This company owned 111 theaters throughout Germany and had its own large distribution organization. In March 1937 the Deutsche Bank, acting for "unnamed parties" (Nazis or others friendly to the party) bought control of Ufa and forced the resignation of all twenty of the company's directors. It was then easy for Goebbels to install his own directors. From that time on, for all practical purposes, Ufa was Nazi-controlled. In Munich a group called the New German Cinema Syndicate bought control of the Bavaria film company and then gradually shut down production so that by early 1938 it was nearly bankrupt. It was then very easy for Goebbels to step in and gain control for the government. As usual, the Nazi government kept its ownership as secret as possible behind a front of banks and publishing houses.

On February 21, 1938, as Riefenstahl completed the editing of *Olympia*, Goebbels established the State Academy of Film at Ufastadt-Babelsberg, where courses were offered in "Nazism as Parent of the New German Screen" and "Nazi Administration." [1] Only Aryans could attend the academy, and Goebbels hoped that in the future all new actors, actresses, and directors in the Nazi film industry would come from this school and no place else. With complete control of the film companies and of the individuals working in the industry, Goebbels felt that he could now control the direction that the Nazi cinema would take.

While Hitler and Goebbels were consolidating their positions, Riefenstahl was working long hours in her glass-walled laboratory at Geyer, editing the 400,000 meters of film her cameramen had taken. Riefenstahl explained the task later as one of her most difficult:

> For *Olympia* I . . . lived in the editing room for a year and a half, never getting home before five o'clock in the morning. My life was tied to the material and the film. In my editing rooms I had glass partitions built, on each side of which I hung filmstrips that went down to the floor. I suspended them one next to the other, very regularly, and I went from one to the other, from one partition to the other, in order to look at them, compare them, so as to verify their harmony in the scale of frames and tones. [2]

She assembled and reassembled the filmstrips until she had the footage she wanted in just the proper sequence. But it wasn't easy and it was very time-consuming.

> It is a little like the foundation of a house. There is first of all the plan; the rest is the melody. There are valleys, there are peaks.

Some things have to be sunk down, others have to soar. And as soon as the montage takes form, I think of the sound. Is the image strong? Then the sound must stay in the background. Is it the sound that is strong? Then the image must take second place to it. This is one of the fundamental rules I have always observed.[3]

Riefenstahl has been accused of cleverly manipulating her audience's attitude toward her subjects through editing. There is no doubt that she took the events out of the order in which they actually occurred and arranged them to maintain the continuity and unity she sought while at the same time distorting the roles of Hitler and the Nazi party. Her great skill in editing kept her films from being obvious propaganda and permitted her to control viewers' emotions while she entertained them. In this subtle manner she was invaluable to Hitler.

After editing the 400,000 meters of film, Riefenstahl ended up with a final cut of 6,151 meters. The first part, *Fest der Völker*, was 3,429 meters long, while the second part, *Fest der Schönheit*, was 2,722 meters. Riefenstahl managed to have the film ready for its premiere on Hitler's birthday, April 20, 1938. It was shown at the Ufa-Palast-am-Zoo, the same theater used for the premiere of *Triumph des Willens*. The two intervening years between the filming of the Olympic Games of 1936 and the premiere of *Olympia* had changed the attitudes of many about Nazi Germany. In 1936, while it had been documented that Hitler was brutal in furthering his ambitions, visitors to Germany had seen little evidence of it, and the joyous activities surrounding the games made them forget much of what they had heard. By 1938, however, there was little doubt outside Germany that Hitler wanted to control all of Europe and that he was an inhumane monster to those he did not like. Consequently, international critics reviewed *Olympia* with a very critical eye.

Nazi reviewers were favorable, of course, whatever their personal opinions: On November 27, 1936, approximately three months after the games ended, Goebbels abolished criticism. At a meeting of the Bureau of Culture he announced:

Because this year has not brought an improvement in criticism of the arts, I forbid once and for all the continuance of criticism in its past form, effective today. In the future, the reporting of art will take the place of criticism that sets itself up as a judge of art—an overall perversion of the concept of criticism which dates from the time of Jewish domination of the arts. The critic is to be replaced by an editor of the arts. The reporting of art should confine itself to description, and such reporting should give the public a chance to form its own opinion about artistic works through its own attitudes and feelings.[4]

Later Captain Wilhelm Weiss, who was in charge of the Reich Press Association, explained further:

If a work of art and its presentation contain a National Socialist idea, we favor it. If the opposite is true, we have not only the right but the duty to oppose it. Art criticism is not primarily an aesthetic question but a political one. Until recently, most theater critics have ignored this fact. Only a short time ago emphasis was always placed on the question of whether a play or film was good from a purely artistic standard. The critic must now understand that what he sees on the stage is politics in the broadest sense of the word.

The art of observation does not differ from the criticism of the arts. Everything does not have to be accepted as good. The newspapers make a serious mistake when they believe that the prohibition of criticism means praising everything. This error must be corrected.[5]

What he really meant was that the critics could write bad reviews of foreign films, but not of German films that were approved and often financed by the Nazi government. Not surprisingly, *Olympia* received fine reviews in Germany. Most of the praise was justified. *Olympia* was a creative contribution to the cinema as well as brilliant propaganda. When it was reviewed by the censorship board on April 14, 1938, it received a high rating: "Politically valuable, artistically valuable, culturally valuable, suitable for the education of the common people, educational film."[6]

The review the Nazis most often quoted was the one by Nazi journalist Erwin Goelz, under his *nom de plume* of Frank Maraun, in the May 1938 issue of *Der Deutsche Film*. He called *Olympia* a "triumph of a documentary that succeeded where the film the Americans tried to make at Los Angeles during the previous Olympic Games failed." Goelz explains why he—and all Nazis—thought it so successful:

> It had to succeed here because Germany created for the Olympic Games of 1936 in Berlin a wonderfully perceived, symbolic framework that from the very beginning elevated the games above a mere sport report. This is not only a creation of the film, which illuminates and animates. It is a result of National Socialism, which is penetrating the total life of the nation with its ramifications, its directional force, and which makes us see reality and idea together. Only in the ideological structure of National Socialism could this great documentary film have come into being as an artistic achievement.[7]

Goelz describes the feelings many viewers had when they first saw *Olympia*. He praises Riefenstahl for her creativeness in turning reality into art in a film that is more stirring than the games themselves were. He also praises her editing:

> Leni Riefenstahl had enough material to select in such a manner that no frame or theme was repeated. She proved to have restraint in the face of this large amount of film. No overloading, no accumulation of shots in short sections. The clarity of the delineation, the uncluttered approach, the precisely measured sequence of events, and the excellent spacing of the peaks and valleys of interest are an outstanding achievement of cinematic structural skill. It is supported very well by the impressive and varied handling of the sound track and the musical background of Herbert Windt as well as the speakers. It is really a Festival of Nations and a Festival of Beauty that one experiences in this film. It is one of the greatest works of art that the German film has produced up to now—filled with a spirit that we sense not only as the spirit of the games but also as the spirit of the German reality of today.[8]

Other German reviews were comparable. Goebbels sent Riefenstahl a congratulatory telegram on May 2, 1938, when *Olympia* received the State Prize for 1938 for the best film of the year.

> Frau Leni Riefenstahl:
> It is a particular pleasure for me that you were awarded the highest recognition in the area of filmmaking in the year 1938 for the towering achievement of the film *Olympia*, "Festival of Beauty" and "Festival of Nations." I extend to you in addition my heartiest and most sincere congratulations.
> Heil Hitler!
>
> REICHSMINISTER DR. GOEBBELS [9]

In addition to the Nazi State Prize, *Olympia* won the Grand Prize in Paris, the Polar Prize in Sweden, and the first prize, nicknamed the Mussolini Cup, at the International Moving Picture Festival in Venice, where she was seen parading arm in arm with Goebbels on the sunlit terrace of the Hotel Excelsior. The award in Venice wasn't given without opposition, however. Harold Smith, an American delegate to the film festival, and Neville Kerney, a British delegate, protested the decision of the international committee on the grounds that *Olympia* was not a feature but a documentary, and a film they considered inferior to any of half a dozen American and British films exhibited at the festival. It was rumored at the festival that pressure had been exerted by Berlin. Smith and Kerney were overruled, and both walked out of the meeting of the international committee.[10] The film *Olympia* ousted from first place was *Snow White and the Seven Dwarfs*.

In the United States *Olympia* met favorable but not overly enthusiastic reviews. When *Fest der Völker* was shown at the 86th Street Garden Theatre in New York City, the critic for the *New York Times* wrote:

> . . . Americans will enjoy watching the numerous victories of our representatives in the track and field events. Assembled under the guidance of Leni Riefenstahl, the shots of the contend-

ing athletes from fifty-one countries and the reactions of the spectators in the huge stadium give the audience many vicarious thrills. [11]

Later, when *Fest der Schönheit* was shown at the same theater, the critic reported:

> . . . While it gets off to a rather slow start, Part II speeds up when the exciting military riding competition hits the screen and continues at a lively pace through the field hockey, polo, soccer and cycling events and the Marathon Race to the thrilling finale of the Decathalon where Glenn Morris, the American, won the title of the greatest all-around athlete in the world. The photography is always effective and sometimes brilliant. There is an adequate account of the doings spoken in English. [12]

Many reviewers agreed that *Olympia* was not only a factual film record of the Olympic Games of 1936 and an outstanding example of how artistic a documentary can be, but also excellent soft-core propaganda for the Nazis. Some thought it was brilliant propaganda, especially the opening twenty minutes, when the international tradition of the Olympic Games is exploited by shots of the Nordic torchbearer lighting the flame in Hitler's new stadium followed by shots of the Führer.

After the war, Ulrich Gregor, a German film expert and director of the Deutsches Kinemathek in West Berlin, said:

> Leni Riefenstahl's film about the Olympic Games, even in their purified versions when the mention of Hitler and the other Nazi leaders is cut out, is still fascist in spirit. The film treats sport as an heroic, superhuman feat, a kind of ritual. This is especially apparent in the narration, which constantly repeats the words "fight" and "conquest," and also in shots of marathon races through the forest, which emphasize the Nordic mystery. Even *Tiefland* contains that demagogic contrast between the noble mountain people and the enchained, civilization-ill people of the lowlands. Arnold Fanck's mountain films are based on this contrast. These few illustrations should suffice to demonstrate the difficulty of separating Leni Riefenstahl's seemingly unpolitical

films from her blatant propaganda works. Both emanate from a unified mind. [13]

Riefenstahl, of course, denies that *Olympia* was a propaganda film or that any part of it was intended for this purpose. In a position paper about the film published in 1958, Riefenstahl tries to explain the facts from her viewpoint. She insists that it was not true that she often had the swastika photographed for an "ideological under-painting of the Olympic Games."

"I actually showed the German flags much less than those of other nations," she said, "and I only showed foreign winners with the swastika twice, and these scenes were later cut out of the film." [14]

She also deals with the accusation that her film included a great deal of propaganda:

> It has been asserted that the *Olympia* film was a propaganda film for National Socialism. The truth is, that Leni Riefenstahl was granted the Olympic Gold Medal at the session of the IOC on June 8, 1939, by the International Olympic Committee upon application of the present president Brundage, USA, and the French Navy Minister, A. D. Pietri. This would have been completely impossible if the film had included National Socialist propaganda.
>
> Also, the kings of Norway, Denmark, Rumania and Belgium and other high-ranking personalities showed by their presence at the premieres of the *Olympia* film that it was free of any National Socialist propaganda. [15]

Riefenstahl did not receive any Olympic gold medal from the International Olympic Committee. The highly prized gold medals are awarded only to the athletes participating in the games. She did receive an Olympic diploma of merit, but it cannot be equated with a gold medal, and the year was 1948, not 1939. [16] And no one who attends the premiere of a film has any clear idea what the film will include, so the notables who attended the first showings of *Olympia* could not have known whether it contained propaganda or not.

Much of the remaining part of her position paper deals with

obstacles she says Goebbels placed in her way as she tried to film the games. Despite the official documents on file at Koblenz, Riefenstahl insists that the newsreel cameramen were not permitted to cooperate with her, and in fact hampered her. The Koblenz documents, issued by Goebbels' office, officially put the newsreel cameramen and their film at her disposal if she wanted or needed them. She also states that shortly before the opening ceremonies of the games, SS troops tried to seize her only sound camera, and she was forced to drop what she was doing and go to protect it. One can only wonder how one man or woman, including Riefenstahl, could prevent the SS troops from taking the camera or anything else they so desired.

She also says that Goebbels issued an order prohibiting her from setting foot inside the Olympic Stadium.[17] If he did give such an order, Hitler or someone with more authority than Goebbels certainly rescinded it quickly, because she and her crew did not miss a single day at the games. She also claims that Hans Ertl made a sworn statement that SS troops acting under orders from Goebbels' office stopped him and his assistant from filming several scenes of the games. Riefenstahl insists that Goebbels did not want her to show any footage of Jesse Owens in the final cut. Since Owens is featured prominently in the first section of *Olympia*, either Goebbels' orders were overruled by Hitler—unlikely, one would think—or he never gave them. When she refused to remove the footage of Owens from the film, she said, Goebbels cut off all further financial credit from the Film Credit Bank;[18] but the official documents quoted in Chapter 10 indicate that Goebbels never approved any money from the Film Credit Bank because he did not want a private bank to know the secret details of the arrangement between the Nazi government and Riefenstahl's company.

Riefenstahl has a ready explanation for a widely publicized photograph of Goebbels giving her a bouquet of flowers in the garden of her home. She says that Goebbels gave her so much trouble while she was making *Olympia* that she decided to stop work on the project and go abroad. When Hitler heard about her plans and discovered the reason for them, he ordered Goebbels to present the flowers to her in her garden so that pictures of the occasion could be distributed to counteract the rumors that Goebbels and Riefenstahl were enemies.[19] If her explanation is true, Hitler must have valued her services more than Goebbels. If it is not true, she and Goebbels must have been friendly despite her later statements to the contrary. Either way, it is difficult for her to deny that she was not friendly with the leading personalities of the Third Reich.

Her claim that she secured the financing for *Olympia* by a distribution contract with Tobis poses further problems. If all the official evidence on the formation of the Olympic Film Company do not show convincingly that the German government funded the company, the documents of its liquidation do. On November 5, 1938, seven months after the premiere of *Olympia*, the General Accounting Office wrote to Goebbels' Ministry for People's Enlightenment and Propaganda to inquire when the liquidation of the Olympic Film Company could be expected. If the Olympic Film Company had been privately owned by Riefenstahl, the inquiry would have been sent to her. Goebbels' office replied that the firm's business would be completed by the end of fiscal year 1939. It wasn't, and the correspondence continued.

On May 17, 1940, after the start of World War II, Goebbels' office notified the Finance Ministry that all the money "needed for the production of *Olympia* and advanced by the government has been repaid in full to the Reich. Future revenues from the film will, as up to now, be paid into a holding account of the Reich Treasury." [20]

Actually the Olympic Film Company was not liquidated officially until February 1, 1943, and the firm's balance, 114,066.45 reichsmarks, was transferred to the Reich. The last paragraph of the report on the liquidation gives no impression of ill feeling between Goebbels and Riefenstahl: "The further utilization and administration of the two films of the Olympics have been transferred to the Riefenstahl Film Company, which will report quarterly about the financial status." [21]

Copies of *Olympia* were made in sixteen languages, each version including triumphs of the athletes of the nation for which it was intended. The British version was never seen by British audiences. It was seized at the German embassy in London when war started, and later the British Army Cinema Corps cut it into short features that were used for physical-training films— an ironic use for a production made with Nazi funds.

After the war, when Riefenstahl presented *Olympia* to the German Voluntary Self-Control (FSK) in Wiesbaden in an attempt to get permission to show the film in Germany, she had to agree to cut the following scenes from the German version:

1. Hitler's official address at the opening of the Olympic Games.
2. Various spectator shots of members of the Nazi government.
3. Two German victory presentations.
4. A scene showing Reichssportsführer Hans von Taschammer und Osten accepting the Olympic bell. During this ceremony he stated that the bell's tones "shall not merely summon the youth of the world but shall remind us constantly of those who gave their lives for the fatherland." [22]

It was obvious that postwar German government censors thought these scenes were propaganda or they would not have ordered them cut.

Otto Skorzeny, SS *Sturmbannführer* who rescued Mussolini from the Italian partisans in 1943 and rounded up the Germans who attempted to assassinate Hitler in 1944, survived the war and became one of the most famous of Hitler's former close associates. In his opinion, "the films of Leni Riefenstahl helped to make propaganda. Hitler was convinced that Leni Riefenstahl was making at this time the best film he could also use as propaganda." [23]

Others who were either Hitler's close associates or prominent in the Nazi regime call *Olympia* a great artistic achievement with no propaganda tinge to it. Hanna Reitsch, the renowned German flier who flew into Berlin shortly before the end of the war and offered to fly Hitler to safety and exile, says that "her films were not made for propaganda but for art, her films were never done to further the aims of the Nazi party." [24]

Karl Ritter, a prominent Third Reich film director now living in Argentina, agrees with Reitsch. "She had only an artistic role in the Third Reich. The artistic assignments fascinated her, not politics. Hitler admired her as he admired and esteemed all women of great achievement. I am convinced that Hitler was fascinated by Leni Riefenstahl's ability." [25]

There is no question that *Olympia* was a remarkable film, one of the best ever made of a sports event. It confirmed the skill and ability Riefenstahl had shown previously in *Das blaue Licht* and *Triumph des Willens*. As we have seen, official documents on file in Koblenz also leave little doubt that the Nazi government arranged for the filming of the Olympic Games of 1936, financed the project with government funds, and selected Riefenstahl to make the film. The government's aim was propaganda for Nazi Germany and Hitler, and Riefenstahl, either consciously or unconsciously, fulfilled this aim successfully.

part three

The War Years

13

The Woman

"I was never Hitler's mistress—though I was dazzled by him. These are nothing but lies," [1] Riefenstahl says.

> It is senseless to call me the queen of the Nazis. I have never spoken a word about politics. It is all lies and forgeries. . . . If I had really been a Nazi I would have killed myself like Eva Braun. . . . I have never said that Hitler was handsome and intelligent. I'm not an idiot. . . . I have never seen mass executions and I have never seen a concentration camp. [2]

Yet it is known that Riefenstahl spent a great deal of time in Hitler's company in Berlin, Munich, and elsewhere, that she always consulted him directly when she had a problem in her work, that he chose her to make his most important films. Frau Anni Winter, the housekeeper who took care of Hitler's apartment in Munich, said during an interview in 1948 that Leni Riefenstahl loved Hitler deeply. Frau Winter claims that before Riefenstahl married during the war, she told Frau Winter that the Führer was her great love and that she would even be happy to stay with him only as a friend, but that Hitler did not want her. [3] Since Frau Winter knew many of Hitler's intimate secrets, Riefenstahl presumably was trying to get the housekeeper's opinion as to whether or not she should marry the "other man." She finally did marry Peter Jacob, a decorated major in the Wehrmacht, in 1944. The marriage didn't last long, however.

Jacob divorced her shortly after the war when he fell in love with actress Ellen Schwiers.

The truth? There are of course no witnesses to anything that happened between them when the two were alone, but it is known that they did not live together. She was never Hitler's mistress. Yet it is very difficult to verify or refute her statements about the extent of her relationship with Hitler and the other Nazi officials. There are stacks of photographs showing Riefenstahl with Adolf Hitler, Joseph Goebbels, Julius Streicher, Martin Bormann, Heinrich Himmler, and Hans Frank, head of the party's legal division and later governor of occupied Poland. There are telegrams indicating that she was very fond of Hitler, but whether her words of affection were expressed for reasons of love or reasons of ambition, only Riefenstahl knows for certain. In August 1938, after Hitler sent her flowers for her birthday, she sent the following telegram of appreciation to the Chancellery in Berlin:

> The good-luck wish my Führer sends me is capable of coming true. For that reason my heart is filled with gratitude. Today I hold in both arms roses as red as the mountains around me in the caresses of the last rays of the sun. I look up to the rose garden, to its shining towers and walls, and run my hands over the red flowers and know only that I am inexpressibly happy.
>
> Your
> LENI RIEFENSTAHL [4]

Such a telegram is not the type sent to a casual acquaintance. Like the other telegrams she sent to Hitler over the years, it expresses a fondness shared only by intimate friends. It also reveals the warmth of a person who needs and craves attention, and knows how to acknowledge such attention gratefully when it is received.

Leni Riefenstahl was her own woman in many ways, closely associated with Hitler but not completely subjugated to his will. She was an independent beauty, much admired by men, who had a masculine spirit in a feminine body. She was assertive, outspoken, determined, a woman in a male-dominated industry who did not permit men to dominate her. Her talent for film-making gave her an edge, and she used it to advantage at all times. If she felt Hitler or anyone else was trying to make her do something she did not want to do, she did not hesitate to speak her mind. When the Wehrmacht harassed her to make the short army film *Tag der Freiheit* (*Day of Freedom*) because so much of the footage of the Wehrmacht shot for *Triumph des Willens* had been cut from the movie of the Nuremberg rally, Riefen-stahl was not afraid to tell Hitler she did not want to do it. Bor-mann, Himmler, Speer, Goebbels—none of the Führer's associ-ates ever spoke to him the way Riefenstahl did that day. The fact that he later persuaded her to make the film after all does not detract from the courage she displayed at the time.

When she wanted something, she went after it, despite any obstacles placed in her path. A memo sent her by Judge Pfen-nig, the legal counselor of the Film Bureau, is evidence that at times she ignored Nazi principles for personal desires:

From: Pfennig
To: L. Riefenstahl (carbon copy to Film Association)
Date: March 10, 1937
The district leader VII of the Berlin *Gau* writes to me on the eighth of this month:
According to a report received here of the German Workers' Front, District Authority VII, commerce section, your member, the well-known cinematographer Leni Riefenstahl, is said to have made purchases in the Jewish fashion studio Götz, Berlin, 213 Kurfürstendamm. Since this occurrence has caused great offense due to the close relationship of the artist with the movement, I request that you inform your member of it.

Heil Hitler!
I. A.[5]

The letter confirms that everyone in Nazi Germany was constantly under surveillance, that Riefenstahl was not averse to buying something she wanted in a Jewish shop, and that she had a "close relationship" with the Nazi movement. The official files contain no further letter of reprimand, so evidently one warning was sufficient.

Riefenstahl's name was linked with the names of many men over the years. Her sensual beauty and extroverted personality attracted a large number of suitors and would-be suitors. Her star status in the German cinema, her fame as a director, and her prestige as a close confidant of the Führer made her a much-sought-after woman, both by those interested in her personally and by those interested in the assistance she in her position of power could give them.

"I know that she was once engaged to Luis Trenker," Jaworsky said after the war. "She was with him a long time, I know that. But it ended in hate." [6]

Trenker was a very popular star before the Nazi takeover and during the first years of the Third Reich. Hitler lavishly praised him in *Berge in Flammen* (*Mountains in Flames*). Later, however, he became irritated with him. In 1939 Hitler abandoned his plans to annex the South Tyrol, largely German-speaking but officially a part of Italy, and permitted its inhabitants to choose between German and Italian citizenship. Hitler expected Trenker, who owned a farm in the South Tyrol, to apply immediately for German citizenship, but Trenker refrained from making a decision as long as possible. Finally, under pressure from Goebbels, Trenker did choose German citizenship, but too late to escape Hitler's displeasure. From this time on, Hitler was cool to him. After World War II a large file on Trenker was found in the Chief Reich Security Office, showing that Hitler had had him under constant surveillance.

Riefenstahl admits that she was fond of Trenker when they worked together, but she can't understand his actions since the end of the war. "Many things he has given out, so that I suffered much, because he gives the wrong rumors. On television he tells a lot of wrong things," she said. "I remember him as a very nice man. He was friendly with me. All the people knew this. I can't believe what he says now." [7]

On a recent television show, Trenker said that one of the men who worked with Riefenstahl on *Tiefland* died in a concentration camp because she had reported him to the police. Riefenstahl denied this; the man lived until the early 1970s, she said, and died of food poisoning in his mountain home. Trenker also wrote after the war that Riefenstahl often danced nude in her apartment for Hitler's enjoyment.

"The tale that I supposedly performed naked dances is really senseless and laughable," Riefenstahl said. "I subsequently went to court in Munich and had this story banned." [8]

Her nude dancing is much easier to believe than the story that she had an actor sent to a concentration camp because he displeased her. Despite the many accusations that have been made about her behavior, her support of Hitler and the Nazi party, and her lack of moral responsibility, no one else has ever accused her of vindictiveness or any acts of direct brutality. The action she took in regard to Emil Schünemann, the cameraman who refused to work with her on *Triumph des Willens*, is the closest she ever came to seeking revenge against someone who opposed her. Naturally, her support of Hitler and the Nazi regime *indirectly* ties her to their brutality and inhumane treatment of the Jews and others, and is one of the reasons many scorn her.

Harry Sokal, the influential German film producer, was very close to Riefenstahl. "In the summer of 1924 we spent a few weeks together in a fashionable hotel in the Dolomites," Sokal relates.

There one night we saw the picture *Berge in Flammen* by Arnold Fanck with Luis Trenker. When she later made *Der heilige Berg*, it was a co-production of Ufa-Sokal. After about three weeks' shooting I began to realize that financially the production threatened to become a very dangerous venture. Our own liaison had ended some time before the picture started but there remained my interest in her as an artist and a highly fascinating personality. The reason for my anxiety was threefold: three lovers! It had started with Arnold Fanck. It soon began with Luis Trenker to be followed with cameraman Hans Schneeberger. It would be too easy to deduce that her only interest in them was to further her career. No, she was interested in all three of them, as such, at the same time. She had told me herself one night when she left Trenker, who made her unhappy and crying, and was seeking consolation in the arms of Schneeberger. I knew production couldn't have smooth sailing under these circumstances so I made an arrangement with Ufa and quit.[9]

Sokal also tells of an experience he had during the filming of *Die weisse Hölle vom Piz Palü*.

One night the entire crew was sitting in the dining room of the small Morteratsch Hotel, which we had to ourselves. I was sitting in one corner with my wife Agnes Eszterhazy, Fanck, and Leni. In the far corner Schneeberger, Leni's lover at the time, was playing cards with another fellow with whom I knew she had been a couple of nights before. All of a sudden we heard pistol shots and I saw Schneeberger sprawling on the floor with his companion standing over him, the gun still in his hand. Leni let out a scream. My own first thought was, My god, how can I replace my most important cameraman?

It was a hoax! A hoax to entertain us on a rainy night. Underlying, however, I felt there was a subconscious menace.[10]

Another prominent leader in the Nazi hierarchy whose name was linked with Riefenstahl's for years was Ernst Udet, the famous World War I ace who became a high-ranking officer in Göring's Luftwaffe. Udet, a short, thick-set bachelor, was a free spirit who loved to drink and eat at leather-paneled gourmet restaurants in Berlin and chase beautiful women. Boisterous and likable, Udet met Riefenstahl when he piloted the plane supposedly flown by Riefenstahl in *S.O.S. Eisberg*. He was an expert flier who between the wars became internationally known for his aerial stunts, such as plucking pocket handkerchiefs from the ground with a hook fastened to the wing tip of his aircraft. Udet was fascinated with the beautiful and talented Riefenstahl and they became very good friends, some say lovers. The same year that Riefenstahl filmed *Olympia*, Göring persuaded the playboy flier, who had shot down sixty-two enemy planes in World War I, to join the Luftwaffe. Udet was not a devoted Nazi or a fanatic admirer of Hitler, but the Führer, recognizing Udet's immense popularity with the German people, promoted him regularly. During the years between 1933 and 1941 Udet

Leni Riefenstahl during the filming of Olympia, *Berlin, 1936.*
(BUNDESARCHIV)

The famous pilot Ernst Udet, Leni Riefenstahl's friend, standing beside a sailplane bearing the 1936 Olympic Games symbol. (COLLECTION OF FOREIGN RECORDS SEIZED, 1941–   , NATIONAL ARCHIVES)

Willy Zielke (sitting on stand) in Greece filming the prologue for Olympia. (WILLY ZIELKE)

In 1936 Willy Zielke, a famous German cameraman, traveled to Greece and East Prussia to film the prologue for the Riefenstahl production Olympia. The following nude photographs are from his private collection of studies made at this time of various actresses in the film. "Riefenstahl has been silent on the fact that the prologue is my intellectual and artistic work," Zielke says. "On that account I will never forgive Frau Riefenstahl for her intolerance. At that time—in 1936—I was in Greece (Athens-Acropolis) and in the Kurischen-Nehrung (East Prussia-Germany). There for the first time in the history of cinematography I filmed nudes." Zielke lives in the outskirts of Berlin today. (WILLY ZIELKE)

(WILLY ZIELKE)

(WILLY ZIELKE)

(WILLY ZIELKE)

(WILLY ZIELKE)

(WILLY ZIELKE)

(WILLY ZIELKE)

(WILLY ZIELKE)

(WILLY ZIELKE)

(WILLY ZIELKE)

Martin Bormann in uniform. As Hitler's deputy, Bormann was in a position to help Leni Riefenstahl. She inferred in her correspondence that he took care of many of her problems. (COLLECTION OF FOREIGN RECORDS SEIZED, 1941–   , NATIONAL ARCHIVES)

Telegraphie des Deutschen Reiches

Telegramm aus   Peradifassa 556 80 W 24/8 1735

funk Rom - Bln

An den Führer des deutschen Reiches

Adolf H i t l e r Reichskanzlei Berlin.

Ein Glückwunsch den mein Führer mir schenkt ist
Erfüllung möglich;darum hat mein Herz mich zum Danke ge-
bracht. Heute halte ich mit beiden Armen die Rosen so rot
wie die Berge ringsum in Rosen der letzten Sonne. So
schau ich hinauf zum Rosengarten zu seinen leuchtenden
Türmen und Wänden und streiche mit meinen Händen über
die roten Blumen hin und weiss nur, dass ich unsagbar
glücklich bin.

Ihre Leni R i e f e n s t a h l.

A telegram from Leni Riefenstahl to Adolf Hitler thanking him for the roses he sent her on her birthday.

Adolf Hitler, Reich Chancellery Berlin

The good-luck wish my Führer sends me is capable of coming true. For that reason my heart is filled with gratitude. Today I hold in both arms roses as red as the mountains around me in the caresses of the last rays of sun. I look up to the rose garden, to its shining towers and walls, and run my hands over the red flowers and know only that I am inexpressibly happy.

Your Leni Riefenstahl

Karl Ritter (left), one of the most prominent film directors during the Third Reich and a director of Ufa, talks with visiting U.S. film star Gary Cooper in 1938 in Germany.

Telegram from Leni Riefenstahl to Adolf Hitler congratulating him on the entry of German troops into Paris.

From: Leni Riefenstahl
To: Hitler

With indescribable joy, deeply moved and filled with warmest thanks, we experience with you, my Führer, your and Germany's greatest victory, the entry of German troops into Paris.

You accomplish deeds beyond the powers of human imagination, deeds without equal in the history of humanity. How are we to thank you? To merely congratulate you is not enough to show you the feelings that move me.

Your Leni Riefenstahl

Badisches Staatskommissariat
für politische Säuberung

Spruchkammer Freiburg

2. Abteilung

A b s c h r i f t .

Akt.-Zeichen U 19 Nr. 753
Lfde. Nr. 1/35 R. 5 Beiakte

ENTSCHEIDUNG
DECISION

im politischen Säuberungsverfahren / dans la procédure d'épuration politique

gegen
à l'encontre de

Herr-Frau-Frl. Riefenstahl-Jakob, Leni geb. am 22.8.02 zu Berlin
M. Mme. Mlle. Filmschauspielerin né (e) à

Hauptberuf Filmregisseurin Wohnort Königsfeld/Schw. Straße Friedrichstr. 24
profession principale Geschäftsführ. domicile rue

Die 2. Spruchkammerabteilung hat in ihrer Sitzung
La section de la Chambre d'Epuration a statué dans sa séance

vom 15. Dezember 1949 erkannt:
du comme suit:

Der – Die Betroffene wird in die Gruppe der
Le – La susnommé(e) est classé(e) dans la catégorie des

MITLÄUFER / SYMPATHISANTS

eingereiht. – Folgende

Sühnemaßnahmen
les Sanctions ci-dessous

werden auferlegt:
lui sont imposées:

Der – Die Betroffene ist nicht wählbar.

außerdem:
en outre:

Die Kosten des Verfahrens trägt der – die Betroffene.
Der Streitwert wird auf 25.000.–DM RM festgesetzt.

bitte wenden
tournez s. v. pl.

*Decision of the "State Commission of Baden-Baden for Political
Purification" naming Leni Riefenstahl a "Sympathizer" in her relationship with Hitler and the Nazi party.*

and Riefenstahl were often seen together, a popular couple who attracted attention wherever they went. But as Riefenstahl became more and more popular with Hitler, Udet fell from favor. There were several reasons.

"I flew with Udet," Jaworsky said.

It was later, after the Riefenstahl mountain films, during the war. He pulled me out during this period after I had a disaster with the Nazis. I was discovered to be part Jewish, but Udet, who was a high-ranking general by this time, pulled me out to do two movies which had to do with flying. So I got a year off from military service. [11]

The Nazi leaders did not like to have their generals protecting "mixed Aryans." Nor did Hitler like to have one of his favorite women so intimate with one of his subordinates. According to Captain Otto Wagner, a test pilot who worked closely with Udet in developing new aircraft during this period, Eva Braun was very jealous of Riefenstahl and through Himmler's staff leaked the information to the Führer that Udet had an "interesting arrangement" with the film queen. Hitler was furious, knowing that Udet was the type of freewheeling individual who would delight in telling fellow officers about his amorous escapades. While he never mentioned the Udet-Riefenstahl affair publicly, Hitler began harassing Udet about his work as chief of the Technical Department of the Luftwaffe. Udet's health finally failed and he changed from a happy-go-lucky flier to a very depressed officer. He went into seclusion and finally, on November 17, 1941, he shot himself. Hitler told the nation that the hero Udet had died in an aircraft accident and gave him a full military funeral. Hitler's intimate associates, as well as Udet's friends, knew the true story.

Riefenstahl does not deny her long affair with her cameraman Hans Schneeberger.

"I had a long friendship, a very strong, deep feeling for Schneeberger," [12] she admits.

Schneeberger was born in Brandberg im Zillertal in the Tyrol seven years before Riefenstahl. He studied architecture.

Later he became one of the most important cameramen on Fanck's mountain films, where he met the actress. After they became inseparable, he worked on her films and became not only her lover but a valued adviser. They vacationed together and often went on skiing trips together. But Schneeberger started flying as cameraman in Udet's plane in various films, and the "flying clown" soon introduced him to the carefree life that Udet loved. It wasn't long before Schneeberger and Riefenstahl drifted apart.

"I lost my friend through Udet," [13] she explained simply.

It would be a mistake to think that Riefenstahl's affairs and rumored affairs were unique among the Führer's intimate circle. They were not. Goebbels was a well-known womanizer who compensated for his physical handicap by seducing as many women as he could—and his list of successes was quite long. His opportunities were many, since he associated with actresses and society women who fawned over him in attempts to gain movie roles or added prestige. Riefenstahl's name was never romantically linked to Goebbels'—it was Hitler who was rumored to be her special friend—but nearly every other actress of the period was either suspected or known to have been involved with him.

In 1936 Goebbels made a mistake that nearly cost him his position in the Hitler hierarchy. He had fallen in love with Czech actress Lida Baarova and decided to leave his wife and six children. When Goebbels became acquainted with Baarova, two years earlier, she was living in the luxurious home of the famous film star Gustav Froelich on the island of Schwanenwerder, where Goebbels also had a home. For the next two years they were together as often as Goebbels could escape from his official duties, and naturally Berliners were well aware of the affair. Neither Baarova nor Goebbels cared—but Magda Goebbels and Adolf Hitler did. With the help of Karl Hanke, one of her husband's staff members who was devoted to her, Magda began gathering documentation of Goebbels' affair so she could file for divorce. Hitler was furious when he learned about the situation and immediately sent for Goebbels. Goebbels admitted the truth, vowed he loved Baarova, and offered to resign his position and go abroad.

Goebbels was given a *Führerbefehl* (a command that could not be ignored): He was not to see Baarova again. Count Wolf von Helldorf, the Berlin police commissioner, summoned the Czech actress to his office and gave her the news. Baarova stayed in Berlin for a short time and then returned to her native country. Her films were withdrawn from German distribution and all her acting contracts were canceled. It wasn't until near the end of 1939 that Goebbels finally got back into Hitler's good graces. Riefenstahl has nothing to say about this affair. She, as well as many others, is well aware that there were many furtive alliances among the Nazi leaders and women of the Third Reich.

In fact, Riefenstahl is only one of many beautiful women who were rumored to be Adolf Hitler's mistresses. Goebbels and his wife were determined to provide female companionship for Hitler, thinking that it was one way to make him more human and less prone to rages. With the help of Putzi Hanf-staengl, the party foreign press chief, they arranged for Hitler to attend parties, concerts, movies, and other affairs with such women as Gretl Slezak, the vivacious blonde daughter of opera singer Leo Slezak and sister of actor Walter Slezak; Unity Mitford, daughter of the British Lord Redesdale, David Bertram Ogilvy Freeman-Mitford; Erna Hanfstaengl, Putzi's sister; Winifred Wagner, daughter-in-law of the composer Richard Wagner; Henny Hoffmann, daughter of Heinrich Hoffmann, Hitler's official photographer; and Olga Tschechowa, a well-known actress. And there were others. Frau Winter, Hitler's housekeeper, said that for a long time he was enamored of a girl named Ada Klein, and that he also was in love with a Munich cabaret dancer, Lola Epp, and with Renate Müller, a beautiful and talented actress whom Goebbels admired greatly. Renate Müller ignored Hitler's romantic advances but did succumb to his compliments. When Hitler was informed that she had a Jewish lover, he went into a rage and ordered Himmler to have his men keep her under surveillance. Frightened and in despair, Renate Müller leaped to her death from her third-floor apartment.

Of all the women linked romantically with Hitler, the two that were known to have lived with him and whom he loved as much as he was capable of loving anyone were Geli Raubal and

Eva Braun. Geli Raubal was the daughter of Hitler's half-sister, Angela. A voluptuous blonde girl who was nineteen years younger than Hitler, Geli Raubal gave him some of his most enjoyable hours and was later the cause of his deepest despair. Her mother had brought Geli with her when she was summoned to Hitler's Obersalzburg mountain retreat south of Munich to keep house for him. At first Hitler ignored the skinny girl but as she matured into a zestful young woman, more beautiful than most of the women surrounding him, he took notice. Before long he had Geli and her mother living with him in his Munich apartment, and the relationship quickly developed from an uncle-niece one to that of lovers. He and Geli lived in adjoining sections of the Prinzregentenstrasse apartment and Angela conveniently looked the other way while they visited one another. But as Hitler became more demanding of Geli and virtually kept the young girl a prisoner, she became depressed and tried to break off the relationship. When this failed, she shot herself.

"Hitler never mentioned her name to me again," Dr. Karl Brandt, Hitler's physician, said after the war. "But I remember that the emotions with which Hitler spoke of her later amounted to the worship of a Madonna. Her room in Hitler's Munich apartment was preserved and left untouched. Moreover, Hitler requested that an exact replica of the room be built in his new home in Munich." [14]

Eva Braun was a close friend of Hitler's even before Geli Raubal committed suicide. There is some speculation that one of the reasons Geli was so frustrated was that she was aware of Hitler's friendship with Eva Braun. Hitler first met Eva when she was working in Heinrich Hoffmann's photography shop in Munich in 1929, and while their affair developed slowly, she remained his mistress until they both died by their own hands in 1945 as Berlin was falling to the Allies. She was often called the "Mystery Woman of the Third Reich," just as Riefenstahl was often called the "Film Goddess of the Third Reich." Hitler never permitted the public to know he had a mistress. He felt that it would hurt his image as a great leader if it was known that he had any concern other than the Reich. Consequently, while

Riefenstahl was often seen with him at public affairs, Eva Braun never was.

Eva Braun, who was twenty-three years younger than Hitler, was the daughter of a Munich schoolteacher. Her parents, Fritz and Franziska Braun, opposed her affair with Hitler, but their daughter refused to listen to them. Later, when they realized they could not stop her from living with him, they insisted that Hitler marry Eva, but he would not—not so long as it mattered to anyone but Eva. There is no question that Hitler was devoted to her, but at the same time his public appearances with Riefenstahl, Anny Ondra, the actress wife of fighter Max Schmeling, and others caused her frequent depressions. Twice she tried to kill herself. On the night of November 1, 1932, she could no longer control her loneliness and despair and shot herself with her father's 6.35-mm. pistol. Her aim was not accurate and the bullet lodged near her neck artery. Quick action by doctors saved her life. Her second attempt to end her life was made on the morning of May 29, 1935, and it is thought that she felt another woman was taking her place with Hitler. Her diary entry for the previous day reveals her feelings:

May 28, 1935: I have just sent him a letter, one that is decisive for me. Will he consider it as important as I do? Well, I'll see. If I don't get an answer by ten o'clock tonight I'll take my twenty-five pills and lie down peacefully. Is it a sign of the terrific love of which he assures me that he hasn't spoken a kind word to me for three months? Agreed, he has been busy with political problems, but haven't things eased off? And how about last year when he had lots of worries with Röhm and with Italy and still found time for me? True, I'm not in a position to judge whether the present situation isn't much worse, but after all, a few kind words at Hoffmann's would hardly have taken much time. I fear there is another woman, although I doubt that it is the *Walküre*. But there are many others. What other reasons could there be?

Lord, I'm afraid I won't get an answer today. If only someone would help me. Everything is so hopeless. Maybe my letter reached him at an inopportune time or maybe I shouldn't have written it at all. Whatever it is, uncertainty is much worse than a sudden end would be. Dear God, please let me speak to him today. Tomorrow will be too late. I have decided on thirty-five pills so as to make it dead certain this time. If he would at least have someone call up for him. [15]

She received no reply from Hitler by the deadline she had set, and, with her diary lying on the bed beside her, she swallowed two dozen Phanodorm tablets. Within a few minutes she was unconscious, and only the fact that her sister decided to pay her an unexpected visit saved her life. Ilse Braun was unable to rouse Eva and summoned medical help. Within two hours the doctor had purged her of the drug and she was on the way to recovery. This second suicide attempt brought Hitler closer to her than ever before because he realized that she really loved him. But the question that was never answered is: Who was the *Walküre*? There are many women who could be considered, and prominent among them is Leni Riefenstahl.

"Hitler once told me," Otto Skorzeny said, "that Leni Riefenstahl was a great artist, an important woman to Germany. There is something fascinating about her. She has a cold sensuality that attracts me. She is also the most ambitious woman I have ever known.' " [16]

Captain Otto Wagner, Udet's associate who was also on Göring's staff for several months, once heard Göring refer to Riefenstahl jokingly as the "crevasse of the Reich." Hitler overheard the remark and was furious.

"Hitler was very fond of Leni Riefenstahl," Wagner says, "and nobody could ridicule her in front of him without being sharply rebuffed. I think he considered her a very important woman but I never could find out whether there was any romance between them or not." [17]

Eva Braun knew from newspaper pictures and from the conversational jibes she heard around Munich and Berchtesgaden from Magda Goebbels, Emmy Göring, and Hitler's secretaries, who liked to provoke her, that Hitler often escorted Riefenstahl around Berlin. In 1935 Riefenstahl had already filmed *Triumph des Willens* and the short Wehrmacht film, *Tag der Freiheit*. When Eva compared Riefenstahl's public adulation to her own secret status, there is little wonder that she became frustrated and despondent. Whether or not Riefenstahl was the cause of the despair that drove her to try to commit suicide is a secret that died with Eva Braun. If Riefenstahl knows the answer, she isn't telling.

Hitler's close female friends had tragic lives. Geli Raubal killed herself; Unity Mitford went into the English Gardens in Munich shortly after England declared war on Germany and shot herself; Renate Müller jumped from her apartment window; and Eva Braun tried to commit suicide twice before she finally succeeded. In fact, when Hitler was involved in a love affair, either as a participant or as an arbitrator, the results were often painful for one or more of the individuals concerned. He ended Lida Baarova's film career and forced her to leave Berlin when he learned about her liaison with Goebbels. He ordered his chauffeur, Erich Kempka, to divorce his wife because he heard she was a former prostitute. Nor was he adverse to using someone else's love affair for his own advantage. He was even willing to invent one if it would serve his purposes. Werner von Blomberg and Werner von Fritsch learned this the hard way.

Blomberg, the minister of defense and commander in chief of the armed forces, played an important role in Hitler's appointment to the chancellorship in 1933, but Hitler showed little gratitude five years later when he decided he wanted to control the German military might himself. When Blomberg opposed a new war, Hitler decided to replace him. His chance came when Blomberg remarried in 1938. (Blomberg's first wife had died in 1932.) His new wife, Erna Grühn, was a twenty-three-year-old secretary in Blomberg's office when the sixty-year-old general married her. He had received approval from Göring, who assured him that it was perfectly all right for a member of the German General Staff to marry again, even if his new bride was a commoner almost young enough to be his granddaughter. Hitler would be delighted with the marriage, Göring said, because it would show the German citizens that the Nazi party and the Führer had done away with the priggish prejudices of the aristocratic old officer corps. Hitler did indeed approve, and he and Göring were chief witnesses at the wedding.

Titillating rumors began to circulate, and at length the Berlin police chief felt it his duty to lay the unsavory facts before Göring: Erna Grühn had a police record for prostitution and had been convicted of posing for pornographic photographs. Further investigation disclosed that the new Frau von Blomberg had grown up in a Berlin massage parlor, operated by her mother, which provided questionable rubdowns. Göring took the damaging documents to Hitler, and the Führer exploded in rage. Blomberg had made him, an official witness at the wedding, look like a fool. Nazis and army officers alike were outraged when it became known that the highest-ranking German military officer had married a common whore. Hitler demanded his resignation. When it was not forthcoming, he dismissed him. It was suggested to Blomberg that the only honorable solution was suicide. Blomberg was not a complete fool. He went with his wife to live a life of comparative ease in a small Bavarian village south of Munich.

Blomberg's deputy, Werner von Fritsch, fully expected to assume the role of commander in chief of the armed forces, but Hitler had already decided that he was going to take the position himself. He had Himmler file trumped-up charges of homosexuality against Fritsch, which were proved false in military court long after Fritsch had been disgraced. Hitler was able to strip him of his post as chief of the army command without repercussions. His career ruined, Fritsch took an assignment in Poland and died during a battle in the suburbs of Warsaw. As he did for Udet, Hitler ordered a full military funeral for Fritsch.

Leni Riefenstahl is the only close female associate of Adolf Hitler still alive, and she too has suffered because of her association with him.

Another troublesome name associated with Riefenstahl's is that of Julius Streicher, the *Gauleiter* of Franconia, the fanatic hater of Jews. At the Nuremberg trials of the Nazi war criminals after World War II, the court stated:

> . . . for his 25 years of speaking, writing, and preaching hatred of the Jews, Streicher was widely known as "Jew-Baiter Number 1." In his speeches and articles, week after week, month after month, he infected the German mind with the virus of anti-Semi-

tism, and incited the German people to active persecution. . . .
Streicher had charge of the Jewish boycott of April 1, 1933. He
advocated the Nuremberg Decrees of 1935. He was responsible
for the demolition on August 10, 1938, of the synagogue in
Nuremberg. And on November 10, 1938, he spoke publicly in
support of the Jewish pogroms which were taking place at that
time. But it was not only in Germany that this defendant advocated his doctrines. As early as 1938 he began to call for the an-
nihilation of the Jewish race. . . . With knowledge of the extermination of the Jews in the Occupied Eastern Territories, this
defendant continued to write and publish his propaganda of
death. . . . Streicher's incitement to murder and extermination
at the time when Jews in the East were being killed under the
most horrible conditions clearly constitutes persecution on political and racial grounds in connection with war crimes, as defined
by the Charter, and constitutes a crime against humanity.
Verdict: GUILTY
Sentence: DEATH BY HANGING [18]

This is the man who wrote Leni Riefenstahl from Nuremberg on July 27, 1937:

Dear Leni,
I must also tell you in writing: The hours we spent in your
house were an experience for all of us. With this creation you
have confirmed anew what we already knew within ourselves:
The place that a good person occupies is consecrated! Anyone
who wants to be acquainted with you in your innermost being
must go through the rooms of your house; and anyone who goes
through them and departs without being deeply impressed is
without feeling and will never fully grasp you and your creative
work in all their greatness.
You, too, will always be lonely, always remain a lonely person, and must remain so. That is your fate as well. But that you
are surrounded by the simplicity and naturalness of these people
is again your fate, and this fate is your happiness.
Remain misunderstood by those lacking judgment, let them
make jokes and let them mock! Go this way laughing, the way of
a great calling. Here you have found your heaven, and through it
you will gain immortality.

Your
JULIUS STREICHER [19]

Riefenstahl did not appear lonely when she attended the many parties and official events in Berlin, often with Hitler. She was friendly with many men, sought after by many more. Riefenstahl traveled in Hitler's intimate circle, had his complete confidence. She sought his company because it gave her prestige to be seen with him in public. He fascinated her, just as she fascinated him. What they did during those hours together in his quarters behind closed doors is known only to Riefenstahl. She says they discussed her artistic achievements.

14
No Triumph in the United States

The following news item appeared in the *Chicago Tribune* on November 3, 1938:

> Berlin, November 2 (AP) Leni Riefenstahl, a plumber's daughter who became Germany's film queen and who has been considered one of Adolf Hitler's few women friends, was said by friends today to have left last Saturday for New York to launch her film of the 1936 Olympics. The friends said they tried to dissuade her on the grounds of unfavorable feeling in the U.S. against Germany but she said she was convinced the film would speak for itself. She was said to have sailed aboard the liner *Europa*.
>
> In 1933 Hitler authorized Miss Riefenstahl to make films of all Nazi party conventions. She received, too, the commission to put the Olympic games into a supertalkie. Her assistants shot 1,700,000 feet of film at a cost that remains a finance ministry secret. She started her career as a dancer in Munich at the age of 14. Hitler's automobile used to be seen parked outside her apartment in a fashionable part of Berlin.[1]

Whether Hitler ordered Riefenstahl to make the trip to the United States in the hope that the popular German actress and director could improve relations between the two countries and give him more time for implementing his plans of conquest is not known. It is obvious that he approved of the trip, because no German citizen, especially one prominent in the Nazi inner circle, could go abroad without government approval. Hitler was

175

well aware of Riefenstahl's whereabouts at all times. There is a belief that he wanted her to make the trip to divert attention from the new *Aktionen* he was planning against the Jews and that he hoped her appearance with her film, with its extensive footage of Jesse Owens, would take attention from the uproar over his outrages.

Certainly Hitler had no warm feelings for either the United States or President Franklin D. Roosevelt. He considered Roosevelt an impostor with a "sick brain." [2] During one of his long monologues Hitler said, "What repulsive hypocrisy that arrant Freemason, Roosevelt, displays when he speaks of Christianity! All the churches should rise up against him—for he acts on principles diametrically opposed to those of the religion of which he boasts." [3] This from the man who eventually was responsible for the death of six million Jews.

Nor did he have any praise for the American people. The nation and its citizens had no future, he said; the United States was a decayed country with the same defects that caused the downfall of the Roman Empire. "Everything about the behavior of American society reveals that it's half-Judaised and the other half negrified. How can one expect a state like that to hold together?" [4]

One indication that Hitler favored, if he did not actually order, Riefenstahl's trip is his affectionate treatment of her when she returned to Germany after her disastrous visit. It was as though he took responsibility for the fiasco and exonerated her completely. This was not the case when Putzi Hanfstaengl, the party foreign press chief, visited the United States earlier and aroused much ill feeling among Americans. Hitler had not suggested Hanfstaengl's trip; it was Putzi's own idea. He wanted to attend a reunion of his Harvard classmates. The trip was a public relations disaster and Hitler was furious. His ill-fated trip, along with other actions, later forced him to flee for his life.

Riefenstahl arrived in New York aboard the liner *Europa* on November 4, 1938, and was met by a large group of newsmen. One of the first questions asked her—and it was to be asked often—was about her personal relationship with Hitler. Was she or was she not Hitler's romantic interest?

Riefenstahl laughed and denied that there was anything romantic about her friendship with Adolf Hitler. "Because I work in films, I have to see Hitler sometimes," she said. "He is not difficult to see. I have known him since 1932. He saw one of my pictures and liked it." [5]

There were many actresses, actors, directors, and others working in German films who had never conferred with the Führer and who desperately wanted at least to be introduced to him. And except for members of his intimate circle, the Führer was all but impossible to see and talk with. Even his ministers and generals complained that they could not get past Martin Bormann, Hitler's deputy, who arranged most of his appointments. But no one has ever suggested that Riefenstahl was exaggerating when she said that Hitler was "not difficult to see"; for her, he was not.

On the same day that she arrived in New York, the protests began. The joint councils of the American Jewish Congress and the Jewish Labor Committee announced that they would picket any theaters that showed *Olympia*. The council sent a telegram warning of the picketing plans to all leading film distributing companies and exhibitors:

> Seeking your cooperation as in the past to stop possible showing of Nazi Olympic film brought to this country by Leni Riefenstahl. This production is part of Nazi propaganda attack on American institutions and American democracy. Council will picket all houses booking this Fascist picture. [6]

There was some criticism leveled against the American Jewish Congress and Jewish Labor Committee for their plans to picket *Olympia* and Leni Riefenstahl. Initially, many Americans thought the action these organizations planned against the beautiful actress and director were unfair. Just because the Olympics had taken place in Berlin and been filmed by a friend of Hitler's, was that sufficient cause to picket the picture? Riefenstahl was a good director, wasn't she? Who cared who her friends were? Many Americans were not yet convinced that Hitler was as inhumane toward the Jews and others he disliked as reports indicated. The thousands of miles between the United States and Germany took the edge off the monstrous actions Americans heard or read about and in many cases these reports were ignored.

Hitler was putting together the final details for new actions against the Jews while Riefenstahl was on the liner *Europa* headed for New York, actions that would once and for all convince even the most reluctant American that Hitler intended to destroy the Jews. He planned to announce his new measures on November 9, 1938, at the Bürgerbräukeller in Munich on the fifteenth anniversary of the abortive Beer Hall Putsch. A secret message was sent by Heinrich Müller, head of the Gestapo, to all Gestapo stations:

> Berlin No. 234 404 9.11.2355
> To all Gestapo stations and Gestapo district stations
> To Officer or Deputy
>
> 1. At very short notice *Aktionen* against Jews, especially against their synagogues, will take place throughout the whole of Germany. They are not to be hindered. In conjunction with the police, however, it is to be ensured that looting and other particular excesses be prevented.
>
> 2. If important archive material is found in synagogues, this is to be taken immediately into safekeeping.
>
> 3. Preparations are to be made for the arrest of about 20,000–30,000 Jews in the Reich. Wealthy Jews in particular are to be selected. More detailed instructions will be issued in the course of this night.
>
> 4. If in the forthcoming *Aktionen* Jews should be found in possession of weapons, the most severe measures are to be taken. SS reserves as well as the German SS can be mobilized in the total *Aktionen*. The direction of the *Aktionen* by the Gestapo is in any case to be ensured by appropriate measures.
>
> Gestapo II, Müller
> This teleprinter message is secret [7]

Two days before Hitler's target date for the pogrom, a seventeen-year-old Polish Jew, Herschel Grynszpan, had slipped into the German embassy in Paris and shot Ernst vom Rath, the third secretary. Rath died two days later. His death inflamed Hitler and his associates even further and the pogrom, known as *Kristallnacht* (Night of Broken Glass), was one of the most diabolic actions of the Nazi regime. Nearly a hundred Jews were murdered in one night and over 26,000 were taken to concentration camps the next day. Synagogues were burned, shops were looted and then set on fire, and in less than twenty-four hours approximately $25 million worth of damage was done. It was enough to make any American doubt that Hitler could be dealt with rationally at the negotiating table.

After the news of the pogrom reached the United States, the press asked Riefenstahl what she thought about it. She said she did not believe the reports.

"I didn't know anything about it at the time," she says now, "and denied everything. I took Hitler for a great and good man." [8]

Most Americans believed that Riefenstahl knew a great deal more about Hitler's plans than she revealed and that she supported him completely. As she prepared to travel to Hollywood, where she expected to be feted and entertained by the elite of filmdom, the protests against her visit became more frequent. Ed Sullivan said in his syndicated newspaper column, "Leni Riefenstahl, Hitler's honey, will get a chilly reception out here." [9]

On November 29 the Hollywood Anti-Nazi League ran an advertisement in *Daily Variety*, the trade paper of the film industry:

> Post this on your bulletin board!
> Over a year ago, on September 24, 1937, this league called attention to the presence in Hollywood of Vittorio Mussolini, son of Il Duce, collaborator of Adolf Hitler. Hollywood demonstrated its unwillingness to entertain emissaries of fascism.
> Today, Leni Riefenstahl, head of the Nazi film industry, has arrived in Hollywood.
> There is no room in Hollywood for Leni Riefenstahl. In this moment when hundreds of thousands of our brethren await certain death, close your doors to all Nazi agents.
> Let the world know there is no room in Hollywood for Nazi agents. Sign the petition for an economic embargo against Germany.

The advertisement was signed by many of the most prominent names in Hollywood. Donald Ogden Stewart, president of the league, did his best to ensure that Riefenstahl's reception would be a chilly one, and he succeeded. After the advertisement appeared, Riefenstahl retired to the seclusion of a Beverly Hills apartment with the comment: "It is all rumors." [10]

As more and more information became known about the *Kristallnacht*, Riefenstahl's stay in Hollywood became less and less enjoyable. Many German refugees and expatriates were now working in Hollywood, among them Fritz Lang, who had made three well-received films in Hollywood after leaving Germany, *Fury* (1936), *You Only Live Once* (1937), and *You and Me* (1938); Josef von Sternberg, who left before the Hitler takeover and now would not go back; Marlene Dietrich; and Ernst Lubitsch. All of them ignored Leni Riefenstahl.

Hal Roach, producer of the *Our Gang* series, Harold Lloyd's films, and the Laurel and Hardy pictures, planned a party for Riefenstahl and invited the notables of Hollywood. Later Riefenstahl said it was a "wonderful party," but Budd Schulberg described it differently. He said that the anti-Nazi community of Hollywood bitterly resented the party and organized a telephone campaign, urging other celebrities invited not to attend. As a result the party was very poorly attended.

Walt Disney, whose *Snow White and the Seven Dwarfs* had lost out to *Olympia* for the first prize at the International Moving Picture Festival in Venice in 1938, welcomed her to his studios as a fellow artist. He was the only Hollywood notable other than Roach to welcome her cordially.

She did meet some Germans who were not unfriendly to the Nazi regime and desired to return to Germany. Her secretary sent a letter to the Reich Film Board in an effort to help one such actor:

From: Leni Riefenstahl's secretary, Höcht
To: Reich Film Board
Date: July 22, 1939

On the occasion of her trip to America, Frl. Riefenstahl was asked by the film actor Ferdinand Geigel, presently at 5815 Irving Street, La Crescenta, California, to intercede for him here, since he wishes to return to Germany and be active here. At the request of Frl. Riefenstahl I am sending you a short biography of Herr Geigel and a list of films in which he has appeared in the U.S.A. I have asked Herr Geigel to send photos of himself, which I will likewise forward to you. Please investigate this matter and let me know whether there may be a possibility of work here for Herr Geigel.

Heil Hitler!
HÖCHT, Secretary [11]

But a few friendly faces could not make up for the contempt displayed by most people in the American film industry and by American audiences. When it was revealed that Goebbels, whose ministry controlled the German film industry, had played an important role in the *Kristallnacht*, U.S. resentment of Riefenstahl as a representative of that film industry heightened. At his press conference the day after the pogrom, Goebbels tried to play down the action against the Jews. He claimed that the accounts of the wanton destruction of Jewish property by Nazi hooligans, events that the foreign press had actually witnessed, were lies. "Not a hair of a Jewish head was disturbed," [12] he insisted. Yet the foreign press correspondents present at the conference knew that less than three minutes away from the ministry building, the rubble from stores destroyed by the frenzied Nazis covered Leipzigerstrasse.

After the war, when documentation on the *Kristallnacht* was presented at the Nuremberg trials, the magnitude of Goebbels' lies was revealed. Most of the documentation came from the minutes of a meeting in Göring's ministry on November 12, 1938:

Göring: How many synagogues were actually burnt down?

Heydrich: A total of 101 synagogues have been destroyed by fire, 76 demolished, 7,500 shops destroyed in the Reich. . . .

Goebbels: Then the Jews must pay for the damage. . . .

Heydrich: Damage to property, equipment, and stock is estimated at several million reichsmarks.

Göring: I wish you had killed 200 Jews instead of destroying so many valuables.[13]

Later on in the meeting Goebbels and Göring discussed the question of the segregation of the Jews.

Goebbels: I consider it imperative to eliminate the Jews completely from appearing in public, especially whenever such appearances have a provocative effect. Do you know that even today it is possible for a Jew to share a compartment in a sleeper with a German? I believe the Reich Minister for Transport should issue an order whereby Jews would have to have special compartments, indicating that when that particular compartment is filled, no Jew would be entitled to claim any other seat; that Jews should not be permitted under any circumstances to intermingle with Germans in the train. In fact, they should not even be seated at all unless every German in the train has a seat. And rather than have a Jew sitting in one compartment filled or half-filled with Germans, I would have him stand out in the aisle.

Göring: Would it be simpler and more reasonable just to give them compartments of their own?

Goebbels: Maybe, but certainly not when the train is crowded.

Göring: Well, what of it? There would have to be just one Jewish coach in each train, and when that one is occupied, the other Jews will just have to stay behind.

Goebbels: Very well, but then suppose there aren't that many Jews who want to get on the Berlin–Munich Express, say? Suppose there are only two Jews in their coach or compartment but all the other coaches and compartments are filled? In a case like that, those two Jews would be sort of privileged. Perhaps the ruling should be, Jews may only claim a seat when all Germans have seats.

Göring: I don't think it's necessary to put all this into an edict. Suppose that particular situation arose—a Jew or two seated in an empty compartment of an otherwise full train—well, what the hell! They would just be kicked out, wouldn't they, even if they had to sit in the lavatory for the rest of the trip? We don't need any legislation for that, do we?

Goebbels: There's another point we should consider. Isn't it about time to stop Jews from entering German woods and forests altogether? Nowadays Jews still run around the Grünewald in droves. I would think that is provocative, and incidents may, and certainly do, occur.

Göring: Very well, then, let's give the Jews a certain part of a certain woods for their own, and Alpers can see to it that certain dumb animals are settled there, too—I mean animals who look like Jews. I'm thinking of elks, who have that sort of a hooked nose, haven't they? [14]

These discussions were taking place in Germany while Riefenstahl, in the United States, was insisting that the rumors about the mistreatment of Jews in her country were entirely false. The anti-Semitic signs that had been removed before foreign visitors arrived for the Olympic Games of 1936 were all back in place. New decrees were issued monthly. In April, June, July, August, September, and October of 1938, the months before Riefenstahl's departure for the United States, at least ten important edicts seriously affected the Jews:

April 22	Decree prohibiting the "camouflage of Jewish industries"
April 26	Decree ordering reporting of Jewish assets
June 14	Decree on the registration and identification of Jewish factories
June 15	Regulations against "antisocial" elements: arrest of all previously convicted Jews, including those convicted of traffic and similar offenses
July 23	Introduction of identity cards for Jews
July 25	Decree that licenses of Jewish doctors would expire on September 30
August 17	Decree making Jewish first names (Sarah, Israel, etc.) mandatory for Jews
September 17	Decree ordering retirement of Jewish lawyers by November 30
October 5	Decree ordering passports of Jews to be marked with the letter "J"
October 28	Decree ordering expulsion of 17,000 "stateless" Jews across the border into Poland [15]

Since all these decrees were given widespread publicity, it is difficult to see how Riefenstahl failed to hear about them, even if most of her thoughts were on filmmaking.

When she realized that she was being snubbed in Hollywood, Riefenstahl left the film capital on December 1, 1938. Ernest Jaeger, her manager, who was accompanying her, vehemently denied to the press that Riefenstahl had come to the United States to study the film industry or to exhibit *Olympia.*

"She was here only to view the scenery," [16] he said.

That's about all she did see. One night club had "no accommodations" for her party of twelve after the owner learned that she was to be the guest of honor. A spokesman for Warner Brothers said that a request had been made for her to tour its studio, but the request had been turned down. Riefenstahl denied she had made such a request, and Dr. George Gysling, the German consul, said that no official request had been made to any studio and there had been no rebuffs. But it was obvious to her that she was not welcome, that her admiration for Hitler was not appreciated or condoned, and that her talent was not great enough to overshadow her association with the Nazi hierarchy. She went back to Germany and the man who "fascinated" her, Adolf Hitler.

When Riefenstahl arrived at Cherbourg on January 27, 1939, she gave an interview to the press corps at the dock. Two days later the *New York Times* reported:

> Leni Riefenstahl, friend of Chancellor Hitler and prominent directorial figure in the Nazi film industry, returned to Europe with resentment at Hollywood's treatment of her. She objected strenuously to "being trailed" continuously by two detectives who, she said, had been paid by an American anti-Nazi organization. She asserted that they not only interfered in her walks about Hollywood but "were actually rude to me a couple of times."
>
> Another thing she said she did not like was an alleged order from studio directors prohibiting their stars from talking to her. She said she was positive such an order had been issued.

She still didn't realize—or at least admit to herself—that the reason she was rebuffed and scorned was because she championed a man who was fast becoming known around the world as the "Monster of the Century." Most people couldn't understand her support for someone as inhumane as Hitler. They were convinced that anyone who publicly defended and praised him must agree with his policies.

When she arrived in Germany, a "source close to the government" issued a statement in retaliation for Riefenstahl's treatment in the United States. It was obvious that Hitler approved—probably ordered—the statement.

> Incessant agitation against the Third Reich in the United States, which among other things has hampered the showing of the Olympics film otherwise received throughout the world with the greatest applause, and which forced Hollywood film artists to sign an inflammatory declaration against Germany, has brought an understandable reaction in the film industry in Germany.
>
> It is pointed out that the American film industry stands under predominating Jewish influence and it may be stated that the number of American films in Germany has declined.[17]

So ended Leni Riefenstahl's attempt to endear herself to the American people in 1938.

15

The War Years

Leni Riefenstahl returned to a Germany that was preparing for war. The Munich agreement had given Hitler the Sudetenland and opened the path for his troops to march into Czechoslovakia. The Nazis, as expected, entered Prague on March 14, 1939, and two months later Hitler ordered the German General Staff to prepare for war with Poland. On May 22 he and Mussolini signed their "Pact of Steel," and on August 23 the German-Soviet pact was signed in Moscow. During this tense period the German film industry concentrated more and more on military subjects. Riefenstahl had other ideas.

Shortly after her return from the United States she made plans to film *Penthesilea*, a drama by Heinrich von Kleist about the queen of the Amazons, slain by Achilles when she came to the aid of the Trojans after Hector's death. Riefenstahl intended to play Penthesilea herself. She had been waiting to play that role ever since Max Reinhardt offered it to her in 1924.

"We kidded her," Jaworsky said. "Leni Riefenstahl was well-built and we told her she would have to have her right breast amputated or otherwise she couldn't pull the arrow." [1]

Hans Schneeberger and Albert Benitz, her favorite cameramen, had agreed to work with her on the production, and Riefenstahl was gathering together the remainder of her crew and seeking financing and approval for the film when the war broke out.

On September 1, 1939, Hitler ordered his troops to invade

Poland. At nine o'clock on the morning of Sunday, September 3, Ambassador Sir Nevile Henderson delivered the British ultimatum to the German Foreign Office:

> If His Majesty's Government has not received satisfactory assurances of the cessation of all aggressive action against Poland and the withdrawal of German troops from that country by 11 o'clock British Summer Time, from that time a state of war will exist between Great Britain and Germany.[2]

Shortly afterward France submitted its own ultimatum to Hitler. He ignored them both and World War II was declared. The start of the war prevented Riefenstahl from continuing with her plans to film *Penthesilea,* and she wasted no time in volunteering to film the German troops in action. On September 5, only four days after war began in Poland, Riefenstahl was photographed in the Polish city of Konsky.[3] She was wearing a uniform similar to that of the SS, complete with sword belt, shoulder straps, and a pistol in a holster. She rode around in a large shiny Mercedes-Benz driven by a Nazi soldier. On September 5 in Konsky, while Riefenstahl watched, thirty-one Jews were murdered in one of the first blood baths of the new war. Some Jews had been ordered to dig with their bare hands a grave for four German soldiers killed in the attack on Konsky. When the grave was deep enough, the Jews were instructed to climb out of it and run across the Konsky town square to a house on the opposite side. As they did so, a German officer ordered his soldiers to shoot into the cobblestone pavement and the richocheting bullets killed thirty-one of the Jews. Riefenstahl stated later that she complained to General Walter von Reichenau about the events in Konsky and immediately returned to Berlin.

This didn't stop her from continuing to support the Nazi troops, however, or to vow her devotion to Hitler. A short time later she wrote to him:

> My admiration for you, my Führer, stands above all that I am otherwise capable of thinking and feeling.
>
> Your LENI RIEFENSTAHL—bound to you in loyalty [4]

Riefenstahl was delighted when Nazi troops entered Paris in 1940. A copy of a telegram to which her name is signed is in the official archives:

> From: Leni Riefenstahl
> To: Hitler
> With indescribable joy, deeply moved and filled with warmest thanks, we experience with you, my Führer, your and Germany's greatest victory, the entry of German troops into Paris. You accomplish deeds beyond the powers of human imagination, deeds without equal in the history of humanity. How are we to thank you? To merely congratulate you is not enough to show you the feelings that move me.
>
> Your LENI RIEFENSTAHL [5]

Today she denies sending the telegram, but there is no denying that she remained on close terms with Hitler throughout the war.

Deciding that the glamour of filming combat troops in action had its disadvantages, Riefenstahl began her long and arduous attempt to film Eugen D'Albert's opera *Tiefland*, the production she had started in Spain before making *Triumph des Willens* in 1934. With the war in progress and Hitler occupied with military matters, she lacked the immediate support she had been accustomed to having, and *Tiefland* was a project that had little priority with Goebbels. Now that the fighting was under way he had no time to help or hinder Riefenstahl. Even the mention of *Tiefland* seemed to irritate him. An entry in his diary dated December 16, 1942, stated:

> Leni Riefenstahl reported to me about her motion picture *Tiefland*. It has become involved in innumerable complications. Already more than five million marks have been wasted on this film and it will take another whole year before it is finished. Frau Riefenstahl has become very ill from overwork and worry, and I urged her earnestly to go on leave before taking up further work. I am glad I have nothing to do with the unfortunate case and hence bear no responsibility. [6]

The entry is particularly interesting for his statement that he had nothing to do with the film. Since he controlled all film production in Germany, this assertion is confusing—unless Hitler himself circumvented Goebbels and personally gave the necessary approval. Goebbels' statement that Riefenstahl was spending a great deal of money was true, as a letter to Dr. Max Winkler, the ministry's economic adviser, indicates:

Berlin, March 9, 1944
From: Dr. Dahlgrun
To: Dr. Winkler
Re: Leni Riefenstahl film *Tiefland*
          Acquisition of film rights by Tobis for 40,000 RM
Through further inquiry with Schwerin, the attorney, I have determined that the amount of expenditure for compensation by Tobis is not disputed. Frau Riefenstahl is presently short of funds and would like to approach her financial backers only for such expenditures as are at the moment absolutely necessary for the completion of the film, while she will bring and submit a summary of all the other work involved with this film project at the conclusion of the shooting. Several weeks ago Frau Riefenstahl was supposed to have calculated the date of completion of *Tiefland* for autumn 1944. Under these circumstances, Tobis will be advised to be patient for the time being in regard to its statement of compensation for 40,000 RM, since it has waited so long already.[7]

Since the Nazi government controlled Tobis, the "advice" was actually an order. Riefenstahl still had her influence, obviously, and a later letter indicates that she usually went after what she wanted—and even more important, usually got it.

From: Leni Riefenstahl-Jacob
To: Dr. Max Winkler
June 18, 1944
Dear Dr. Winkler:
          I am so thankful to you for helping me to procure the necessary studio space in Prague; I believed that with that I had seen the greatest difficulty for the finishing of my *Tiefland* removed.

Now today I receive a "Job's message" that seriously threatens the finishing of my film once more. My production chief, Herr Traut, told me that Herr Teichs of the Terra-Filmkunst GmbH could not place my cameraman Albert Benitz at my disposal for the concluding scenes, since he wants to employ him in a new Terra color film. . . . Terra has always known that Benitz is indispensable for the concluding scenes of *Tiefland*, and it was possible for us to release Benitz to Terra for a film only under this stipulation. Now this film is to be finished in a few days; all terms for studio, actors, and other necessary staff have been set at this time for six months. The film has already had to be postponed for a year because the state theater would not release Minetti for the filming in Spain. It is not possible to postpone it again.

Before I communicate this new threat to Herr Reichsleiter Bormann, I would like to ask you, dear Herr Dr. Winkler, to use your influence so that such a catastrophe may be prevented. Meanwhile, with hopes that everything will still turn out to the good, I remain with best greetings and

Heil Hitler
Your
LENI RIEFENSTAHL-JACOB [8]

The veiled threat to tell Martin Bormann about the attempt to take her cameraman actually meant that she intended to tell Hitler. By 1944 Bormann was the most powerful Nazi in Germany next to the Führer. He was a coarse, rude man who operated on fear. He had great power and had made himself indispensable to Hitler. He decided who would see Hitler, whose correspondence would be forwarded to Hitler, and whose verbal messages would be given to Hitler. Consequently, if, as indicated in her letter, Riefenstahl was on friendly terms with Bormann, she had a very influential ally. Since Hitler had always aided her with her filmmaking plans, there is little doubt that Bormann was well aware of the Führer's relationship with Riefenstahl and would help her, too.

The hint that she would notify Hitler through Bormann was all that was necessary to keep Albert Benitz with her crew. Dr. Winkler wrote to Herr Reich Film Director Gruppenführer

Hans Hinkel at the Reich Bureau of Culture and enclosed a copy of Riefenstahl's letter. The second paragraph of the note he sent with the copy of her letter discloses the status Riefenstahl enjoyed with both Hitler and Goebbels' ministry: "As far as it has been in my power—for example, assignment of studio space—I have thus far been able to fulfill the wishes of Frau Riefenstahl to a great extent. . . ." [9]

On July 5, 1944, Riefenstahl was notified that Benitz was placed at her disposal for the final shots of *Tiefland* at "considerable sacrifice." [10] Hinkel's office explained that with Benitz working with Riefenstahl, the color film at Terra could not be made, and therefore one less film in the total program would be the result. Riefenstahl's influence had once again asserted itself.

This was not a happy summer and fall for Riefenstahl, however. Personal tragedy and the strain of trying to complete *Tiefland* while the war raged throughout Europe took their toll of her health. She actually directed some of the scenes from a stretcher, and fellow filmmakers G. W. Pabst and Veit Harlan shot some scenes for her without credit. In August 1944 her father died, and a few days after his death she received news that her brother had died in battle; or, as she said, "died a hero's death in the firm belief in his Führer and in Germany's victory." [11] Even in a time of failing health, Hitler's friendship was a comfort: The Führer's personal physician, Dr. Theodor Morell, prescribed medicine for her. [12]

By October 1944 her health had improved and she was back at work trying to complete *Tiefland*—and facing another problem. She now needed Hermann Storr, the chief sound technician who had previously worked on the film, but Storr was working with Veit Harlan, another of Adolf Hitler's favorite directors. In 1940 Harlan had shot one of the most infamous films in history, *Jud Süss (Sweet Jew)*, about a criminal Jew who raped a German woman. He had used every emotional and rhetorical means possible to inflame the audience's hatred of Jews, and the advocacy of mass murder was unmistakable. But Riefenstahl didn't allow Harlan's actions to affect her friendship with him, as this letter written four years after the filming of *Jud Süss* indicates.

From: Leni Riefenstahl
To: Prof. Veit Harlan
October 22, 1944

Dear Veit Harlan,

I am writing this letter to you with a heavy heart. I know that you, as an enthusiast and artist, would fight for everything that would increase the quality of your work. That I have also done before, and it is for that reason that I understand you so well. Now I can fight no more. The illness that has destroyed my body in the past four years, the hard blows of fate that have struck me recently, and in addition the constant anxiety about my husband, who for months has been in constant danger on the Italian front, and I never know—all of this together has broken my strength.

In spite of that, it is my duty to finish my *Tiefland* film, which is very, very difficult for me in my present condition. Having ended my shooting in Prague a short time ago, I face the musical arrangement, which is more difficult with my film than with others, since this film, like my previous films, is very much oriented toward the optical, and on that account had to be filmed to a great extent without speech. Up to now all speech and sound shots for *Tiefland* have been made by Storr. You know better than anyone else what it would mean if I had to take another sound chief now. Storr is so well acquainted with my work that he could relieve me by working independently, so that I and therefore the film could be protected from further interruptions due to the condition of my health. I have worked with no other sound chief besides Storr. For this reason I secured him for myself for the *Tiefland* film by contract with Tobis. The director at the time, Lehmann, made the contract. Herr von Demandowsky knew nothing of this agreement, and on that account has recently placed Herr Storr at the disposal of your film company.

I ask you now, dear Veit Harlan, out of human consideration and out of the appreciation that you have previously had for my work, to give me Storr for the completion of my film. I need him from November 25 to the end of January. I will never forget you for this kind service if you will help me, and perhaps in the future I can also show my thanks in a similar manner. Awaiting your answer, I remain with friendly greetings, also to Kristina,

Your
LENI RIEFENSTAHL [13]

Riefenstahl sent a carbon copy of this letter to Reich Film Director Gruppenführer Hinkel and asked him to intercede with Harlan in her behalf. The fact that in October 1944 the Allies were moving toward Germany, that Hitler had forced the famous German military officer Field Marshal Erwin Rommel to commit suicide, and that thousands of Jews were being gassed daily in concentration camps did not deter Riefenstahl from her filmmaking. There is a possibility that she did not know the details of the fighting or of the concentration camps, but, as active as she was in the German film industry during the Nazi regime, she surely knew about the fate of some of the performers who were in disfavor with the Führer.

The tragedy that befell Joachim Gottschalk was well known throughout Germany. Gottschalk was one of the most popular actors of the period. He appeared in such nonpropaganda films as *Ein Leben lang* (*For a Lifetime*) a big box-office hit, and *Das Mädchen von Fanö* (*The Girl from Fano*), and played the part of Hans Christian Andersen in *Die schwedische Nachtigall* (*The Swedish Nightingale*). Unfortunately for his career and for his family, Gottschalk was married to a Jewish woman whom he loved very much. When the Nazi film officials suggested he divorce her, indicating that he would attain even greater fame because then the party would smooth the way for him, Gottschalk refused. Eventually Goebbels gave him an ultimatum: divorce his wife or be banned from his profession.

Gottschalk not only refused to comply; he took his wife to the reception held after the premiere of *Die schwedische Nachtigall*. There he introduced her to many high-ranking Nazis who were unaware that she was Jewish. When Goebbels learned about the incident he had the Gestapo give Gottschalk's wife and child one day to pack and join the exodus of Jews to the east. Gottschalk was forbidden to go with them. At the end of the twenty-four-hour period the Gestapo went to the Gottschalk home to make certain the family had complied with the order, only to discover that Gottschalk had killed his wife, his child, and himself. The beloved actor was mourned all across Germany by his fans, and Goebbels tried to put the blame on Himmler, but was unsuccessful.[14]

Another victim of the Nazi regime was film director Herbert Selpin, whose greatest successes were comedies and adventure films starring the great German actor Hans Albers. Unfortunately, he became associated with screenwriter Walter Zerlett-Olfenius, a devoted Nazi. Goebbels assigned Selpin and Zerlett-Olfenius to produce the film *Titanic,* the epic story of the British liner that sank on its maiden voyage. Zerlett-Olfenius loaded the script with propaganda until the story was pure fiction. Selpin became very unhappy with his Nazi associate and welcomed the chance to send Zerlett-Olfenius with a crew and several extras to Gdynia to shoot some exterior scenes on a real vessel. Arriving at Gdynia several weeks later, Selpin discovered that Zerlett-Olfenius had not shot a single scene. When Selpin berated him, the Nazi fanatic merely shrugged his shoulders and muttered that the German naval officers who were supposed to cooperate with the filmmaking were too busy romancing local women. Selpin, angry, said the medals these naval officers were wearing on their chests must have been awarded for the number of women they seduced.

Zerlett-Olfenius immediately reported Selpin's remark to Goebbels, and Selpin was ordered back to Berlin under SS guard. In front of Goebbels, Hinkel, Demandowsky (vice-president of the Bureau of Culture), and Fritz Hippler (*Reichs-filmintendant*), the stubborn Selpin conceded that he had made the statement about the naval officers, even though Goebbels gave him a chance to say that he had been misquoted. Taken to jail by SS guards, Selpin was forced to stand on a bench while his suspenders were wrapped around his neck. The guards then removed the bench and Selpin "committed suicide." Everyone in the film industry knew the truth, however, and Zerlett-Olfenius was given the silent treatment. After the war he was sentenced in absentia to five years' hard labor for his actions.[15] Hans Hinkel, who was with Goebbels when Selpin was arrested and taken to jail, is the same man who later helped Riefenstahl get her favorite cameraman for *Tiefland.*

The fates of Gottschalk and Selpin were evidence that only those artists who cooperated with the Nazi leaders were able to succeed in their endeavors; and in most instances, the endeavors in which they succeeded were not projects of their own choice. While Riefenstahl was cajoling Hitler, Harlan, Winkler, Hinkel, and others to help with her film *Tiefland,* another member of the German film industry, Kurt Gerron, was having a much more difficult time.

Gerron, a German actor who had appeared in Sternberg's famous *Der blaue Engel,* worked for Max Reinhardt, E. A. Dupont, and Anatole Litvak, and had appeared with Hans Albers, the actor with whom the doomed Selpin had been associated earlier. He was a director with Ufa when Hitler came to power. Because he had ridiculed Hitler many times from night-club stages and because he was a Jew, he fled Germany. It was his misfortune to be in Holland in 1940 when the German army overran the country. Because of his fame in prewar Germany, however, the Nazis at first allowed him to direct at the Joodsche Schouwburg, a Jewish theater in Amsterdam, a curious action the Nazi regime never explained. But by 1943 the situation had changed. Gerron was in the Westerbork concentration camp and later the Terezin camp, where most prisoners were left to die of malnutrition. His film industry friends back in Germany knew of his fate but were unable to help him.

In 1944, when Riefenstahl was writing her letters to Veit Harlan and Max Winkler about her problems with *Tiefland,* Goebbels selected Gerron to direct a special film. The prominent leaders of the Nazi regime, worried about military losses to the Allies, decided that as a safety measure they should start a propaganda campaign to convince the world that the reports of atrocities and mass murders over the years were only rumors. They decided that since films such as *Triumph des Willens* and *Olympia* had served the nation so well in the past, a special propaganda film to show to the International Red Cross, the pope, the king of Sweden, and people in noninvolved countries would be ideal. The film was to be called *Der Führer schenkt den Juden eine Stadt (Hitler Presents a Town to the Jews).* Gerron was taken from Terezin and ordered to direct it.

The ghetto city of Theresienstadt was chosen as the town to be given the Jews. It was cleaned up, disinfected, and painted; the electricity was turned on. All the sick and injured were removed from the city, the buildings along the main street were decorated with flowers, and banners and swastikas were hung all over the area. The concentration camp inmates received clean clothing and were forced to pose at a huge banquet where the tables were loaded with food. Gerron was commanded to show how well the Jews were treated by the kindly Nazis. Gerron had no choice but to do as Goebbels ordered. Neither he nor the other starving concentration camp prisoners were permitted to touch the food heaped on the banquet tables. [16] Immediately after the completion of the film, Gerron, the entire crew, and all the actors were sent to Auschwitz and executed. [17]

Despite such incidents, Riefenstahl maintained her steadfast loyalty to Hitler. Nor did her influence dissipate during this period. In 1943 a friend of hers at Babelsberg heard that Albert Speer, minister of armaments and war production, intended to refuse her request for sound tables (control panels). At the time Speer was in complete charge of production and resources in the nation, one of the most important positions in the Nazi government and vital to the war effort. But Riefenstahl had no intention of allowing the needs of the battlefield to prevent her from obtaining the equipment she needed for her films. Evidently Speer learned that even a man in his exalted position did not give orders to close associates of Hitler. A memo issued a few days later by the Film Bureau shows that Riefenstahl received the sound tables.

Re: Sound tables for Riefenstahl production
The Ufa Ag itself possesses no sound tables. Herr Hölas will call on Herr Orlich of Wochenschau GmbH to place a table at the disposal of Riefenstahl immediately. The table will be sent to Riefenstahl's residence at Kitzbühel. [18]

Although the war situation was deteriorating and Hitler had a multitude of problems to consider, he had not forgotten about his favorite filmmaker. When he heard that she was very friendly with an officer in the Wehrmacht he had his security officers provide him with details about the romance. The officer was Major Peter Jacob, winner of the *Ritterkreuz* (Knight's Cross). Before she married the major in 1944, they often traveled together, and Hitler knew where she was at all times as this 1943 report from a Gestapo agent indicates:

> To: SS Gruppenführer and Lieutenant General of Police Müller, Head of Office IV of Reich Security Headquarters
> Berlin SW 11
>
> Dear Comrade Müller,
> On October 29, 1943, Frau Leni Riefenstahl was in Nuremberg with her fiancé, Major Jacob, bearer of the Knight's Cross, and stayed at the hotel Der Deutsche Hof. She got in touch at once with *Gauleiter* Julius Streicher in the Plotzkershof and visited him there. I request that you get further details from connection NN-29240 of October 30, 1943. With best greetings and Heil Hitler!
>
> I am your
> JPD [19]

As the fortunes of war turned against Germany, it became extremely difficult to produce films. Riefenstahl shelved *Tiefland* and went to her home at Kitzbühel, occasionally visiting Berlin and attending some party functions there. There is evidence that at this time, late 1944 and early 1945, Riefenstahl was aware that Hitler might lose the war. Jaworsky went to her for help late in the war when it was learned that his grandmother was Jewish. She did what she could for him and she also gave him some advice.

"She told me to do exactly what they told me to do, shut up, and try to survive the war," Jaworsky explained. "I believe she thought the war was lost. She still was devoted to Hitler but she thought he was surrounded by gangsters." [20]

There is evidence that she tried to keep some of her other crew members and actors out of military service, knowing that they would face almost certain injury or death if forced to join the German army in its last stand. In a letter to Hinkel late in 1944 she praised the actor Franz Eichberger, who had a role in *Tiefland:*

> . . . I point out that this concerns a quite extraordinary gift of Franz Eichberger, who was discovered by me, which has not

been seen in German films until now, and I think this discovery represents a unique gain for German films. I suggest consideration as to whether there are possibilities of keeping this excellent performer in the armor of German culture production through nonrelease to the Wehrmacht.

Handwritten across the top of the letter is a note signed with Hinkel's initials: "Everything refused." [21]

After the Russian army crossed the border of Germany and moved toward Berlin while U.S. and British troops crossed the Rhine and drove toward the capital from the east, the need for men to defend Berlin became critical. Many males who were not able-bodied, as well as the aged and the very young, were recruited for the final stand. On April 18, 1945, only three days before Russian troops reached the outskirts of Berlin, the Film Bureau received the following letter:

From: Reich Film Board
To: Film Department, Frl. Schreiber
Date: April 18, 1945
Re: Riefenstahl-Film

According to a communication to me from the Riefenstahl-Film GmbH, the following male members of the staff have become available owing to the dissolution of their Berlin office:

Walter Siebert, assistant director of photography
Born: November 13, 1919 Residence: Berlin N018
                                        Bornimstr. 14

Richard Scheinpflug, archive compiler
Born: January 9, 1902 Residence: Berlin-Grünewald
                                        Berkaerstr. 27a

Walter Riml, cameraman
Born: September 23, 1905 Residence:——

Hermann Winter, archive compiler
Born: March 26, 1892 Residence: Landhaus Höff
                                        Schwangau/Füssen

Herbert Kiehne, production cutter–assistant
Born: December 25, 1909 Residence: Höchenschwand/Schwarzwald

Dieter Schwaebl, technical aid
Born: December 8, 1928 Residence: Berlin-Friedenau
Offenbacherstr. 27

Dr. Arnold Fanck, producer
Born: March 6, 1889 Residence: Berlin-Wannsee
am Sandwerder 39

Wilhelm Corsalli, film operator
Born: July 4, 1891 Residence: Schwanebeck/Krs. Zepernick
Bergwaldstr. 4, Kolonie
Gehrenberge

It is to be assumed that some of these staff members are still classified as essential for films and remain on the film list. I request that their "essential positions" classification be lifted and that they be deleted from the film list. Riefenstahl cannot give the reference numbers of those named. However, it is possible that the cameraman Riml and the producer Dr. Fanck were recently classified as essential through the Reichsministerium Speer.

Heil Hitler!
DR. BAUER [22]

Reclassification of men to make them available to the army was a futile gesture. On April 30, 1945, twelve days after this letter was written, Adolf Hitler and the Third Reich died in the elaborate bunker near the Chancellery in Berlin. Leni Riefenstahl was in her mountain retreat the day Hitler, Eva Braun, Goebbels, and his family killed themselves. She had escaped the Russians who swept into Berlin, but there was no way she could escape the many questions that her status as "film queen of the Third Reich" would provoke.

part four

The Postwar Years

16

No Peace

By late spring of 1945 many German film studios were in ruins because of the Allied air and ground attacks. Ufa and the large studios in Prague survived, but the film industry itself was practically nonexistent. The actors, actresses, directors, and producers were too worried about their own immediate futures to be concerned about new movie projects. Karl Ritter, one of the most popular directors during the Third Reich, decided that he would be safer in South America. While most of his films had a certain artistry, they were primarily political and propaganda projects. He fled to Argentina. Heinrich George, director of the Schiller Theatre in Berlin and one of the greatest actors in German cinema, was captured by the Russians and died in a Soviet prison camp in 1946. Ferdinand Marian, who had gained overnight fame in the title role of *Jud Süss*, was overcome by feelings of guilt and killed himself in a car crash. Other performers and directors tried to fade from sight when the war ended, hoping that their roles in the Nazi film industry would soon be forgotten. Among this group was Leni Riefenstahl.

After giving up plans to complete *Tiefland* during the war years, Riefenstahl had returned to her home in Kitzbühel, a small Austrian village at the foot of the Kitzbühler Alps. Gingerbread houses, painted arches over the main street, and men wearing leather breeches, white knitted stockings, and Tyrolean hats with feathers made Kitzbühel a picture-postcard Alpine village. Riefenstahl lived in a large white hunting lodge set about a hundred yards from Schwarzee (Black Lake), against a backdrop of towering snow-covered peaks. It was a scene reminiscent of her mountain films. Here Riefenstahl planned to live comfortably until the ashes of the war had blown away and she could resume her career. It was a dream that would have made a good movie plot, but it was not realistic. She had been much too close to Hitler to be forgotten.

Her first encounter with Allied troops must have made her think that while everything would not be as easy as she had thought, her intimate friendship with the Führer was not going to be taken too seriously. One day shortly after the fighting ended there was a knock at the door of her mountain home. When she opened the door she came face to face with a Boston Irishman of the Forty-second (Rainbow) Division wearing sergeant's stripes. He stared at her a few seconds and then asked, "Who are you?"

"Why, I am Leni Riefenstahl," she answered, as if that settled matters.

"Never heard of you. What do you do?" the sergeant bellowed.

"I act, write, produce films," the startled Riefenstahl answered.

The American sergeant laughed. "Baby, I've been going to the movies for a long time and I never heard of you."

Riefenstahl, who didn't want to be known as a close friend of Hitler, who wanted to go unnoticed now that the war had ended, couldn't stand the thought of being a nobody. Tears welled up in her eyes, but the sergeant, accustomed to all sorts of emotional reactions when Germans first encountered the occupying troops, was not impressed. "Now get going. We need this house." [1]

She had no choice but to leave. She moved to a house that had once belonged to Joachim von Ribbentrop, Hitler's foreign minister. Her own beautiful home was turned into a G.I. rest center. It would be many years before she regained ownership of the mountain house.

It was at Kitzbühel that Budd Schulberg finally caught up with Leni Riefenstahl when he was searching for motion pictures that could be used as evidence against the major war criminals at Nuremberg. She and her husband, Major Peter Jacob, met with him in an oak-paneled study that contained the leather-bound scenarios of many of her films, several volumes of still photographs of herself, and several large books of clippings about her career. Schulberg, who was searching for information and, he hoped, copies of *Sieg des Glaubens* and *Tag der Freiheit* to use as examples of Nazi propaganda films at Nuremberg, noticed that there was no material about these movies in the study. As a young writer in Hollywood in 1938, Schulberg had witnessed the hostility toward her during her visit there. He already had a copy of *Triumph des Willens* to exhibit at Nuremberg, but Riefenstahl was not aware of the reason he wanted it. She thought he was obtaining copies of all her films for the National Film Archives in Washington. Still, she was suspicious.

"Why do you want that one?"

"Well, after all, it's a good documentary," Schulberg said. "The photography. The use of music."

"Exactly," Riefenstahl said quickly. "That's the way I meant it. Not propaganda but, well, after all, a party congress in Nuremberg was something important, whether you were for it or not." [2]

She showed him the prize the French gave *Triumph des Willens* in 1937, and she emphasized that her art, all art, must be international. When Schulberg, convinced that *Triumph des Willens* was more propaganda than art, had the temerity to tell her that he didn't think Hitler was an advocate of art, Riefenstahl immediately disagreed.

"Oh, but Hitler had a tremendous interest in art. He was very artistic himself, and sensitive," she said.

Schulberg then asked her why so many people thought she had been Hitler's mistress if there was no truth to the story.

"They were jealous, and they didn't understand," Riefenstahl said. "I could get in to see him alone. I couldn't stand talking to him with all those adjutants and SS around, so I'd ask Hitler to send everybody away. And once or twice we were seen out together—when my films opened, for instance—but that was purely professional, there was nothing personal about it. He just respected me as an artist." [3]

Riefenstahl denied that she knew anything about the concentration camps and said that it wasn't until after she returned from the United States in 1938 that she became aware of Hitler's treatment of the Jews. Similar statements were, of course, made quite often by Germans during the immediate postwar period in an attempt at self-defense, and sometimes, in a vain attempt to ease a tormented conscience. Riefenstahl would not give Schulberg any help in locating copies of *Sieg des Glaubens* or *Tag der Freiheit.* She obviously didn't want her name connected with these two films now that Germany had lost the war.

"Those are nothing," she said. "They really wouldn't interest you. The first one was just a short on the first party congress after Hitler came to power; it was just something I had to do. And it was on such short notice, all I could do was a rush job. After all, when the head of a state orders you to make a film . . ." She shrugged her shoulders. "*Tag der Freiheit* was just a little picture I had to make for the Wehrmacht in 1935. Von Blomberg didn't think there was enough about the army in *Triumph des Willens*. It was just a little tribute I had to make for the army to keep them quiet. It wouldn't interest you really." [4]

With these innocent-sounding statements she passed over two Nazi documentaries that were very important at the time to the Führer and helped him to achieve his dictatorship. Riefenstahl also tried to impress Schulberg with the fact that *Triumph des Willens* had no propaganda value. But she convinced neither Schulberg nor her other critics that she had not aided Hitler and the Nazi party with her film productions.

While Riefenstahl stayed in Austria and pondered her fate in the film industry, the Allies and Germans began to establish an uneasy relationship in order to act together to get the country back to work. Railways and highways were repaired, bridges were rebuilt, rubble was cleared away, new buildings were constructed; some industries began limited production. Food was in extremely short supply and fuel for automobiles still in running condition was rationed when it was available. One industry that never shut down completely was the film industry. At the end of the war 10 theaters were still in use in Munich. Before the war there had been 80. In Bavaria 100 of the 500 movie houses were operating; Hamburg had 20 of its previous 80; and in the French zones of Germany and Austria 370 theaters were still usable. The same condition existed all over Germany and Austria.

In 1945 at Potsdam, the Allied occupation forces divided Germany into four zones. The Allies differed in their approach to postwar film production. The Soviet Union's zone of occupation included the important film studios at Babelsberg, near Potsdam, and the Russians were able to begin producing movies more quickly than the British, French, or Americans. Soviet occupation officials formed the DEFA (*Deutsche Film Aktiengesellschaft*), a state-owned company, which scheduled ten feature films in 1946.

Shortly after DEFA was established, British occupation officials licensed a German production company called Studio 45, with headquarters in Berlin. Other firms licensed in the British zone were the Central Cinema Company, Berlin; Camera Film, Hamburg; and Real Film, Hamburg. The British-zone companies had to rely on their own financial resources, while the Russians supplied huge sums of money to DEFA. Film writer Ernst Hasselbach, who was part owner of Studio 45, explained some of the problems they faced when they tried to shoot a film. Shooting had to be done mainly at night because of frequent electric failures during the day. There was a shortage of material for sets and no cloth for costumes, so film stories had to be selected with these shortages in mind.[5]

By the end of 1946 only four films had been completed in Germany. The total went to seven in 1947, twenty-six in 1948, and more than seventy before the end of 1949. During these first years after the end of the war, German-produced films could be placed in three categories: entertainment and escapist stories; films depicting contemporary problems such as the marital difficulties of returning military men and their wives, the adjustment of youth to postwar life, and so on; and productions with political themes, such as racial discrimination, war guilt, and morality under stress.

In the immediate postwar period actors and actresses had to be acceptable to the occupying authorities before they could be cast in a film, and this often presented problems. Some performers were permitted to go back to film work immediately; others were blacklisted. This caused animosity among artists and chaos throughout the industry.

Among those blacklisted was Leni Riefenstahl. On May 30, 1945, the Seventh Army Interrogation Center published a "confidential" report based on an investigation of her by its German Intelligence Section. The report was the basis of her blacklisting.

PWB–CPT–HQ 7th Army
German Intelligence Section
Special Interrogation Series No. 3
(This Report is published in cooperation with Seventh Army Interrogation Center)

Leni Riefenstahl, film star and producer, Hitler's alleged mistress

Leni Riefenstahl (wife of Wehrmacht Major Jacob) was arrested by American troops in a house in Kitzbühel, where she has been living and working for years. It is difficult to recognize the leading actress of the films *Das blaue Licht, Die weisse Hölle vom Piz Palü, Stürme über dem Montblanc,* and *S.O.S. Eisberg* in this aging, seriously ailing woman. Arrest, interrogations, and internment have strongly affected her mental state, and she gives one the impression of a broken human being. Her greatest worry is the film *Tiefland,* a movie on which she worked for many years and which was nearing completion. She now thinks that the film is lost "as everything in Germany has come to a stop."

Since her visit to the USA in November 1938 she knows that the international movie world boycotts her and considers her finished. She expected this boycott, although she could not understand why it was done. Here is what she had to say in her defense and to the clarification as far as her relations to Hitler and the party are concerned. She says that it is a "gross injustice" when she is being told again and again that "she only made the grade by going to bed with Goebbels." She states that she had never had any sexual relations with either Hitler or Goebbels. She says further that she had a reputation as a movie artist before the world ever heard the names Hitler and Goebbels. Even after 1933 she never tried to maintain relations with party offices (according to her statement). Mrs. Riefenstahl states that during her entire career she was never obliged to take any assignments from anybody, and, as a matter of fact, rejected more offers than she accepted. "If I, as so many other colleagues, would have worked for the sake of money, I could have become a millionaire. But money was of no importance to me. I worked on a film for years until I thought it artistically perfected. I was my own boss, nobody could tell me what to do. Had I ever had the impression that my freedom as a creative artist would be limited, I would have gone abroad."

Her relations to Hitler:

About her first meeting with Hitler and about her later connections with him she says the following: "Beginning in 1933 I received a phone call from the Reichs Chancellery asking me to appear at Hitler's house for tea. We were sitting on the terrace of the Chancellery, and during the conversation Hitler stated: 'I have great respect for your knowledge, but I believe that you could accomplish something in the organizational field, too. That is why I should like to see you take charge of the entire German film production.' This offer I rejected without even bothering to think about it because my main interest was to retain my freedom as a creative artist. This freedom I have kept until the last day of my work. At a later date Hitler again approached me and asked me to take over the production of the Horst-Wessel-Film. This offer, too, I rejected emphatically. During 1934 I only met Hitler at occasional receptions in the Chancellery. Early 1935, after my return from Madrid where I had been ill for a long time, I was again called to Hitler and this time he gave me the task of the production of the party rally film *Triumph des Willens.*" [6]

It is obvious that Riefenstahl has omitted any mention of the film she made for the Nazi party in 1933, *Sieg des Glaubens.* Since this film of the 1933 party rally at Nuremberg, the one she told Schulberg "was nothing," was a propaganda film that refuted her statement that she was interested only in artistic perfection, Riefenstahl wanted to forget it and wanted everyone else to forget it. The Seventh Army Interrogation Center report continues with Riefenstahl speaking about *Triumph des Willens:*

"He [Hitler] stated that the Party Film Authority could not accomplish this task the way he wanted it. He would like to see the party rally filmed 'as the artist sees it.' I accepted this offer under the express condition that I'd be my own boss as far as the production of the film was concerned and that I would not have any consideration of persons, position, and rank. Hitler agreed to these terms. Had I known, however, what difficulties I would encounter in Nuremberg, and how much aggravation I would have with this film, I would have rejected this offer of the Führer, too. The people of the Party Film Authority, who were envious of my independence and of the production of the film, tried to sabotage my work in Nuremberg with all means. It came to regular fights between my cameramen and those of the party; some of my cameras were destroyed and several of my employees were even arrested. I had the greatest difficulties to even finish the production. Shortly afterward I was ordered to appear before Hess, who received me as if I was a criminal, and questioned me on account of my behavior during the party rally. I then intended to complain to Hitler about this treatment, but for weeks it was impossible for me to get an audience, as the party men around him made things difficult for me. Finally I was able to present my complaints at a reception, with Goebbels present; Hitler was furious and promised to investigate the matter. The following day I was asked to appear before Goebbels, who received me with the following words: 'How dare you complain about my men to the Führer? If you were not a woman I would throw you down the staircase.' Then the activities against me began. Everybody was insulted because my film did not contain sufficient propaganda for the individual party—and Wehrmacht—leaders. Shortly after these incidents I met Udet, with whom I had friendly relations. He said to me: 'Leni, watch out, I believe those people are after your life.' Again I was called to Hitler, who proposed that I come to a compromise. I ought to call together all the people who had not been considered in the film, take their pictures, and paste them in front of the already completed filmstrip. It came to a rather heated discussion during which Hitler insisted that I compromise. In the heat of the discussion I jumped to my feet, stamped my foot, and shouted that I wouldn't do it! Hitler replied: 'Are you forgetting who you are talking to?' There was no addition to the film, however, and it was performed the way I had filmed it." [7]

Once again Riefenstahl tries to mislead the U.S. army interrogators by not telling all the story. While *Triumph des Willens* was not changed, she did shoot another short film, *Tag der Freiheit*, to appease the Wehrmacht officers. This was the second propaganda film that she wanted the Allied authorities to ignore. No prints of this film or of *Sieg des Glaubens* were ever found. She says that a representative of the Ministry for People's Enlightenment and Propaganda came to her house near the end of the war and took the prints and negatives of these two films to be stored in a secret archive. They have never been seen since. Some critics believe she may have destroyed them herself.

In the interrogation report of 1945, Riefenstahl tells of her last visit to Hitler.

Mrs. Riefenstahl claims that she last saw the Führer on March 21, 1944, at the Berghof. Mrs. Schaub, the wife of the Führer's adjutant, had told Hitler about Mrs. Riefenstahl's marriage to Major Jacob, and he wanted to meet Mrs. Riefenstahl's husband. The conversation supposedly lasted for 45 minutes. Mrs. Riefenstahl admits that she entertained a certain admiration for the personality of the Führer. (She added, "If that was a crime, then many people in the democratic countries are guilty, too, because they have committed the same crime during the years 1933–1939.") She further says that she had never thought about the Führer's policy because she does not have the slightest idea about these things. Mrs. Riefenstahl claims that she had refused all offers to join the party, although Hitler had advised her to do so. Her personal impression of Hitler was the following: "He was always polite and helpful, but never asked her about her parents or other personal or family matters. He spoke only of objects, or problems, of work, of the future; everything was presented in a way as if he were speaking to a great mass of people. I could not imagine that great people could stand being around him" is the closing remark of Mrs. Riefenstahl. But once more she emphasizes strongly that her relation to Hitler could at no time and in no form be considered intimate.

Hitler's attitude toward her and toward other persons could only be explained by a certain "complex of faithfulness," she says, and it was very hard for Hitler to part with people whom he had once chosen as friends or collaborators. In the case of Röhm, he only then made up his mind to take action when he had definite proof that Röhm and his friends had betrayed the Führer and the party.

On Goebbels and other party leaders:

Her statements about Goebbels are made in a disparaging and contemptuous way. "I always was in bad standing with him, he was cold and forbidding toward me. I almost hated him. With all other party men I had no contact whatever. I saw them occasionally at official celebrations. I never received an invitation from any party man, and if I had I would have rejected every one of them. The only decent man whom I met in these circles was Dr. Speer." Her opinion about the other party men, whom she does not know personally, as she claims, are based on those of the flier Udet, who told her that the Führer was surrounded and isolated by men who do not grasp the scope of their actions. "This Bormann was such a primitive man." [8]

Her statement that she had "no contact whatever" with any party men except Hitler and Goebbels is not true, as official documents and letters prove. She was well acquainted with Julius Streicher, the Jew-baiter supreme of the Nazi party. Documents indicate that he helped her at Nuremberg when she made *Triumph des Willens;* she hired his legal services in a lawsuit; she visited with him in 1943 when she traveled to Nuremberg with her fiancé, a fact reported by Hitler's security officer; and Streicher visited her at her home. As for Bormann's being "such a primitive man," Riefenstahl did not seem to find this objectionable when she threatened to tell him if Dr. Max Winkler failed to return her favorite cameraman, Albert Benitz, to the *Tiefland* production crew.

Riefenstahl was also asked her opinions about other artists of the Third Reich.

She is not prepared to pass judgment about other artists who had close connections with the party, and only reluctantly admits that there were many who would have done anything for money. She reports about a conversation with the well-known actor Veit Harlan, who was scheduled for the role Jud Süss in a film of the same name. He was in desperation about this assignment but saw no possibility to turn down the role. Riefenstahl claims to have told him: "Who can force you to have anything to do with such trash; you are a man, aren't you? I would rather die than play a role which I despise." Harlan, according to Riefenstahl, could not make up his mind to fight the issue and finally played the role.[9]

Her accusations against Veit Harlan in the interrogation report are in direct contrast with the "Dear Veit Harlan" letter she wrote him on October 22, 1944, when she wanted to obtain the services of her former chief sound man, Hermann Storr. But the war was over now, and it was every artist for himself.

Naturally, the Seventh Army intelligence officers queried her about the persecution of the Jews and the concentration camps.

During all these years Riefenstahl had heard of KZs [Konzentrationslager: concentration camps] now and then but had no actual conception of what they really meant. She thought them to be a kind of prison where criminals had to serve their sentences. "Otherwise I knew nothing about them. Today, when I hear all these dreadful things which happened in Germany, I could cry. And I cannot grasp how any of the people who shared Hitler's political ideas have the courage to continue living. I would have committed suicide had I felt that I shared the responsibility for these crimes."

Similarly, Riefenstahl claims never to have represented anti-Semitic ideas. She claims to have worked together with many Jews, to have been on very friendly terms with the director Sternberg, and to have maintained these friendships with Jews even during the Nazi regime. In a number of cases she states that she placed sums of money at the disposal of Jewish artists who had become penniless. She mentions the case of the editor of Filmkurier [a film publication], Ernst Jaeger, who, because of his Jewish wife, was expelled from the Schrifttumskammer [Writers' Bureau] and fell into debt. She says that she supported him financially on several occasions and finally succeeded to persuade

Goebbels to permit Jaeger's readmission into the Schrifttumskammer. She also engaged him as press chief for the *Olympia* film and had him accompany her on her trip to America. She
goes on to say that he borrowed money in her name and then
decided to stay in America where he released scandal stories
about her in which, she claims, there was no truth whatsoever.
She says that before their trip to America Jaeger watched over
her wherever she went and took notes on everything she said or
did.[10]

Riefenstahl does not mention that her book *Hinter den Kulissen des Reichsparteitagfilms* (*Behind the Scenes of the Reich
Party Day Film*), published in 1935 to promote *Triumph des
Willens*, was actually written by Ernst Jaeger,[11] although she
took the credit. Her admission that she "persuaded Goebbels" to
readmit Jaeger to the Writers' Bureau indicates that she and
Goebbels were not always at odds. And while she professes to
have many Jewish friends, the only one she mentions by name is
described as dishonest and treacherous. She attempts to explain
her views on the Jews in more detail later on in the interrogation:

> The pogroms against the Jews took place as she found herself
> on the trip to America [November 1938]. As she left the ship she
> saw the headlines in the newspapers. She considered the reports
> so fantastic that she refused to believe them. Questioned by re-
> porters about her opinion on the matter, she explained that she
> did not believe that the reports were correct. After her return to
> Berlin she asked Hauptmann Wiedemann whether there was any
> truth in these reports. Wiedemann replied that unfortunately ev-
> erything had taken place just as the foreign papers reported it.
> She was terribly upset over this but calmed down when she
> learned that those responsible for the pogrom had been pun-
> ished.[12]

Those responsible for the "Night of Broken Glass" were not
punished, of course, but rewarded. This was the beginning of
the final solution to the Jewish problem: Death to all Jews.

Olympia Film

The production of the *Olympia* film was another assignment given her personally by Hitler. She states that she dedicated herself with all her strength and faculties to this work. It never entered her mind that the event of the Olympic Games could have been a grand propaganda enterprise of the National Socialist regime. [13]

Her statement in 1945 that "the production of the *Olympia* film was another assignment given her personally by Hitler" is ample proof that *Olympia* was a production sponsored by Hitler and his government not for artistic purposes but for propaganda. Her later statements that Hitler had nothing to do with the assignment are contradicted by official documents that indicate conclusively that the film was indirectly financed by the Nazi regime. The interrogation report continues:

She saw in the Olympic Games youth, strength, and beauty—in the same sense as it had been pictured by the majority of the world press. In this film, too, she wanted to express no more than her art, her artistic interpretation, and her desire to erect a monument to the youth and beauty of all lands and races. She points out that she received no directives of any sort for the production of this film and could select her own co-workers. The premiere of the film, for which she received many international awards, was not preceded by any kind of censorship. The film did not favor any race or nation in particular. The American Negro sportsmen were given all the credit due them and Jesse Owens is mentioned in the introduction as well as pictured together with other Negroes in the book about the Olympic Games which she published. The entire book contains not the slightest shade of propaganda, she goes on to say, and the word "Deutschland" received not a single mention. "If I have a conviction, then it is expressed in my conception of the art to which I have dedicated myself and for which I have lived." [14]

The two questioners, Hans Wallenberg and Ernst Langendorf, then sum up their impressions of Leni Riefenstahl:

One may or may not consider Riefenstahl's statements reliable. Nevertheless, they give one the impression of honesty, and dread which she expresses about the regime and its leaders seems sincere. It is possible that she actually was not aware of what went on. That was her sin of omission, which appears all the more serious due to the fact that she, more than any other person, had the opportunity to get the truth. She is a product of the moral corruption which characterizes the regime. But it would be false to picture her as an ambitious female who wanted to attain fame and wealth on the NSDAP bandwagon. She is certainly no fanatical National Socialist who had sold her soul to the regime. Admiration for Hitler had closed her eyes to all that his regime meant for Germany. His protecting hand insured her artistic activities—contrary to those of so many others. His hand offered protection from the political clutches, and built a dream world for her in which she could live with "her art." Now and then this dream was interrupted by a flicker of reality. One may judge her reaction, which perhaps has not always been without strength of character, as being unimportant when compared to her lack of moral poise. However, one fact remains. This moral poise did obviously not spring from opportunistic motives but from the desire to continue dreaming her dream of a life "fully dedicated to art." If her statements are sincere, she has never grasped, and still does not grasp, the fact that she, by dedicating her life to art, has given expression to a gruesome regime and contributed to its glorification. [15]

After further questioning by the Seventh Army personnel in Bärenkeller, near Augsburg, Riefenstahl was released by the American occupation forces as "unchargeable." She returned to her temporary home in the mountains.

She was not, however, issued a work permit that would have enabled her to resume her filmmaking activities. Further investigations were planned, investigations that were to continue for years.

17
Art, Politics, and Morality

The indictment handed down by the International Military Tribunal at the trials of Nazi war criminals in Nuremberg in 1945–1946 was divided into four counts: (1) the *common plan* or *conspiracy* to acquire totalitarian control of Germany; (2) *crimes against peace*, which included violation of international treaties and agreements; (3) *war crimes*, such as murder and ill treatment of civilians and prisoners of war, slave labor, murder of hostages; and (4) *crimes against humanity*, which included persecution for political and racial reasons.

The war criminals on trial at Nuremberg included Albert Speer, whom Riefenstahl considered a "decent man," and Julius Streicher, with whom she associated during the years of the Third Reich. Also a defendant was Joachim von Ribbentrop, the Nazi foreign minister, who formerly owned the home into which Riefenstahl moved when the Seventh Army evicted her from her mountain retreat in 1945. If she felt alone at this time, she certainly had reason. Both Hitler and Goebbels had died by their own hands in the bunker in Berlin; Bormann, whose name she used to help her get what she wanted for filmmaking, had disappeared; Himmler, who had aided in the production of *Triumph des Willens*, had committed suicide; Streicher and Speer were in jail at Nuremberg; and she herself was still under investigation by the French and German authorities. Nor was it any comfort to know that Veit Harlan was scheduled to go on trial in Hamburg for his filmmaking activities. To add to her misery and frustration, Riefenstahl was prohibited from working in the German film industry.

Gradually the interrogations and trials came to an end. Streicher was sentenced to death by hanging for counts 2, 3, and 4 of the indictment, while Speer, convicted on the same three counts, received a twenty-year prison sentence. If there was any encouragement for Riefenstahl during this dark period of her life, it was the acquittal of Hans Fritzsche. Fritzsche, chief of German radio propaganda under Goebbels, was tried for crimes against humanity on the grounds that his radio broadcasts had incited such crimes among his listeners. The verdict, in part, read:

> The Radio Division, of which Fritzsche became the head in November, 1942, was one of the twelve divisions of the Propaganda Ministry. It appears that Fritzsche sometimes made strong statements of a propagandistic nature in his broadcasts. But the Tribunal is not prepared to hold that they were intended to incite the German people to commit atrocities on conquered peoples, and he cannot be said to have been a participant in the crimes charge.[1]

This was the first of many indications that it was extremely difficult, under law, to prove that an artist was directly responsible for any type of crime against the people who experienced the finished artistic production. In 1948 Veit Harlan was tried for his film activities, which many people considered to constitute crimes against humanity. His performance in *Jud Süss* was one of the reasons for his arrest. The indictment stated that *Jud Süss* was an inflammatory film that slandered the Jewish people and thereby provoked actions against them. Harlan's defense was that it was not an inflammatory film but a presentation of the Jewish question in artistic terms, an expression of important matters, of human concerns. His critics were convinced that he would be found guilty because there was ample proof that the film had encouraged viewers to persecute the Jews. Thousands of men, women, and children had been arrested by SS troops after Himmler had required them to view *Jud Süss*. The critics were wrong, however. After two sensational hearings, Harlan was acquitted for lack of evidence.

Riefenstahl was having difficulty proving that her own film work was not inflammatory. She was accused of being a political opportunist, a Nazi collaborator, and was even suspected of taking part in the execution of the Polish Jews at Konsky. The French, who had acclaimed *Triumph des Willens* and had given her a prize at the 1937 Paris International Exhibition, now had reservations about her work. She was turned over to the French after her arrest by American forces in the French zone—they took her into custody and questioned her periodically. Her own government also had doubts about her. A decision handed down by the State Commission of Baden-Baden for Political Purification at Freiburg in 1949 shows the complexity of the problem surrounding the activities of performers and directors during the Third Reich. To prove in court that they had committed crimes against humanity was extremely difficult. In part, the decision states:

> Leni Riefenstahl, divorced Jacob, actress, film producer, and businesswoman in Königsberg in the Black Forest, was born on August 22, 1902, in Berlin; divorced and childless. She was neither in the party nor in any other organization, group, or association. The hearing chamber in Department 2, Freiburg/Breisgau, has, in its session of July 6, 1949, classified the above-named as "not covered by the law."
>
> In respect to form, it is established that Frau Leni Riefenstahl, born August 22, 1902, was a member of neither the NSDAP nor any of its organizations, so that no presumption of guilt exists according to directive 38. It remains to be investigated, however, whether and to what extent Frau Riefenstahl, in some way other than through membership in the party or its organizations, furthered the National Socialist despotism, or whether she is prominent as a beneficiary of it. For this part of the investigation, a presumption of guilt may not be made, but on the contrary, at any given time the complete evidence for the existence of a guilty act is required. . . .
>
> The investigation of the relationship of Frau Riefenstahl to the leading personalities of the Third Reich—in contrast to the

widespread rumors and contentions among the public and in the press—has shown that it is impossible to determine her relationships with any of these persons beyond the framework of the professional performance of the tasks given the artist. In particular, no evidence could be found that could justify the assumption of a friendly or even intimate relationship with Hitler. Repeated thorough investigations by the American and French occupation authorities have similarly come to no clear conclusion. There was not a single witness or other evidence to be found that would indicate a closer relationship between Frau Riefenstahl and Hitler. On the contrary, there are several sworn statements, partly from the group around Hitler, which support these findings.[2]

Many Germans challenged this finding of the State Commission, especially the statements concerning her friendship with Hitler. In consideration of the charges that she had made propaganda films, the commission said:

> To propagandize for the NSDAP was completely foreign to her. The taking of both film commissions [Party Day and *Olympia*] does not constitute evidence to the contrary . . . the taking and fulfilling of both commissions does not constitute subjective evidence of propaganda activity for the National Socialists. Without consideration of the fact that Frau Riefenstahl at first refused to take both of the commissions with firmness and carried them out only after the repeated and irrevocable determination of Hitler. . . .[3]

This statement contradicts Riefenstahl's own contention that Hitler never asked her to film the Olympic Games of 1936, nor did he have the authority to do so, since this decision was in the hands of the International Olympic Committee. Documentation, of course, proves that the Nazi government did finance *Olympia*, but evidently when she testified before the State Commission at Baden-Baden she admitted that Hitler asked her to film the games.

> The task that was given to her was not intended to be the creation of a propaganda film but rather of a so-called documentary

film. That the film was judged by the party to be a useful propaganda tool for National Socialism both in Germany and foreign countries . . . cannot be accounted as guilt on the part of its producer. . . .[4]

The State Commission appeared to conclude that Nazi party leaders were more expert film analysts than Riefenstahl. Hitler and his compatriots knew that it was a propaganda film, but Riefenstahl, whose expertise in the film industry was unquestioned, did not. This, of course, was very hard for her critics to believe in 1949, and it is still very hard to believe today.

The State Commission, however, had certain reservations about completely clearing Riefenstahl of all charges. The final paragraph of the decision states:

> The Baden-Baden State Commission for Political Purification . . . has directed a renewed examination of the case and forwarded the documents to the Hearings Bureau, Department 2. It has given its reasons for the directive—that classification in the group "not affected by the law" is not in accord with the law. Even if the accusation of gaining benefits cannot be supported, it must still be noted that according to Article 2, Section 4, of the LVO, nonmembership in the party or its branches, organizations, or associations is not sufficient to eliminate political responsibility, when it is demonstrated that the party concerned was active in the sense of the LVO. An essential furthering of the National Socialist despotism is indeed not established, so that Article 5 is excluded; the assistance with the films used as propaganda tools [Party Day film and *Olympia*] is sufficient to require her to be viewed as a "sympathizer." The person concerned was not charged. In its action today the bureau has adopted the findings of the Baden-Baden State Commission and accordingly placed the person concerned in the group of:
>
> SYMPATHIZER
>
> without further optional reparation.[5]

The classification "sympathizer" carried a stigma that was to affect her future. In 1952 the French courts finally ruled that her filmmaking activities for the Nazi regime did not bring her political favors and did not justify sanction. That same year the Berlin

Senate declared her "not charged." This decision, seven years after Hitler's death, caused an uproar in Germany. A typical reaction was voiced by Harry Richard in *Das freie Wort* (Düsseldorf) on May 10, 1952:

> Leni Riefenstahl is on the scene again. The 49-year-old actress, director, and film producer has it in black and white. After she was already classified in 1949 in Freiburg/Breisgau as "sympathizer without propitiation measures," now the Hearings Bureau of the Berlin Senate finds the creator of the Nazi Party Day film *Triumph des Willens, Olympia,* and other brown-colored documentary films is to be considered as "not charged."
>
> Hearings Bureau Chairman Levinsohn takes pains to find a just verdict, and, bound by laws incomprehensible to many, had to determine after a four-hour session that the new evidence could be refuted. Frau Riefenstahl experienced in Berlin the triumph of her own will. . . .
>
> The pictorial material submitted, not disputed in its authenticity by Frau Riefenstahl, proved that she was present and an eyewitness as a photographer in September 1939, in the Polish city of Konsky, to the murder of 31 Jews by a firing squad of German soldiers. The victims had to dig their own graves with their own hands. Yes, Frau Riefenstahl indeed drew her conclusions from this inhuman occurrence. She did not take a position against the murder system of Hitler, however. No, she complained to the responsible General von Reichenau and requested an investigation of the incident. She herself was so shocked at the events experienced at the scene of the murder of innocent men, so she says today, that she returned to Berlin and divested herself of her activity as war photographer, just as she did of the SS-like uniform with sword belt, pistol, and shoulder straps that she had worn at the blood bath at Konsky.
>
> Her conscience seems to have been relieved with the complaint to the general. It is understandable in a different way when she, Frau Riefenstahl, wrote to Hitler a few months later: "My admiration for you, my Führer, stands above all that I am otherwise capable of thinking and feeling."
>
> The unwanted "relationship" of six million Jews and innumerable honest fighters for a democracy and against totalitarian striving for power are condemned by murder and perishing in gas chambers and concentration camps. Not condemned is Frau Leni

Riefenstahl, for her relations with the controlling offices of the Third Reich were only of a commercial nature, she herself declares. But in order to become the beneficiary of a regime, the relationships of well-endowed film contracts were not enough. "I have not denied having believed in Hitler, yet I have never worried about politics," said Frau Riefenstahl before the Hearings Bureau.

She has achieved her atonement exactly like the circle of persons to which she belongs, who were presumably nonpolitical but never opponents of Hitler. The release of her confiscated villa in Berlin-Dahlem—peacetime value 140,000 DM—confronts no more Nazistic condemnation. Frau Riefenstahl also now has her peace for further work, for renewed entry into the large film industry. The beginning has already been made. During the Hearings Bureau proceedings the film cameras hummed and the flashbulbs of the numerous press cameras flared around the confident, bent-for-action Leni Riefenstahl. Whether the poor German film and still poorer Germany are richer for it . . . ?

After being officially cleared, Riefenstahl traveled throughout Europe retrieving her films, which had been dispersed, mostly in Paris and Rome. Once she obtained copies, she hoarded them; she was proud of those films, no matter who had sponsored them. Erwin Leiser, a German film director who fled Berlin after the November pogrom of 1938, discovered how proud she was of her Hitler-backed films. In 1960 Leiser completed a documentary titled *Mein Kampf*, which was released in ninety countries. In addition to winning awards in Germany, Poland, Austria, and France, the film received the Golden Gate Award at San Francisco for "revealing the face of fascism and for its warning to humanity." Leiser used parts of Riefenstahl's *Triumph des Willens* to illustrate the use of film to glorify Hitler and the Nazi party, an act that infuriated Riefenstahl.

Was she ashamed that she had made the film? Did she request that the footage of *Triumph des Willens* be deleted from the documentary so that her name would not be associated with the scenes of Nazi horror depicted in *Mein Kampf?* No, but she did bring suit for a share of the box-office receipts, because, as she stated, she was "part-creator" of the film. Leiser answered this startling claim at a press conference by remarking that "old National Socialist enthusiasts are evidently getting so bold again as to demand financial gain from the denunciation of crimes they had helped to bring about." [6] Late in December 1960, a trial took place in Hamburg to settle the Riefenstahl rights claim. The final decision, not handed down until 1969, after many appeals, is very interesting in view of the position Riefenstahl has taken during the postwar years in regard to the films she made during the Third Reich. A summary of the decision in this suit, brought by Friedrich A. Mainz, a former Riefenstahl associate to whom she had vested her film rights, states:

> Minerva [a Swedish film company] produced *Mein Kampf* in the spring of 1960. About 10 percent of this film is from *Triumph des Willens*, and Leni Riefenstahl claims rights to this part. She was paid 35,000 DM by Neuen Filmverleih GmbH [a film distributing company]. Mainz demands payment from Minerva as reimbursement, and this claim is based on Leni Riefenstahl's claims that she holds all German and foreign rights to the film. Minerva's position is that the NSDAP produced the film.
>
> Mainz maintains the following:
>
> 1. The film was made at Hitler's request.
> 2. Leni Riefenstahl financed it herself through Ufa with a loan of 300,000 RM. Ufa was to get 70 percent of the profit, Leni Riefenstahl 30 percent.
> 3. It is an artistic creation of Leni Riefenstahl.
> 4. Minerva is bound to recompense him by an 1886 law that protects works of literature and art.
> 5. Mainz demands 50,000 DM based on the profits of *Mein Kampf*. This represents approximately 11 percent of the profit.
>
> Minerva maintains the following:
>
> 1. In 1945 the Russian army confiscated the film *Triumph des Willens* and later turned it over to the DDR [German Democratic Republic]. Therefore the DDR has legal rights to it.
> 2. Leni Riefenstahl was never owner of the rights to *Triumph des Willens*. It was produced for the NSDAP. The rights belonged to the party. This is

based on various communications concerning the film.

3. *Mein Kampf* did not use unchanged whole parts of *Triumph des Willens*. The parts that were used do not fall under protection of the copyright laws.

Evidence in the preceding case came from several witnesses and from documents from the Koblenz archives and the Deutsche Institut für Filmkunde in Wiesbaden. The appeal of the plaintiff was denied.

Reasons for the decision:

1. No error in law was found in the original decision.

2. The court views *Triumph des Willens* as a protected work under law but is not convinced that Leni Riefenstahl is, in the meaning of the law, the producer of the film and entitled to rights. The reason for this is: Although Leni Riefenstahl received no money from the Reich Treasury for the film, Ufa recognized her as "agent of the Reich leadership" in the contract, "in the name of the Führer." Therefore, Ufa intended to make a contract with the NSDAP, not Leni Riefenstahl solely. The NSDAP is listed as sole producer on the censor card. In the beginning of the film itself, it says: "Reich Party Day Film of the NSDAP." In Leni Riefenstahl's own book, *Behind the Scenes of the Reich Party Day Film*, it is not said that she or her film company is the producer of the film. In the reference work *Das Archiv*, Leni Riefenstahl is mentioned only as director.

It is considered from the above that the party and Leni Riefenstahl were agreed that Leni Riefenstahl should have artistic and organizational freedom in the making of the film. The fact that she had such freedom has nothing to do with the agreement between her and the party. The burden of proof that Leni Riefenstahl was the producer rests on the plaintiff, and there is insufficient evidence to show this. The court has established that the party received part of the profit of the film.[7]

Riefenstahl's reaction? "Leiser was very hateful, yes? He was Jewish and he was hateful and maybe he has thought the

same things others have heard about me." [8] She explained that
she had given the rights to *Triumph des Willens* to Mainz, her
former associate, because he was penniless, but she did not
explain her pride in a film that was incorporated in a documentary on the brutality of the Nazi regime.

This court decision came many years after she was cleared
of crimes by the occupation forces and her work permit was restored by the verdicts of many denazification boards. Once she
received her work permit, in 1952, Riefenstahl was confident
that her former popularity and prestige would be automatically
restored. She gathered together the cast and crew that she had
used in her earlier attempts to film *Tiefland* and completed the
film. It was not a success, and after a tour in Germany and Austria to present it, Riefenstahl withdrew the film from distribution. Even the name of Jean Cocteau, who wrote the subtitles
for the French version, could not save the production. Later
Riefenstahl and Cocteau began collaborating on a film tentatively
titled *Friedrich und Voltaire*, but before it could go into production, Cocteau died.

Other Riefenstahl projects that never got off the planning
board during these years were *Die roten Teufel* (*The Red Devils*)
and *Ewige Gipfel* (*Eternal Summit*) in 1954; *Drei Sterne am
Mantel der Madonna* (*Three Stars in the Robe of the Madonna*),
Sol y Sombra (*Sun and Shadow*), and *Tanz mit dem Tod* (*Dance
with Death*) in 1955; and a proposed film about contemporary
slave traffic in Africa. None of her plans were realized, not even
an English-language version of *Das blaue Licht* that was scheduled to be shot in London. This project was canceled when it
became evident she was not welcome in England—the film
trade unions protested her attempts to join, and the house
where she was staying in London was smeared with swastikas.

Slowly disillusionment set in. Riefenstahl realized that for
some reason the clearances she received from the officials of the
occupation forces and the denazification boards were not
enough. She was not accepted by the film industry in Germany
or in any other country. Financing was extremely difficult to
find, and many performers declined to join her company. She
displayed her clearance papers to anyone who would look at

them, professed her innocence of any wrongdoing during the Third Reich, denied any intimate friendship with Adolf Hitler, vowed her friendliness toward the Jews. . . .

She was still scorned, ignored, insulted.

Unable to mount any successful projects in Europe, Riefenstahl decided to make a film in Africa, in the Sudan, a documentary titled *Schwarze Fracht* (*Black Cargo*), but misfortune followed her there, too. In Northern Kenya the Land Rover in which she was riding slid into a dry river bed and she was critically injured. At the hospital in Nairobi it was discovered that she had a compound fracture of the skull and several broken ribs. That ended her first attempt to make the documentary, and in subsequent trips other problems prevented her from completing the film. The final disaster occurred in a processing laboratory, where her material was placed in the wrong chemicals and ruined.

In 1972, twenty years after she was cleared of any unlawful acts during the Third Reich, Riefenstahl was scheduled to show her film *Olympia* in Berlin at the Ufa-Palast-am-Zoo, where *Triumph des Willens* had first been shown to Hitler. So many people protested, however, that the showing was canceled, and Riefenstahl was warned to leave the city immediately because her life was in danger. The incident was further evidence that the adages "art transcends the artist" and "politics and art must never be confused" no longer suit the times. The adages lost their meaning in Germany when Hitler used art and artists to produce political propaganda in his persecution of mankind.

It was not the courts that issued the final decision on Leni Riefenstahl. It was the common citizens of the world who passed sentence.

18
Triumph of
Whose Will?

In the ballet *Swan Lake* Leni Riefenstahl had danced both Odette, the white-swan heroine, and Odile, the black-swan sorceress. After she left the stage for films, Riefenstahl continued to exhibit these two sides of her personality. The romantic heroine she played in the mountain films, a pure, innocent, and simple girl who had mystic and beautiful goals, made her fans believe that Riefenstahl herself had the same character and ambitions. To them she was the symbol of the naive mountain girl trying to rise above the sins of the valley people. Cast in this type of role, Riefenstahl was trusted by those who adored her on the screen and tried to follow her example.

As the State Commission of Baden-Baden said in its 1949 denazification hearing decision:

> In answer to the charge of opportunism, it is sufficient to point out that Frau Riefenstahl was already an internationally recognized film star before the seizing of power, drew her main income from her earlier films, and did not seek out commissions through the party or National Socialist government, but on the contrary took those commissions only under pressure. . . .[1]

In 1933, however, Riefenstahl stopped making mountain films. It would not be correct to say that no more pure entertainment films were produced during Hitler's years in power; many were made, and in fact Hitler encouraged such films in

228

order to help maintain morale among the German people. Yet Riefenstahl switched from entertainment films to documentaries proclaiming the absolute unity of Germany under the new Führer and depicting the greatness of Adolf Hitler. After the mountain film *Das blaue Licht*, Riefenstahl set about directing *Sieg des Glaubens*, a film about the first Nazi party rally held after Hitler took power. She made this major change in her career because Hitler asked her to do so. Her postwar claims that she was "pressured" into taking the assignments do not stand up under the evidence of her long friendship with Hitler and her admiration for him. Harry Sokal, the producer of some of her early films and one of her lovers, tells of an incident that occurred in 1932 when he and Riefenstahl lived in penthouse apartments opposite each other in the same building.

"She came over to my apartment one day," Sokal says, "holding a book high above her head, and said: 'Harry, you must sit down and read this man's book through. I must meet him!' It was *Mein Kampf*. Up to that day she was as much interested in and knew probably less about politics than my housemaid." [2]

Her reading of *Mein Kampf* must have influenced her, because when some of the critics wrote unfavorable reviews of *Das blaue Licht*, which premiered shortly after her visit to Sokal's apartment, her remarks echoed Hitler's writings. Sokal says:

> Riefenstahl blamed the Jewish critics for trying to wreck her career. She said that they were "foreigners" who didn't understand her art and when Hitler came to power he would not permit them to do such things. She seemed to have completely forgotten or otherwise eliminated from her mind the fact that I was of Jewish descent and that Jews had contributed considerably to the artistic quality of the picture, at least to the same extent as she herself. Béla Balász, codirector and writer of the screenplay, was a Jew. So was I, who not only made this production with her first directorial job possible, but also contributed considerably to her entire career and artistic development right from the start. [3]

It is difficult to say that she was "pressured" into the film assignments for the Nazi party; rather, it is obvious that she relished such projects. And because of her fame she had great influence with her fans. Those who idolized her as the pure Alpine heroine who could do no wrong continued to idolize her when she became the film queen of the Third Reich. The Riefenstahl pre-Nazi cult was convinced that if she thought Hitler was a man worth supporting, then it was true. Her status in the Nazi social circle put her in a position to know Hitler much better than they. She visited him personally, was seen in public with him, was praised by him. Obviously she knew him well, and her admiration of him swayed many of her fans. The fact that Riefenstahl's name appeared as director of *Sieg des Glaubens* gave prestige to the production in the eyes of her followers.

Since the war, she has tried to exonerate herself of the charge of deceiving her fans by insisting that her films were not propaganda works. She has claimed that *Triumph des Willens* was a work of art that the Nazis used for propaganda purposes without consulting her. Her claim is unfounded. An artist's work is the result of the artist's emotions, instincts, delicate sense of touch, feel, sight, and sound. The result, regardless of the form, does not express a preconceived, deliberate message, but is a spontaneous expression of the artist's own convictions. Once the artist decides to create a piece of work that will express a message or portray an image at variance with the artist's convictions, the artist is prostituting his or her artistic talents. This can be done for many reasons: commercial success, prestige, desire to produce a piece of work that will help someone else at sacrifice of self. An artist must have complete freedom as well as creative ability. If the artist agrees to certain restrictions for any of these reasons, then the result is a compromised work of art. This impure streak in a pure art form is what separates art from propaganda.

Riefenstahl violated the artist's purity of expression in *Triumph des Willens*. She admits it in her own story about the film, published in 1935, when she states:

> The preparations for the party congress were made in concert with the preparations for the camera work—that is, the event was planned not only as a spectacular mass meeting but as a spectacular propaganda film . . . the ceremonies and precise plans of the

parades, marches, processions, the architecture of the halls and stadium were designed for the convenience of the cameras.[4]

The truth is that *Triumph des Willens* is manufactured art, produced to project an image of the Nazi party and of Hitler that was predetermined by Hitler and carried out by Riefenstahl. Her propaganda techniques closely follow the techniques outlined by Hitler in *Mein Kampf:*

> The function of propaganda does not lie in the scientific training of the individual, but in calling the masses' attention to certain facts, processes, necessities, etc., whose significance is thus for the first time placed within their field of vision. The whole art consists in doing this so skillfully that everyone will be convinced that the fact is real, the process necessary, the necessity correct, etc.[5]

Riefenstahl did exactly this in *Triumph des Willens.* She introduced National Socialist policies, National Socialist military might, National Socialist popularity, and the National Socialist leader, Adolf Hitler, to the masses—the masses in this case being the German citizens and the citizens of the world who had previously dismissed Hitler and the Nazi party as insignificant. She did it in an exceptionally skillful manner, just as Hitler advocated in *Mein Kampf.* She convinced those who saw *Triumph des Willens* that what they were seeing on the screen was real, that the SS and SA were necessary, that the Führer was Germany and Germany was the Führer. It was conscious manipulation that was propaganda at its highest level. It was false art. *Triumph des Willens* did draw attention to its creator's guiding impulses, and after the war was over and Hitler was dead, the world remembered.

Yet propaganda in itself is not a crime, nor is the creator of propaganda considered an outcast under normal circumstances. Propaganda is not limited to one group or one organization or one political party or one nation. It is universal and used in all media. The fact that actress Shirley MacLaine's film *The Other Half of the Sky: A China Memoir,* based on her experiences during a trip through China, is considered by many to be propaganda does not make her liable to criminal charges or make it necessary for her to defend herself before a board investigating her "political purification," as Riefenstahl was forced to do after World War II. The film expresses her views, draws attention to her political beliefs, and perhaps has convinced many Americans that life in China is not so disagreeable as we have been led to believe. That is no crime against humanity. It is compromised art although it is questionable whether the filmmaking talents of Shirley MacLaine ever ranked her as an artist in this field.

Even Jane Fonda, whose activities border on treason in the minds of many American citizens, has not overstepped the line that would cause her to be charged with "crimes against humanity." Some former American prisoners of the North Vietnamese contradict this assertion because of her actions while they were caged and treated as animals in North Vietnam; however, the United States government never officially charged her. Her film *Introduction to the Enemy*, a straightforward propaganda piece that delivers the North Vietnamese political line, was not banned in the United States. It certainly is not a work of art. The film tries to convince viewers that the United States was backing the wrong side in the Vietnam conflict, and that the average American soldier is ruthless and has no compassion; it proclaims her political beliefs loudly and clearly. It is propaganda in a mediocre film package. It was largely ignored in this country, and Jane Fonda's association with it has been largely forgotten. Her acting talents, which are renowned, keep her in the public eye.

Other propaganda films have been proclaimed artistic productions by their producers. Peter Davis's *Hearts and Minds*, a study of the feelings of the people involved in the Vietnam conflict, is one of the rare films that approach the artistry of *Triumph des Willens*. Did the filmmaker use gestures, facial expressions, words out of context, and other devices to achieve a predetermined theme? Unless the viewer can certify that every frame of film is balanced, accurate, and fair—and obviously the average viewer cannot—such a film, fluctuating between a work of art and the advancement of a political belief or argument, is suspect as far as its integrity is concerned. Yet *Hearts and Minds* is still shown in the United States and other parts of the world, and director Peter Davis is not harassed by the courts or "political purification" boards. Even though Bert Schneider, the producer of the film, used the televised Academy Awards dinner to make a pro–North Vietnamese speech that angered many viewers, he was not ostracized.

Why then, does the world still scorn Leni Riefenstahl? Is she a symbol of the Third Reich, one of the few surviving intimates of Hitler on whom recriminations can be heaped? Or is there a more justifiable reason for her treatment? There is. One sentence in Hitler's writings explains: "The function of propaganda is, for example, not to weigh and ponder the rights of different people, but exclusively to emphasize the one right which it has set out to argue for." [6]

Hitler "set out to argue for" the elimination of all Jews under his control, and anyone who helped him gain a position of power so that he could accomplish this aim is guilty as an accomplice. Riefenstahl's films undoubtedly helped establish Hitler and his party in the early years. Her indirect collaboration in Hitler's brutal policies puts her propaganda efforts in a separate category from the average propaganda film.

Riefenstahl says:

> *Triumph des Willens* brought me innumerable, very hard troubles after the war. It was, effectively, a film made to order, proposed by Hitler. But that was happening, you must remember, in 1934. And, assuredly, it was impossible for the young girl that I was to foresee what was going to come about. [7]

This statement, made twenty years after Hitler died, can be accepted. In 1934 Hitler's policies were not yet clearly defined except in *Mein Kampf,* which few people had read. But during the following years his attitude toward the Jews became perfectly clear to everyone. Once the persecution of the Jews became known, those who continued to support Hitler and his policies with whatever talents they possessed became a part of the policy of persecution, whether they actually joined the party or not. Riefenstahl's profession of ignorance in 1934 can be accepted, but her actions in later years, after the horrendous treatment of the Jews by Hitler and the Nazi party was a known fact, condemns her in the eyes of those who opposed such treatment.

According to Harry Sokal, Riefenstahl's loyalty to Hitler was sincere and long-lasting. He says:

> I left Germany in 1933. In 1935 I met her again in Davos with her brother Heinz, a very likable fellow who referred to her jokingly as *unsere Landesmutter* ["mother of our country"], indicating her close relationship with Hitler. She had invited me to her apartment and I found her in the company of a few young Nazis. Prominently displayed on the wall was a picture of the Führer. She didn't like her brother's remark and gave him an icy look.
>
> When I came back to Germany in 1950 I met her in Munich and from the talk we had I soon noticed that she still mourned the loss of the Führer and the Thousand-Year Reich. I left without another word.[8]

Riefenstahl's acquaintance with Julius Streicher, the Nazi party's leading advocate of persecution of the Jews, is another reason for her repudiation. Documentation proves that she was in contact with him as late as 1943. Any attempt to deny that she knew Streicher's feelings toward the Jews would be ridiculous. Even schoolchildren knew of his Jew-baiting as early as 1935. One schoolgirl wrote a letter to *Der Stürmer* in that year, a letter that indicates to what depths of depravity Streicher was willing to go.

> Dear Stürmer:
>
> Gauleiter Streicher has told us so much about the Jews that we absolutely hate them. At school we wrote an essay called "The Jews Are Our Misfortune." I should like you to print my essay.[9]

The essay that accompanied the letter compared Jews to animals; "vermin are also animals but we still destroy them." The young girl, sure of Streicher's approval, denigrated the Jews because of their supposed half-caste characteristics, their study of the Talmud, their selling of rotten meat, and the trouble the Jews caused in Russia and Germany before Hitler's assumption of power. If Streicher's harangues turned a schoolgirl's mind to such thoughts, it is reasonable to assume that adults—including Riefenstahl, who knew him well—were well aware of his preachings. To say that her acquaintance with Streicher—or Hitler, for that matter—is immaterial because an artist's private life has no bearing on his or her artistic work is not true, not if the artist's work supports a regime that infringes on the rights of others. The statement of a film buff, Hanspeter Krueger, when *Triumph des Willens* was shown at a small art house recently is typical of those who support her, who overlook the big picture of her career and concentrate on the small screen: "One must judge her films on their photographic excellence and what the film conveys, whether good or evil. Even though *Triumph des Willens* is a horror and a preparation for the mass murder of the world, it is a work of art." [10]

Such a statement cannot be accepted by people who feel that an artist is also a citizen of the world, with greater moral responsibility than the average person, not less. An artist's skill, imagination, and creativity give him or her the ability to touch the minds of others much more easily than the less talented person. When an artist loses or ignores his or her ethical compass, artistic techniques fade into insignificance. An aesthetic of mass murder is not possible.

The ability of a film to shape a viewer's opinion should not be minimized. Hitler and the Nazi party understood this very well. In 1933, the year Hitler took office, Hans Traub, a German film writer, said:

> Without a doubt the film as a means of communication has outstanding value for propaganda purposes. Persuasion requires this type of language, which conveys a strong message through simple stories and vivid action. Furthermore, the moving picture occupies second place among all propaganda means. In the first place stands the living word: the Führer in his speeches. . . . Within the great realm of language, however, which approaches the listener through technical means, the most effective method

is the motion picture. It requires constant attention, for it is full of surprises, sudden changes in action, time and space. . . . When we consider that movies are screened once, most twice, and at times up to four times daily in 5,000 cinemas, we realize that the film has the following main characteristics of an ideal propaganda vehicle: 1) the potential subjective appeal to the "world of the emotions"; 2) selective limitations of content; 3) polemic value from the start; 4) repetition in "lasting and regular uniformity," to use Hitler's words.[11]

People who pay their money at a box office are usually in a frame of mind that makes them susceptible to belief in the images they see on the screen. Once the lights go out, viewers are caught up in the action on the screen and tend to accept what they see there as a reflection of life. Most moviegoers are unaware that during half of their time in the theater there is no image on the screen at all. In one second there are forty-eight periods of light and forty-eight periods of darkness. As Amos Vogel, an expert in filmmaking, explains:

During this same infinitesimal period, every image is shown to the audience twice; and as a still photograph; for the film comes to a dead stop in the projector forty-eight times in the course of a single second. . . . Thus during half the time spent at the movies, the viewer sees no picture at all. . . . Without the viewer's physiological and psychological complicity the cinema could not exist. . . . Could it be precisely during the periods of total darkness—45 out of every 90 minutes of film we see—that our voracious subconscious, newly nourished by yet another provocative image, "absorbs" the work's deeper meaning and sets off chains of associations? [12]

Riefenstahl's creative artistry has been praised over the years by most critics, many of whom deplore her association with Hitler and the Nazi party and the propaganda her films spread throughout Germany and other parts of the world. Yet this praise is not universal. Marcel Ophuls, son of the great German romantic Max Ophuls, does not agree that Riefenstahl deserves immortality in the record book of cinema history. Ophuls produced *The Sorrow and the Pity* in 1971, an acclaimed documentary about life in France under the Nazi occupation, and *The Memory of Justice,* an intelligent and thorough study of the Nuremberg trials. Thus he is well aware of the techniques and thought processes required in the complex task of making a film. He says, "I am not a fan of Leni Riefenstahl. I don't think Ms. Riefenstahl is one of the greatest filmmakers in the world, Nazi or not." [13]

Willy Zielke, the expert cameraman who shot the prologue of *Olympia* for Riefenstahl in 1936, states:

> The prologue is the artistic part of the Olympic film. I produced it alone—under my direction. Also I wrote the scenario and filmed the prologue *from a to z* with my camera. . . . At that time I was in Greece and in the Kurischen-Hehrung. There, for the first time in the history of cinematography, I filmed nudes. . . . "Women are harmless when they are undressed and lie in bed. But then so much the more dangerous when they decorate themselves with strange feathers!" On that account I will never forgive Frau Riefenstahl for her intolerable behavior, for "decorating" herself before the film public of the world with my prologue. And she has not to this day had the greatness of soul to confess that I am the author of the prologue! Indeed, in her big red picture book, *Olympiade 1936,* she didn't mention my name, although in this book, right at the front, thirty of my pictures are used as illustrations. Also, at all presentations of my prologue, Frau Riefenstahl has been silent on the fact that it is my intellectual and artistic work! [14]

And Susan Sontag, writer and director of such movies as *Duet for Cannibals, Brother Carl,* and *Promised Lands,* says: "*Triumph of the Will* and *Olympia* are undoubtedly superb films (they may be the two greatest documentaries ever made), but they are not really important in the history of cinema as an art form. Nobody making films today alludes to Riefenstahl. . . ." [15]

Yet the Leni Riefenstahl cult continues to grow. One reason

is the growth of the feminist movement. Riefenstahl is the only important woman director in the history of cinema, and as such, regardless of her ethics or morals, is cherished by some leaders of the feminist movement. Much more important is the current morbid interest in Nazism itself and the resurgence of anti-Semitism in the world. New studies of Hitler, not only as the personification of evil but as a man, have somewhat softened the image of him, and those who surrounded him and worked with him are also sometimes shown in a more flattering light. "If one forgets his treatment of the Jews . . ." is an oft-heard phrase now, as though it were possible to forget about it. Unquestionably there is a new perspective on this man who took the Germans to the heights of power and the depths of degradation, and this, of course, means a new perspective on those who were associated with him, such as Riefenstahl.

The equation is set: As the image of Hitler improves, even an infinitesimal amount, anti-Semitism increases by the same amount. When on November 10, 1975 (the anniversary of the Nazi "Night of Broken Glass"), the United Nations General Assembly voted 72–35 to label Zionism "a form of racism and racial discrimination," the world once again understood that Hitler's policies against the Jews were not universally rejected.

Perhaps the next time Riefenstahl goes to Telluride there will be no protests. Perhaps, but not likely, because those who believe in freedom have not forgotten her actions during the period when so many men, women, and children were losing their freedom—and their lives.

As she left the Telluride Film Festival in 1974 she remarked, "It has been beautiful for me but it also makes me a little sad. It does not give me back what I lost." [16]

Leni Riefenstahl does not have far to travel from her home in Munich to understand why she lost the adulation and respect of her public. North of the city a few miles, at the concentration camp memorial at Dachau, wherever Hitler's picture appears depicting the events of the Third Reich, it is constantly gouged, cut, and smeared by visitors. And Riefenstahl knows that it was her association with him and her decision to use her genius to glorify his cause that brought her downfall.

The curtains have not completely closed but the chances of a rerun of fame and adulation for Leni Riefenstahl, the film queen of the Third Reich, are unlikely. Time passes but memories remain.

Appendices

Appendix A

A Chronology of
Leni Riefenstahl Film Projects

RELEASE DATE		FILM

1926

Title: Der heilige Berg
Production: Ufa
Director: Dr. Arnold Fanck
Cast: Leni Riefenstahl, Luis Trenker, Friedach Richard, Friedrich Schneider, Hannes Schneider

1927

Title: Der grosse Sprung
Production: Ufa
Director: Dr. Arnold Fanck
Cast: Leni Riefenstahl, Luis Trenker, Hans Schneeberger, Paul Graetz

1929

Title: Die weisse Hölle vom Piz Palü
Production: H. R. Sokal-Film GmbH
Directors: Dr. Arnold Fanck, G. W. Pabst
Cast: Leni Riefenstahl, Gustav Diesel

1929

Title: Das Schicksal derer von Habsburg
Production: Leofilm and Essemfilm
Director: Rudolf Raffé
Cast: Leni Riefenstahl, Erna Morena, Fritz Spira, Maly Debschaft, Alfons Fryland, Franz Kammauf

1930	Title:	Stürme über dem Montblanc
	Production:	Aafa-Film A.G.
	Director:	Dr. Arnold Fanck
	Cast:	Leni Riefenstahl, Sepp Rist, Ernst Udet, Mathias Wieman, Friedrich Kayssler

1931-Die weisse Rausch Dr. Arnold Fanck

1932	Title:	Das blaue Licht
	Production:	Leni Riefenstahl Studio-Film, Sokal-Film GmbH
	Director:	Leni Riefenstahl in collaboration with Béla Balázs
	Cast:	Leni Riefenstahl, Mathias Wieman, Max Holzboer, Beni Führer, Martha Mair, Franz Maldacea

1933	Title:	S.O.S. Eisberg
	Production:	Deutsche Universal A.G., Universal Corporation
	Director:	Dr. Arnold Fanck
	Cast:	Leni Riefenstahl, Gibson Gowland, Rod La Rocque, Walter Riml

1933	Title:	Sieg des Glaubens
	Production:	Propagandaministerium
	Director:	Leni Riefenstahl
	Cast:	NSDAP members at Nuremberg Rally

1935	Title:	Triumph des Willens
	Production:	Reichsparteitagsfilm by Leni Riefenstahl Studio-Film
	Director:	Leni Riefenstahl
	Cast:	NSDAP members and visitors at Nuremberg Rally

1935	Title:	Tag der Freiheit
	Production:	Reichsparteitagsfilm by Leni Riefenstahl Studio-Film
	Director:	Leni Riefenstahl
	Cast:	German army and officers

| 1938 | Title: | Olympia |
| | Production: | Olympia-Film GmbH |

	Director:	Leni Riefenstahl
	Cast:	Olympic Games contestants, Nazi officials, Olympic Committee officials, visitors
1954	*Title:*	*Tiefland*
	Production:	Riefenstahl-Film GmbH
	Director:	Leni Riefenstahl assisted by G. W. Pabst
	Cast:	Leni Riefenstahl, Franz Eichberger, Bernhard Minetti, Aribert Wäscher, Maria Koppenhöfer, Luise Rainer, Frieda Richard, Karl Skramps, Max Holzboer

Uncompleted Leni Riefenstahl Projects

1929	*Die schwarze Katze*
1933	*Mademoiselle Docteur*
1939	*Penthesilea*
1943	*Van Gogh*
1954	*Die roten Teufel*
1955	*Friedrich und Voltaire*
	Drei Sterne am Mantel der Madonna
	Sol y Sombra
	Tanz mit dem Tod
1960	*The Blue Light* (London production proposal)

1956	*Schwarze Fracht*	Both of these projects were undertaken in Africa and have not yet been completed
1973	*Nuba*	

Appendix B

The following letter to the author from Charlotte Keer-Sokal, wife of German film producer Harry Sokal, gives an insight into the attitude of many people who lived through the Nazi period in Germany and whose opinions of Leni Riefenstahl are not influenced by personal tragedy. Frau Sokal, thirty years younger than her husband, summarizes the case against Riefenstahl very well in terms understood by young and old alike. The letter is an analysis of Riefenstahl by a compassionate German woman who has an excellent understanding of the film industry.

Since Leni Riefenstahl has become the Holy Leni of documentary filmmakers, especially in the United States, we have to put her on trial. Should she be burned? I don't think so. I think burning as well as canonizing would be overrating her. Without a doubt she did excellent documentaries on the Olympic Games and on the Reich Party Day. But who, with any talent at all, would not, if he had all the support of a dictator's regime and was supported also by an enthusiastic belief in that regime?

Hitchcock has said: "In feature films the director is God; in documentaries God is the director." If that god is manipulated by a cunning and all-powerful devil in the person of Hitler, Goebbels, or whoever, even a more naive person than Leni Riefenstahl could not fail to make a good picture. Without any doubt she is talented, especially with willpower and the talent to make others believe she is even more talented than she is. And she is naive—though less so than she wants people to believe.

Let us not discuss here the Virgin's talent, let us put the question in another form: What part of her talent is artistic and what part is talent for cooperating with the powerful, for ignoring moral responsibility, consequences? Maybe it's part of a great talent to ignore the rest of the world, but then you cannot blame Hitler or Goebbels any more. They had talent, too. To destroy. To concentrate a whole nation around a false ideal. And Leni Riefenstahl was St. Leni who carried the flag!

Think of the ideal of a superior race—northern, fair-skinned, slender bodies, blue eyes, blond hair—an idol that Leni Riefenstahl did her very best to establish. An idol that gave the superior race a right to kill the inferior—six million Jews, for instance. Young people became intoxicated on that idol, feeling they belonged to the superior race, that they were supermen and the natural masters of the world. They behaved accordingly and they were justified by, among others, Leni Riefenstahl.

If Veit Harlan, by making *Jud Süss*, and Werner Krauss, by acting in that picture, were found guilty after the war of responsibility for the death of millions of Jews because they portrayed with so much talent the "inferior" race, I find Leni Riefenstahl guilty of the same crime because she manifested the idol of the superior race. It is two sides of the same coin.

And the Reich Party Day film? How many youngsters who saw that demonstration of will, willpower, power, the usurpation of all rights for the "superior race" went to war drunk on false ideals that Leni Riefenstahl had so effectively portrayed? And how many of them stayed on the "field of honor"?

Film is a highly political medium and everybody knows it; the Nazis knew it and used it to perfection. Was Leni Riefenstahl the only one not to know? Or did she know and ignore her knowledge because, as she said, "I am a great artist and I want to make pictures"?

Everybody agrees an artist has political responsibility. Why do young American and British and German cinéastes relieve Leni Riefenstahl of that responsibility? Because it was so long ago? It was not—and the question always remains the same, in Vietnam, Greece, Portugal, Spain, Argentina, etc. Because she is old? A living monument now making propaganda for her great past in the same perfect way she had a chance to learn with the Nazis? Emphasizing the fact that she was never a member of the party? A priest of an idol is not a member of a party. Or was it her opportunistic instinct that guided her so well? In any case, the fact is irrelevant; what is relevant is her efficiency and effectiveness.

I thought young people had sobered up. They had for a while. But the tendency to fall for false ideals or idols grows again. That makes me shiver.

Notes

Chapter 1

1. Richard M. Barsam, *Filmguide to* Triumph of the Will (Bloomington: Indiana University Press, 1975), p. 26.
2. Ibid., p. 3.
3. Ibid., p. 67.
4. *New York Times*, January 8, 1960.
5. Ibid.
6. Ibid.
7. *Film Culture*, Spring 1973.
8. *Denver Post*, August 16, 1974.
9. *New York Times*, September 15, 1974.
10. Ibid.
11. Ibid.
12. *Denver Post*, September 3, 1974.
13. Ibid.
14. Ibid.
15. Statement issued by Richard Cohen, director of Department of Public Relations, American Jewish Congress, August 21, 1974.
16. Personal communication, May 12, 1975.
17. *Denver Post*, September 3, 1974.

Chapter 2

1. Fragebogen für die Reichsfilmkammer, July 12, 1938, #02249. This form, which she had to complete for Goebbels' Ministry of People's Enlightenment and Propaganda, is on file at the Bundesarchiv, Koblenz.
2. Interview, British Broadcasting Corporation, June 1972.

3. *Neue Rhein-Zeitung* (Düsseldorf), March 14, 1960.

4. Ibid.

5. Interview, British Broadcasting Corporation, June 1972.

6. Leni Riefenstahl, *Kampf in Schnee und Eis* (Leipzig: Hesse & Becker, 1935), p. 2.

7. Interview, British Broadcasting Company, June 1972.

8. Felix Bucher, *Germany: Screen Series* (London: Zwemmer, 1970), p. 74.

9. Roger Manvell and Heinrich Fraenkel, *The German Cinema* (New York: Praeger, 1971), p. 1.

10. Ibid., p. 4.

11. *Neue Rhein-Zeitung*, March 14, 1960.

12. Andrew Sarris, ed., *Interviews with Film Directors* (New York: Avon, 1967), p. 454.

13. From the classification list of the Academy of Fine Arts, Vienna, 1907.

14. Bucher, *Germany: Screen Series*, p. 46.

15. Riefenstahl, *Kampf in Schnee und Eis*, p. 2.

16. David Gunston, "Leni Riefenstahl," *Film Quarterly*, Fall 1960, p. 4.

Chapter 3

1. Siegfried Kracauer, *From Caligari to Hitler* (Princeton, N.J.: Princeton University Press, 1947), p. 112.

2. Susan Sontag, "Fascinating Fascism," *New York Review of Books*, February 6, 1975, p. 23.

3. Walter Laqueur, *Weimar: A Cultural History* (New York: Putnam, 1974), p. 244.

4. *Neue Rhein-Zeitung* (Düsseldorf), March 17, 1960.

5. Ibid.

6. Ibid.

7. Andrew Sarris, ed., *Interviews with Film Directors* (New York: Avon, 1967), p. 454.

8. Interview, British Broadcasting Corporation, June 1972.

9. Marc Sorki, "Six Talks with G. W. Pabst," *Cinemages 3*, 1955, p. 12.

10. "White Hell," *Close-Up* (Territet, Switzerland, December 1929).

11. *Nation*, October 15, 1930.

12. Sarris, *Interviews with Film Directors*, p. 454.

13. Interview, British Broadcasting Corporation, June 1972.

14. *Filmkritik*, August 1972.

15. Interview, British Broadcasting Corporation, June 1972.

16. *Film Culture*, Spring 1973.

17. Leni Riefenstahl, "Statement on Sarris/Gessner Quarrel about *Olympia*," *Film Comment*, Fall 1967, p. 69.

18. Sarris, *Interviews with Film Directors*, p. 456.

19. *The New York Times*, August 21, 1932, p. 9.

Chapter 4

1. Paul Joseph Goebbels, *My Party in Germany's Fight* (London: Hurst & Blackett, 1935), p. 40.

2. Ernst Hanfstaengl, *Unheard Witness* (Philadelphia: Lippincott, 1957), p. 197. Hanfstaengl was the piano-playing scion of a family of cultivated and prosperous art dealers. He became one of Hitler's earliest followers and most energetic propagandists in the 1920s and early 1930s. He fled Nazi Germany in 1937 when Hitler became angry with him, but returned to Munich after the war. He died there at the age of eighty-eight in the fall of 1975.

3. Roger Manvell and Heinrich Fraenkel, *Dr. Goebbels* (New York: Simon & Schuster, 1960), p. 89.

4. *Neue Rhein-Zeitung* (Düsseldorf), March 12, 1960.

5. Paul Tabori, ed., *The Private Life of Adolf Hitler* (London: Aldus Publications, 1947), p. 24.

6. Hanfstaengl, *Unheard Witness*, p. 203.

7. Glenn Infield, *Eva and Adolf* (New York: Grosset & Dunlap, 1974), p. 64.

8. Hans V. Kaltenborn, "An Interview with Hitler," *Wisconsin Magazine of History*, Summer 1967, p. 286.

9. William L. Shirer, *The Rise and Fall of the Third Reich* (New York: Simon & Schuster, 1960), p. 176.

10. *Hitler's Secret Conversations, 1941–1944* (New York: Octagon Books, 1972), pp. 243–244.

11. *Film*, Spring 1967, p. 14.

Chapter 5

1. *Film*, Spring 1967, pp. 14–17.

2. Gordon Hitchens, *Film Comment*, Winter 1965, p. 8.

3. Andrew Sarris, ed., *Interviews with Film Directors* (New York: Avon, 1967), p. 459.

4. Ibid.

5. Richard M. Barsam, *Filmguide to* Triumph of the Will (Bloomington: Indiana University Press, 1975), p. 11.

6. Sarris, *Interviews with Film Directors,* p. 459.

7. *Film Comment,* Winter 1965, p. 14.

8. Padraic King, "The Woman Behind Hitler," *Detroit News,* February 21, 1937.

9. Ibid.

10. Werner Stephan, *Joseph Goebbels: Dämon einer Diktatur* (Stuttgart: Union Deutsche, 1949), p. 103.

11. Paul Joseph Goebbels, *My Part in Germany's Fight* (London: Hurst & Blackett, 1935), p. 237.

12. Roger Manvell and Heinrich Fraenkel, *Dr. Goebbels* (New York: Simon & Schuster, 1960), p. 134.

13. King, "Woman Behind Hitler."

Chapter 6

1. Dietrich Bonhoeffer, *Letters and Papers from Prison,* ed. Eberhard Bethge (New York: Macmillan, 1953), p. 8.

2. Ibid.

3. Richard Grunberger, *The Twelve-Year Reich* (New York: Ballantine, 1972), p. 27.

4. Ibid.

5. Riefenstahl file, Berlin Document Center.

6. Ibid.

7. Ibid.

8. Ibid.

9. Padraic King, "The Woman Behind Hitler," *Detroit News,* February 21, 1937.

10. *Film Culture,* Spring 1973. Henry Jaworsky, formerly Heinz von Jaworsky, now lives in New York City. He is one of the world's most skilled and experienced cinematographers, having worked behind cameras for more than forty years. He worked with and knew Leni Riefenstahl during the pre-Nazi years and during the Third Reich. Ernst Hanfstaengl wrote in his book of memoirs that Jaworsky was aboard the plane when Hitler tried to murder Hanfstaengl just before he fled Germany.

11. Interview, British Broadcasting Corporation, June 1972.

12. Ibid.

13. Ibid.

14. *Der Stürmer,* no. 41, 1933.

15. Riefenstahl file, Berlin Document Center.

16. Joseph Wulf, *Theatre und Film in Dritten Reich* (Gütersloh: Sigbert Mohn, 1964), p. 284.

17. *New York Times*, April 2, 1933, p. 1.

18. Wulf, *Theatre und Film*, p. 271.

19. Glenn Infield, *Eva and Adolf* (New York: Grossett & Dunlap, 1974), p. 89.

Chapter 7

1. *New York Times*, April 16, 1933, sec. 4, p. 2.

2. Interview, British Broadcasting Corporation, June 1972.

3. Ibid.

4. Ibid.

5. *Film Comment*, Winter 1965, p. 10.

6. Riefenstahl file, Berlin Document Center.

7. Ibid.

8. Ibid.

9. Ibid.

10. Ibid.

11. *Die Welt*, January 25, 1949.

12. Interview, British Broadcasting Corporation, June 1972.

13. Bundesgerichtshof im Namen des Volkes, Munich, IZR 48/67, January 10, 1969.

14. *Film Culture*, Spring 1973, p. 123.

15. Andrew Sarris, ed., *Interviews with Film Directors* (New York: Avon, 1967), p. 460.

16. Albert Speer, *Inside the Third Reich* (New York: Macmillan, 1970), p. 97. I visited Albert Speer at his home high on a mountain overlooking Heidelberg, where he has lived since his release from prison after serving twenty years for war crimes. He has written extensively about his activities during the years when Hitler and the Nazi party ruled Germany.

17. Ibid., p. 100.

18. Leni Riefenstahl, *Hinter den Kulissen des Reichsparteitagfilms* (Munich: Zentralverlag der NSDAP, 1935), Preface.

Chapter 8

1. From print of film at Bundesarchiv, Koblenz.

2. Ernest K. Bramsted, *Goebbels and National Socialist Propaganda, 1925–1945* (East Lansing: Michigan State University Press, 1965), p. 88.

3. Ibid.

4. Hitler's Reichstag speech of July 13, 1934. Bundesarchiv, Koblenz.

5. Andrew Sarris, ed., *Interviews with Film Directors* (New York: Avon, 1967), p. 461.

6. Werner Klose, *Generation in Gleichschritt* (Oldenburg, 1964), p. 109.

Chapter 9

1. Interview, British Broadcasting Corporation, June 1972.

2. Leni Riefenstahl, *Hinter den Kulissen des Reichsparteitagfilms* (Munich: Zentralverlag der NSDAP, 1935), p. 3.

3. Andrew Sarris, ed., *Interviews with Film Directors*, p. 461.

4. Albert Speer, *Inside the Third Reich* (New York: Macmillan, 1970), p. 100.

5. Interview, British Broadcasting Corporation, June 1972.

6. Ibid.

7. *Film Culture*, Spring 1973, p. 103.

8. Paul Rotha (with Richard Griffith and Sinclair Road), *Documentary Film* (London: Faber & Faber, 1952), p. 80.

9. *Westdeutscher Beobachter*, August 16, 1935.

10. Abba Eban, *My People: The Story of the Jews* (New York: Random House, 1968), p. 393.

11. *New York Times*, April 25, 1935, p. 19.

12. *Film-Welt*, May 5, 1935.

13. Sarris, *Interviews with Film Directors*, p. 460.

14. *New York Times*, September 28, 1975.

Chapter 10

1. *Olympic Games 1936: Official Organ of the XI Olympic Games*, no. 2 (Wiesbaden-Biebrich: Deutsches Institut für Filmkunde, July 1935), p. 16.

2. Personal communication, September 9, 1975. Luis Trenker, now eighty-three years of age, lives in Munich. In Fanck's mountain films he created a screen personality similar to that of John Wayne—adventurous, rugged, brave. He made many films in the United States. For many years he was very close to Leni Riefenstahl when both were Hitler's favorites. Later, however, Trenker fell into disfavor with the Nazis, and today he is very critical of Riefenstahl and her work in films during the years of the Third Reich.

3. Bundesarchiv, Koblenz, R43II/731, p. 102.

4. Ibid., R56VI/18.

5. *Film Culture*, Spring 1973, p. 104.
6. Bundesarchiv, Koblenz, R2/4788, pp. 433, 435.
7. Ibid.
8. Ibid.
9. Ibid., p. 437.
10. Ibid.
11. Ibid.
12. Ibid., p. 439.
13. Ibid.
14. Ibid., p. 441.
15. Ibid., p. 445.
16. Ibid.
17. Andrew Sarris, ed., *Interviews with Film Directors* (New York: Avon, 1967), p. 465.
18. Bundesarchiv, Koblenz, RII/4789, p. 103.
19. *Film Culture*, Spring 1973, p. 122.
20. Sarris, *Interviews with Film Directors*, p. 463.
21. Albert Speer, *Inside the Third Reich* (New York: Macmillan, 1970), p. 111.
22. *Der Stürmer*, August 1, 1933.
23. Bruno Malitz, *Die Leibesübungen in der Nationalsozialistischen Idee* (Munich: F. Eher, 1933), p. 21.
24. Letter from S. Brodetsky, November 12, 1935, in *Bulletin officiel du Comité International Olympique, 10ième année*, no. 30 (December 1935), p. 6.
25. Richard D. Mandell, *The Nazi Olympics* (New York: Ballantine, 1972), p. 104.
26. Ibid.
27. Alan Bullock, *Hitler: A Study in Tyranny* (New York: Perennial Library, 1971), p. 191.

Chapter 11

1. Credits from official *Olympia* program at Deutsches Institut für Filmkunde, Wiesbaden-Biebrich.
2. Andrew Sarris, ed., *Interviews with Film Directors* (New York: Avon, 1967), p. 464.
3. *Film Comment*, Winter 1965, p. 9.
4. *Film Culture*, Spring 1973, p. 123.
5. Ibid., p. 126.
6. Ibid.
7. Ibid., p. 127.

8. Richard D. Mandell, *The Nazi Olympics* (New York: Ballantine, 1972), p. 169.

9. Ibid.

10. Ibid.

11. Sarris, *Interviews with Film Directors*, p. 466.

12. Baldur von Schirach, *Ich Glaube an Hitler* (Hamburg: Mosark, 1967), p. 217. Schirach, the son of a German aristocrat and an American mother, was the arrogant leader of Hitler's youth movement. He married the daughter of Hitler's official photographer, Heinrich Hoffmann. At Nuremberg he was sentenced to twenty years in Berlin's Spandau Prison. Schirach died during the summer of 1974.

13. *Film Culture*, Spring 1973, p. 181.

14. *Film Comment*, Winter 1965, p. 9.

Chapter 12

1. David Stewart Hull, *Film in the Third Reich* (New York: Simon & Schuster, 1973), p. 126.

2. Andrew Sarris, ed., *Interviews with Film Directors* (New York: Avon, 1967), p. 467.

3. Ibid., p. 468.

4. *Deutsche Schriftsteller*, 1:12.

5. *New York Times*, March 16, 1937, p. 15.

6. Official production credits for *Olympia*, Deutsches Institut für Filmkunde, Wiesbaden-Biebrich.

7. *Deutsche Film*, no. 11, May 1938.

8. Ibid.

9. Film Archives, Deutsche Institut für Filmkunde, Wiesbaden-Biebrich.

10. *New York Times*, September 2, 1938, p. 21.

11. Ibid., March 9, 1940, p. 19.

12. Ibid., March 30, 1940, p. 11.

13. *Film Comment*, Winter 1965, p. 25.

14. *Frankfurter Rundeschau*, August 5, 1958.

15. *Film Culture*, Spring 1973, p. 174.

16. Personal communication from C. Robert Paul, Jr., assistant director of communications, U.S. Olympic Committee, May 29, 1975.

17. *Film Culture*, Spring 1973, p. 171.

18. Ibid.

19. WCBS-TV interview, 1973.

20. Bundesarchiv, Koblenz, R-2/4789, p. 279.

21. Ibid., p. 287.

22. *Film Comment,* Fall 1967, p. 126. Quotation from Mandell, *The Nazi Olympics* (New York: Ballantine, 1972), p. 143.

23. Personal communication, April 16, 1975. Skorzeny was one of the most famous Nazis to survive the war. He remained a fervent Nazi until his death in 1975. When I visited with him in Madrid, where he lived in exile, he told me that while he did not approve of Hitler's treatment of the Jews, he did think Hitler was an outstanding leader and that Hitler's ideas brought prosperity and status to Germany after the disaster of World War I. Skorzeny was also an admirer of Leni Riefenstahl.

24. Personal communication, April 23, 1975. Hanna Reitsch was the outstanding woman pilot of the Third Reich. She lives today in Frankfurt. She considers Leni Riefenstahl an artist, not a propagandist.

25. Personal communication, May 23, 1975. Ritter was a very influential and busy director during the Third Reich. He was also a director of Ufa until 1945. He was a dedicated Nazi and most of his films were primarily of political and propaganda interest, but he managed to introduce a certain artistry into them. He made more than fifty films, some of them after the end of the Third Reich. Among the stars who appeared in his films were Richard Tauber, Pierre Blancha, Lillian Harvey, Zsa Zsa Gabor, and Françoise Rosay. He is a cousin of Winifred Wagner, the English-born daughter-in-law of composer Richard Wagner and a close friend of Hitler. Frau Wagner recently appeared in a film about the famous concerts at Bayreuth, during which she said, "If Hitler walked through the door today, I would be just as glad to see and have him as ever." Ritter fled to Argentina at the end of the Third Reich and today, at the age of eighty-seven, lives in Buenos Aires. He defends Leni Riefenstahl as being a "pure artist" and insists she never had any erotic interest in Hitler.

Chapter 13

1. *Time,* September 4, 1972.

2. *Abendzeitung* (Munich), December 15, 1960.

3. Interview with Anni Winter, Munich, March 30, 1948, Musmanno Archives, Duquesne University, Pittsburgh, vol. 4. Michael A. Musmanno was a naval aide to General Mark W. Clark at the end of World War II. When he heard so many conflicting stories about the death or escape of Adolf Hitler, he recommended to his U.S. Navy superiors that the matter be fully investigated. Musmanno himself was given the assignment, and from May 1945 until the summer of 1948 he interviewed more than two hundred people who had known Hitler or

were associated with him. Later he was appointed a judge at the Nuremberg war crimes trials by President Harry S. Truman. In 1961 Musmanno was an important witness at the Eichmann trial and helped to convict the former Nazi official. At the time of his death on October 14, 1968, Musmanno was a Pennsylvania State Supreme Court Justice. He is buried at Arlington National Cemetery.

4. Riefenstahl file, Berlin Document Center.

5. Ibid.

6. *Film Culture*, Spring 1973, p. 132.

7. Ibid., p. 116.

8. Personal communication, September 9, 1975.

9. Personal communication, October 20, 1975. Sokal produced many German films through his company, H. R. Sokal Film GmbH. He helped finance Riefenstahl's famous *Das blaue Licht* and, as he says, "I don't think there is one person alive who knows Leni Riefenstahl as thoroughly as I do." Sokal doesn't think she was ever a good actress, but he liked to make films with her because "she was such a perfectionist and with her tireless drive was a good influence on the creative work of picture making." He first met her in the summer of 1922 at Warnemünde, a resort on the Ostsee, and today, more than fifty years later, still lives near Riefenstahl in Munich. He thinks she was very close to Hitler.

10. Ibid.

11. *Film Culture*, Spring 1973, p. 146.

12. Ibid., p. 118.

13. Ibid., p. 119.

14. Interview with Dr. Karl Brandt at Nuremberg, 1946, Musmanno Archives, vol. 4. Dr. Brandt was found guilty during the so-called doctors' war crimes trials and executed.

15. Eva Braun diary, National Archives, Washington, D.C., Record Group 242.

16. Personal communication, February 1973.

17. Personal communication, March 1970.

18. G. M. Gilbert, *Nuremberg Diary* (New York: Farrar, Straus & Giroux, 1947), p. 403.

19. Riefenstahl file, Berlin Document Center.

Chapter 14

1. *Chicago Tribune*, November 3, 1938, p. 3.

2. *Table Talk* (New York: Octagon Books, 1972), p. 147.

3. Ibid.

4. Ibid., p. 155.

5. *Chicago Tribune*, November 5, 1938, p. 10.

6. *New York Times*, November 4, 1938, p. 20.

7. Gerhard Schoenberner, *The Yellow Star* (New York: Bantam, 1973), p. 20.

8. *Film Comment*, Winter 1965, p. 25.

9. Ed Sullivan, "Looking at Hollywood," November 7, 1938.

10. *Los Angeles Daily News*, November 30, 1938, p. 16.

11. Riefenstahl File, Berlin Document Center.

12. Louis P. Lochner, *The Goebbels Diaries* (New York: Doubleday, 1948), p. 26.

13. Nuremberg trials documents, Weiner Library, London.

14. Ibid.

15. Ibid.

16. *Detroit News*, December 1, 1938, p. 46.

17. *New York Times*, January 24, 1939, p. 17.

Chapter 15

1. *Film Culture*, Spring 1973, p. 141.

2. Paul Schmidt, *Hitler's Interpreter* (London: Heinemann, 1951), p. 155.

3. *Revue*, no. 16, 1952, p. 7.

4. *Das freie Wort* (Düsseldorf), May 10, 1952.

5. Riefenstahl file, Berlin Document Center.

6. Louis P. Lochner, *The Goebbels Diaries* (New York: Doubleday, 1948), pp. 246–247.

7. Riefenstahl file, Berlin Document Center.

8. Ibid.

9. Bundesarchiv, Koblenz, R109 III/VORL 16.

10. Ibid.

11. Ibid.

12. National Archives, Washington, D.C., frames 746–748, roll R45 (R roll), Microfilm Publication T-253.

13. Riefenstahl file, Berlin Document Center.

14. David Stewart Hull, *Film in the Third Reich* (New York: Simon & Schuster, 1973), pp. 174–177.

15. Ibid., pp. 222–230.

16. *Film Journal*, vol. 2, no. 7, p. 22.

17. Felix Bucher, *Germany: Screen Series* (London: Zwemmer, 1970), p. 57.

18. Bundesarchiv, Koblenz, R109 I/1593.

19. National Archives, Washington, D.C., frame 60381, roll 57, Microfilm Publication T-81.

20. *Film Culture,* Spring 1973, p. 150.

21. Riefenstahl file, Berlin Document Center.

22. Ibid.

Chapter 16

1. *New York Sun,* May 17, 1945.

2. *Saturday Evening Post,* March 30, 1946, p. 39.

3. Ibid., p. 41.

4. Ibid., p. 39.

5. *Sight and Sound,* Spring 1947.

6. National Archives, Washington, D.C., Interrogation Report PWB/SAIC/3.

7. Ibid.

8. Ibid.

9. Ibid.

10. Ibid.

11. Richard M. Barsam, *Filmguide to* Triumph of the Will (Bloomington: Indiana University Press, 1975), p. 79.

12. National Archives, Washington, D.C., Interrogation Report PWB/SAIC/3.

13. Ibid.

14. Ibid.

15. Ibid.

Chapter 17

1. G. M. Gilbert, *Nuremberg Diary* (New York: Farrar, Straus & Giroux, 1947), p. 409.

2. State Commission of Baden-Baden for Political Purification, *Decision in the Proceedings Against Frau Riefenstahl-Jacob* (Freiburg, December 16, 1949).

3. Ibid.

4. Ibid.

5. Ibid.

6. *Der Abend* (West Berlin), December 10, 1960.

7. *Summary of Judgment of the Dispute Between Friedrich A. Mainz, Plaintiff, and the Minerva Company of Stockholm, Defendant, January 10, 1969* (Munich).

8. *Film Culture,* Spring 1973.

Chapter 18

1. State Commission of Baden-Baden for Political Purification, *Decision in the Proceedings Against Frau Riefenstahl-Jacob* (Freiburg, December 16, 1949).

2. Personal communication, October 20, 1975.

3. Ibid.

4. Leni Riefenstahl, *Hinter den Kulissen des Reichsparteitagfilms* (Munich: Zentralverlag der NSDAP, 1935), p. 176.

5. Adolf Hitler, *Mein Kampf*, trans. Ralph Manheim (Boston: Houghton Mifflin, 1943), p. 176.

6. Ibid., p. 179.

7. Andrew Sarris, ed., *Interviews with Film Directors* (New York: Avon, 1967), p. 459.

8. Personal communication, October 20, 1975.

9. Gerhard Schoenberner, *The Yellow Star* (New York: Bantam, 1973), p. 18.

10. *Variety*, January 31, 1973.

11. Cited in David Stewart Hull, *Film in the Third Reich* (New York: Simon & Schuster, 1973), p. 35.

12. Amos Vogel, *Film as a Subversive Art* (New York: Random House, 1974), p. 10.

13. Personal communication, May 21, 1975.

14. Personal communication, October 16, 1975, and October 20, 1975. Willy Zielke lives in retirement at Vahlbruck, Germany, and he is still uneasy at the notion that a woman might legitimately be active anywhere but in bed.

15. Susan Sontag, "Fascinating Fascism," *New York Review of Books*, February 6, 1975, p. 23.

16. *Newsweek*, September 16, 1974, p. 91.

Bibliography

ALLGEIER, SEPP. *Die Jagd nach dem Bild*. Stuttgart: J. Engelhorn, 1931.

AMENGUAL, BARTHELEMY. *G. W. Pabst*. Paris: Seghers, 1966.

BALÁZS, BÉLA. *Theory of the Film*. London: Dennis Dobson, 1952.

BARSAM, RICHARD M. *Filmguide to* Triumph of the Will. Bloomington: Indiana University Press, 1975.

BONHOEFFER, DIETRICH. *Letters and Papers from Prison*, ed. Eberhard Bethge. New York: Macmillan, 1953.

BRAMSTED, ERNEST K. *Goebbels and National Socialist Propaganda, 1925–1945*. East Lansing: Michigan State University Press, 1965.

BUCHER, FELIX. *Germany: Screen Series*. London: Zwemmer, 1970.

BULLOCK, ALAN. *Hitler: A Study in Tyranny*. New York: Perennial Library, 1971.

COURTADE, FRANCIS, AND CADARS, PIERRE. *Histoire du Cinéma Nazi*. Paris: S.N.I.L., 1972.

DEFA. *20 Jahre Defa-Speilfilm*. Berlin: Henschelverlag, 1968.

Deutschland und der deutsche Film. Berlin: Neue Film-Kurier, 1935.

EBAN, ABBA. *My People: The Story of the Jews*. New York: Random House, 1968.

FRAENKEL, HEINRICH. *Unsterblicher Film*, 2 vols. Munich: Kindler, 1955, 1957.

GILBERT, G. M. *Nuremberg Diary*. New York: Farrar, Straus & Giroux, 1947.

GOEBBELS, PAUL JOSEPH. *My Part in Germany's Fight*. London: Hurst & Blackett, 1935.

GRUNBERGER, RICHARD. *The Twelve-Year Reich*. New York: Ballantine, 1972.

HANFSTAENGL, ERNST. *Unheard Witness*. Philadelphia: Lippincott, 1957.

HARLAN, VEIT. *Im Schatten meiner Filme*. Gütersloh: Sigbert Mohn, 1966.

HIPPLER, FRITZ. *Betrachtungen zum Filmschaffen*. Berlin: Max Hesse, 1942.

HITLER, ADOLF. *Mein Kampf*. Trans. Ralph Manheim. Boston: Houghton Mifflin, 1943.

Hitler's Secret Conversations, 1941–1944. New York: Octagon Books, 1972.

HULL, DAVID STEWART. *Film in the Third Reich*. New York: Simon & Schuster, 1973.

INFIELD, GLENN. *Eva and Adolf*. New York: Grosset & Dunlap, 1974.

KELLER, WERNER. *Diaspora: The Post-Biblical History of the Jews*. New York: Harcourt, Brace & World, 1969.

KLOSE, WERNER. *Generation in Gleichschritt*. Oldenburg, 1964.

KOCH, HEINRICH, AND BRAUNE, HEINRICH. *Von deutscher Filmkunst*. Berlin: Hermann Scherping, 1943.

KRACAUER, SIEGFRIED. *From Caligari to Hitler*. Princeton, N.J.: Princeton University Press, 1947.

LAQUEUR, WALTER. *Weimar: A Cultural History*. New York: Putnam, 1974.

LEISER, ERWIN. *Nazi Cinema*. London: Secker & Warburg, 1974.

LOCHNER, LOUIS P. *The Goebbels Diaries*. New York: Doubleday, 1948.

MALITZ, BRUNO. *Die Leibesübungen in der Nationalsozialistischen Idee*. Munich: F. Eher, 1933.

MANDELL, RICHARD D. *The Nazi Olympics*. New York: Ballantine, 1972.

MANVELL, ROGER, AND FRAENKEL, HEINRICH. *Dr. Goebbels*. New York: Simon & Schuster, 1960.

―――. *The German Cinema*. New York: Praeger, 1971.

MANZ, H. P. *Ufa and der frühe deutsche Film*. Zurich: Sanssouci, 1963.

NEUMANN, CARL; BELLING, CURT; AND BETZ, HANS-WALTHER. *Film "Kunst," Film-Kohn, Film-Korruption*. Berlin: Hermann Scherping, 1937.

PARDO, HERBERT. *Jud Süss: historisches und juristisches Material zum Fall Veit Harlan*. Hamburg: Auerdruck, 1949.

PAYNE, ROBERT. *The Life and Death of Adolf Hitler.* New York: Popular Library, 1973.

RIEFENSTAHL, LENI. *Hinter den Kulissen des Reichsparteitagfilms.* Munich: Zentralverlag der NSDAP, 1935.

————. *Kampf in Schnee und Eis.* Leipzig: Hesse & Becker, 1935.

————. *Schönheit im Olympischen Kampf.* Berlin: Deutsch, 1937.

ROTHA, PAUL (with Richard Griffith and Sinclair Road). *Documentary Film.* London: Faber & Faber, 1952.

SARRIS, ANDREW, ed. *Interviews with Film Directors.* New York: Avon Books, 1967.

SCHIRACH, BALDUR VON. *Ich glaube an Hitler.* Hamburg: Mosark, 1967.

SCHMIDT, DR. PAUL. *Hitler's Interpreter.* London: Heinemann, 1951.

SCHOENBERNER, GERHARD. *The Yellow Star.* New York: Bantam, 1973.

SHIRER, WILLIAM L. *The Rise and Fall of the Third Reich.* New York: Simon & Schuster, 1960.

SISKA, HEINZ, ed. *Wunderwelt Film.* Heidelberg: Hüthig, 1943.

SMITH, HOWARD K. *Last Train from Berlin.* New York: Popular Library, 1962.

SPEER, ALBERT. *Inside the Third Reich.* New York: Macmillan, 1970.

STEPHAN, WERNER. *Joseph Goebbels: Dämon einer Diktatur.* Stuttgart: Union Deutsche, 1949.

TRAUB, HANS ALEX. *Der Film als politisches Machtmittel.* Munich: Münchener Druck- und Verlagshaus, 1933.

VOGEL, AMOS. *Film as a Subversive Art.* New York: Random House, 1974.

WOLF, KURT. *Entwicklung und Neugestaltung der deutschen Filmwirtschaft seit 1933.* Heidelberg: Hermann Meister, 1938.

WOLLENBERG, H. H. *Fifty Years of German Film.* London: Falcon Press, 1948.

WULF, JOSEPH. *Theatre und Film in Dritten Reich.* Gütersloh: Sigbert Mohn, 1964.

Selected Additional Sources

ABENDZEITUNG. "Leni Riefenstahl in England nicht Willkommen." Munich, December 15, 1960.

ALTMANN, JOHN. "Movies' Role in Hitler's Conquest of German Youth." *Hollywood Quarterly*, vol. 3, no. 4.

BARKHAUSEN, HANS. "Footnote to the History of Riefenstahl's Olympia." *Film Quarterly,* Fall 1974.

BARRY, IRIS. "The German Film." *New Republic,* May 19, 1947.

BARSAM, R. M. "Leni Riefenstahl: Artifice and Truth in a World Apart." *Film Comment,* November–December 1973.

BARSKY, ALEXANDER. "Films: The Grafted Narrative." *The Nation,* vol. 131, no. 3406 (October 15, 1930).

BECKLEY, PAUL V. "Nothing Grand About Illusions in Nazi Film." *New York Herald Tribune,* July 10, 1960.

BENTLEY, ERIC. "The Cinema: Its Art and Techniques." *New York Times Book Review,* May 18, 1947.

"Bilder aus dem Olympia-film." *Berliner Illustrierte Zeitung,* February 17, 1938.

BISHOP, CHRISTOPHER. Speech given to the Toronto Film Society at its sixth exhibition meeting, February 3, 1957, Capitol Theatre, Toronto.

British Film Institute clipping files, London. The large number of articles about the German cinema are mostly unidentified and undated.

BROOKS, R. D. "Triumph des Willens." Urbana: University of Illinois Film Society Program Notes, October 12, 1966.

BROWNLOW, KEVIN. "Leni Riefenstahl." *Film,* Winter 1966.

———. "Reply to Paul Rotha." *Film,* Spring 1967.

CLARE, GEORGE P. *A Dream That Has Some Significance.* Deutsches Institut für Filmkunde, November 24, 1948.

CLOSE-UP. "White Hell." Territet, Switzerland, December 1929.

COCTEAU, JEAN. "Four Letters by Jean Cocteau to Leni Riefenstahl." *Film Culture,* Spring 1973.

Control Commission for Germany, Information Services Office. *Catalogue of Forbidden German Features and Short Film Productions Held in Zonal Film Archives of the Film Section Division.* Hamburg, 1951.

CORLISS, RICHARD. "Leni Riefenstahl: A Bibliography." *Film Heritage,* Fall 1969.

DAS FREIE WORT. "My Admiration for You, My Führer . . ." May 10, 1952.

DER ABEND. "Leni Riefenstahl Cashes in on Party Day Film." December 10, 1960.

Deutscher Film-Katalog, 1930–1945 (Ufa, Tobis, Bavaria). Short synopsis of German films in English and German. No date.

DIE WELT. "Flucht vor Leni." January 25, 1949.

————. "Leni Riefenstahl: Not Affected." January 13, 1949.

DONNELLY, BILL. "Olympia: Parts I and II." *Film Notes*, 1960.

ESTES, JIM. "Nazi Film—A Triumph of Evil Genius." *San Francisco Chronicle*, July 28, 1959.

FELDMAN, H., AND FELDMAN, H. "Women Directors." *Films in Review*, November 1950.

FLOT, Y. "Brève rencontre avec Leni Riefenstahl." *Ecran*, November 9, 1972.

FUENTES, CARLOS. "The Discreet Charm of Luis Buñuel." *New York Times Magazine*, March 11, 1973.

GARDNER, ROBERT. "Can the Will Triumph?" *Film Comment*, Winter 1965.

GREGOR, ULRICH. "A Comeback for Leni Riefenstahl." *Film Comment*, Winter 1965.

GUNSTON, DAVID. "Leni Riefenstahl." *Film Quarterly*, Fall 1960.

HITCHENS, GORDON. "An Interview with a Legend." *Film Comment*, Winter 1965.

————. "Leni Riefenstahl Interview, October 11, 1971, in Munich." *Film Culture*, Spring 1973.

————. "Henry Jaworsky Interviewed." *Film Culture*, Spring 1973.

KALTENBORN, HANS V. "An Interview with Hitler." *Wisconsin Magazine of History*, Summer 1967.

KELMAN, KEN. "Propaganda as Vision: Triumph of the Will." *Film Culture*, Spring 1973.

KING, PADRAIC. "The Woman Behind Hitler." *The Detroit News*, February 21, 1937.

LEISER, ERWIN. "La Vérité sur Leni Riefenstahl et Le Triomphe de la Volonté." *Cinema 69*, February 1969.

————. "Dans les coulisses d'Olympia." *Ecran*, November 19, 1973.

LINDER, H. "Filmography of Leni Riefenstahl." *Filmkritik*, August 1972.

LUFT, HERBERT G. "The Screen as a Propaganda Weapon." *Journal of Producer's Guild*, June 1973.

————. "Der Führer Presents a Town to the Jews." *Film Journal*, issue 7, vol. 2, no. 4 (1975).

MACHNER, HANS. "Leni Riefenstahl." *Neue Rhein-Zeitung* (Düsseldorf), March 14–17, 1960.

MARCORELLES, LOUIS. "The Nazi Cinema." *Sight and Sound*, Autumn 1955.

MORRIS, GERALD. "Triumph of the Will." Toronto Film Society Program Notes, February 3, 1957.

MULLER, R. "Romantic Miss Riefenstahl." *Spectator* (London), February 10, 1961.

Olympic Games 1936: Official Organ of the XI Olympic Games, no. 2. Wiesbaden-Biebrich: Deutsches Institut für Filmkunde, July 1935.

PILGERT, HENRY P. *Press, Radio, and Film in West Germany.* Bonn: Historical Division, Office of the Executive Secretary, Office of the United States High Commissioner for Germany, 1953.

PYROS, J. "Notes on Women Directors." *Take One,* November–December 1970.

RICHARDS, J. "Leni Riefenstahl: Style and Structure." *Silent Pictures,* Autumn 1970.

RIEFENSTAHL, LENI. "Statement on Sarris/Gessner Quarrel about Olympia." *Film Comment,* Fall 1967.

———. "Notizen zu Penthesilea." *Filmkritik,* August 1972.

———. "Letter to Gorden Hitchens, June 11, 1972." *Film Culture,* Spring 1973.

———. "Why I Am Filming Penthesilea." *Film Culture,* Spring 1973.

ROTHA, PAUL. "I Deplore . . ." *Film,* Spring 1967.

SARRIS, ANDREW. "Films." *The Village Voice,* May 4, 1967.

SCHULBERG, B. "Nazi Pin-Up Girl: Hitler's No. 1 Movie Actress." *Saturday Evening Post,* March 30, 1946.

SONTAG, SUSAN. "Fascinating Fascism." *New York Review of Books,* February 6, 1975.

SORKI, MARC. "Six Talks with G. W. Pabst." *Cinemages 3,* 1955.

State Commission of Baden-Baden for Political Purification. *Decision in the Proceedings Against Frau Riefenstahl-Jacob, December 16, 1949.* Freiburg.

Summary of Judgment in the Dispute Between Friedrich A. Mainz, Plaintiff, and the Minerva Company of Stockholm, Defendant, January 10, 1969. Munich.

TOBIS FILM-KURIER. *Olympia.* Pressbook, 1938.

UFA FILM-KURIER. *Triumph des Willens.* Pressbook, 1936.

VÖLKISCHER BEOBACHTER. "Das Schwarzbuck." April 3, 1933.

———. "My Name Is Leni Riefenstahl . . ." April 22, 1938.

WEIGEL, H. "Interview mit Leni Riefenstahl." *Filmkritik,* August 1972.

Index